The Complete Idiot's Almanac of Business Letters and Memos Reference Card

Three Steps to Great Memos

Many people find writing difficult because they try to do it in one step. While one step might sound faster than three steps, it really isn't, because that one step usually amounts to a process of slowly muddling through.

It's much better to take the three-step approach of Plan-Draft-Edit.

➤ **Plan:** Clarify your point, anticipate reader response, choose a format, and do a "quick 'n dirty" outline.

➤ **Draft:** Start writing, quickly and without worrying about grammar and punctuation, until you have a complete memo.

➤ **Edit:** Take your draft and edit it for content, grammar, and punctuation, and then make one final check.

At first many people fear that this approach will take longer than the way they were writing before. Actually, doing each of these tasks as three separate steps is faster, for three reasons:

➤ First, you can write the draft very quickly because you've taken time to decide what you will say and to jot that down in a brief outline.

➤ Second, you can write faster and get a sense of "flow" while writing because you stop editing as you write.

➤ Third, this approach helps you manage your writing time better.

That last point is critical. Ideally, you should spend about one-third of the time you have for a writing task on planning, one-third on drafting, and one-third on editing. Even if you have only an hour to write something, try spending about 20 minutes on planning, 20 minutes on drafting, and 20 minutes on editing. It works!

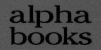

alpha
books

Six Ways to Write with Impact

1. **Talk to the reader.** Don't think that you are supposed to sound lofty or stuffy in order to write well. If you write the way you would talk to the reader, you'll find that you not only enjoy writing more, but that you sound better on paper. Business writing should be clear, crisp, and personal in tone. That's the result of sounding like yourself, which happens if you "talk to the reader."

2. **Have one main point to make.** Too many letters and memos either try to make too many points or don't seem to have a point. Decide in the planning step what your main point will be and then present it to the reader early in the document. Readers are busy and need to know what you are writing about right away.

3. **Present your ideas logically.** You must support your point with logically presented facts. Opinions are fine, but they need to be backed up with facts. Whenever possible, use numbers to support your points.

4. **Use language effectively.** Effective language affects readers. Often business writers will say "sales rose very sharply" when "sales skyrocketed" would be better. Or they might say "profits are really off" when "profits plummeted" would have more impact. Find fresh ways of expressing your ideas.

5. **Get rid of clutter.** In the editing step, get rid of every word that you can without sacrificing clarity. Many people believe that the more words they write, the clearer the message becomes. Actually, the opposite is true: The fewer the words, the greater the clarity.

6. **Proofread like a pro.** Grammar mistakes and typographical errors reflect poorly on you. Always take the extra time necessary to get it right before you get it out.

Writing for Your Boss, a Committee, or a Team

Unless you're self-employed, writing for others will be among your business writing tasks. It can be difficult because the people you write for may not always know what they want until they see it. Also, it can be frustrating to have others edit your writing.

To make writing for others easier:

➤ Understand the goal and the message.

➤ Analyze the audience.

➤ Get ideas—and agreement—on paper.

➤ Write alone.

➤ Get and enter all edits.

➤ Get final sign-off.

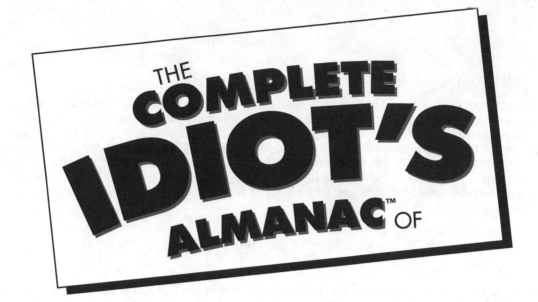

THE COMPLETE IDIOT'S ALMANAC™ OF

Business Letters and Memos

by Tom Gorman

alpha
books

A Division of Macmillan General Reference
A Simon & Schuster Macmillan Company
1633 Broadway, New York, NY 10019

International Standard Book Number: 0-02-861741-x
Library of Congress Catalog Card Number: 97-071180

99 98 97   8 7 6 5 4 3 2 1

Interpretation of the printing code: the rightmost number of the first series of numbers is the year of the book's printing; the rightmost number of the second series of numbers is the number of the book's printing. For example, a printing code of 97-1 shows that the first printing occurred in 1997.

Printed in the United States of America

Clip art used in this book comes from The Corel GALLERY Clipart Catalog.

Editor-in-Chief
Richard J. Staron

Editorial Manager
Gretchen Henderson

Editor
Kate Layzer

Production/Copy Editors
Lynn Northrup
Lori Cates

Cover Designer
Michael Freeland

Cartoonist
Judd Winick

Designer
Glenn Larsen

Indexer
Nadia Ibrahim

Production Team
Angela Calvert
Daniela Raderstorf
Maureen West

Contents at a Glance

Contents

Foreword

I used to be a terrible writer. Now I am a published author. How did I go from being a bad writer to being a good writer? I looked carefully at how successful writers write so well and I practiced their techniques. I analyzed the step-by-step processes they used to write things that I enjoyed reading and that communicated clearly.

I discovered that good writing is a skill that can be learned. I learned that the best way to write well was to copy the style of good and successful writers. It didn't matter what I was trying to write. Whether it was a book, a business letter, or a memo to my associates, I looked for a model that I knew got the job done, then used that model for my own purposes.

We write business letters and memos to get things done. They have to communicate clearly what we have in mind. We expect our readers to understand and act on the ideas and feelings we express. We want them to understand us as we intend them to. Then we will get the results we want from whatever we have written.

In *The Complete Idiot's Almanac of Business Letters and Memos,* Tom Gorman shows you just what to do to write effective letters and memos. No matter what your present skills may be, his step-by-step method will boost your power to communicate and get things done. Using his easy, simple approach, you will learn how to write faster—and better.

This handy guide provides you with clear explanations of the general principles of good writing, along with numerous practical examples of good letters and memos. You can copy these models for your own purposes, or study them for insights on writing from scratch. Either way, you will learn how to write the best letter or memo for the occasion.

As you'll discover, being a good communicator increases your sense of personal worth and confidence in whatever you do. Before long, writing will be a pleasure instead of a chore.

Richard Heyman

Dr. Richard Heyman is professor of communication and education at the University of Calgary and Director of the Discourse Analysis Research Group, an international network of people who study language use in everyday life. He is the author of *Why Didn't You Say That in The First Place?: How to Be Understood at Work* (San Francisco: Jossey-Bass, 1994).

Introduction

Your success in business depends on your ability to express yourself on paper. Whether you're looking for a job or you're on the job—or in your own business—you have to be able to write great letters and memos and express yourself on paper in a professional yet personal and persuasive way.

If you have problems with business writing, you found this book at exactly the right time. That's because written communication skills have become more important than ever in business. The computer and e-mail demand that we write constantly. Meanwhile, most of us can no longer count on secretaries to correct badly written letters and memos, because secretaries are becoming increasingly rare.

I'm a professional writer with over 20 years of business experience. I've used letters and memos to get jobs, make sales, solve problems, hire people, and then help them improve their performance. I've been a corporate writing instructor for a successful training firm, and I ran the editorial and production department for a division of a Fortune 500 company. This is my third book. But before I ever wrote a book, I wrote thousands of letters and memos, most of which did the job they were supposed to do.

I wrote this book because I know how hard it can be to get good, practical guidance for on-the-job writing. Although business people expect you to be able to write professional-sounding letters and memos, no one is born knowing how to do that. It often takes years to learn how.

This book will save you incredible amounts of time as you learn to write great letters and memos. It offers techniques for speeding up the writing process and inside tips on how to avoid mistakes—real time-savers. And the dozens of samples and outlines of letters and memos will make life on the job much easier for you.

Here's the approach we'll take in this book:

Part 1, "The Business of Business Writing," explains what makes a letter or memo great and gives some practical help on solving writing problems and building communication skills.

Part 2, "Writing: It's Easier Than You Think (So Please Relax)," shows you how to write quickly using a simple three-step process, how to handle punctuation, and how to write for bosses and committees.

Part 3, "Taming the Wild and Wooly Memo," helps you express your personal style in your letters and memos and avoid embarrassing mistakes in written English. It also shows you how to format documents.

Part 4, "What Should I Write and When Should I Write It?" is about which letters and memos to use for a variety of different business occasions, from thank-you's to reprimands to requests. It includes outlines and samples that you can use as models, plus a lot of good ways to say things that can be hard to say in writing.

Part 5, "Now What Do I Do with It?" examines the best means of delivery—plus how to handle follow-up and keep track of what you've written.

Part 6, "Screen Writing: Letters, Memos, E-Mail, and Your Computer," tells you how to get more out of your personal computer and how to write effective e-mail messages.

As you go through this book, remember to relax and take time to learn what works. I think you'll find it's well worth the investment.

Signposts Along the Way

You'll find the following sidebars throughout the book. They highlight special points that I want to be sure you catch.

What's That?

These boxes give you definitions of words and terms that might not be entirely familiar to you.

Trick of the Trade
These sidebars provide professional tips on how to write better, faster, or with more impact. Some show you how to handle certain aspects of writing letters or memos.

Watch Out!
These boxes warn you of problems that can occur in business writing and suggest how you can handle sticky situations.

Acknowledgments

Many thanks to everyone who helped to make this book possible: Dick Staron (editor-in-chief), Mike Snell (my agent), Kate Layzer, Lynn Northrup, and Lori Cates (the editorial team on the book), John Hunt (graphics coordinator), Glenn Larsen (designer), my wife Phyllis and my sons Danny and Matt, and all of my past employers, employees, trainees, and clients.

Trademarks

All terms mentioned in this book that are known to be or are suspected of being trademarks or service marks have been appropriately capitalized. Alpha Books and Macmillan General Reference cannot attest to the accuracy of this information. Use of a term in this book should not be regarded as affecting the validity of any trademark or service mark.

Part 1
The Business of Business Writing

You go to your boss with an idea for a new procedure to solve a recurring problem in your department, and she says, "That sounds promising. Please give me a memo on that by next Monday." What's your reaction?

You just met with a potential new customer and need to follow up that meeting with a letter that shows you understand his needs and that asks for an order. Can you write a letter that will do the job?

You are reading an interesting help-wanted ad in the newspaper and see the words, "Must have demonstrated first-rate written communication skills." Will you apply for the position?

There's no doubt about it: Business involves business writing. That writing most often takes the form of a letter or memo. Yet lots of people have trouble writing letters and memos clearly, quickly, and professionally. If you're one of those people, you have a source of real help right in your hands.

Please use one of those hands to turn the page, and let's get started.

Chapter 1

A Memo Is Just a Memo—or Is It?

In This Chapter

➤ How letters and memos move business forward

➤ What makes a great letter or memo?

➤ How to become a better communicator

Why do companies of all sizes create so much paper? Why are there so many people "pushing paper" in business? Why has the personal computer created more, rather than less, paper in most organizations?

Because business runs on paper.

People have to see things on paper in order to make a decision or commitment. Most of us in business need to show someone else ideas or a plan on paper to get that person's opinion or approval. Every business needs a record of what people are doing, of who is responsible for what. People almost always need "something in writing" if they are going to make a loan, start a project, or cut a check. Most often, that "something in writing" is a letter or a memo. In business, letters and memos make things happen.

So if you are going to make things happen in business, you have to be able to write a great letter or memo.

The Characteristics of Greatness

What makes a great letter or memo? I'm glad you asked. A great letter or memo:

➤ Grabs the reader's attention

➤ Makes a recommendation or asks for action

➤ Supports your position

➤ Mentions next steps and deadlines

A great letter or memo does these things in a crisp, professional way, but with a personal touch. A great memo gets results, and creates a positive impression of you with your bosses, co-workers, and customers—or anyone else who might be reading it. Let's take a look at each of these "characteristics of greatness."

Grab the Reader's Attention

Let's face it: We all have too much paper coming at us. (Sure, business runs on paper, but it can get ridiculous!) With so much paper to deal with, how do we decide what we'll spend time reading and what we'll just skim or toss?

Often, we decide on the basis of who wrote the memo. If it's from our boss, we'll probably read it. But even so, if the boss's memos are confusing, most of us would rather go and ask the boss what it's about.

Trick of the Trade
If you ever get phone calls from people asking what your memo means, you need to work on your business writing.

Usually, we'll read a letter or memo if it is clear and interesting to us. If we can't figure out what it says, we move on to the next one. And if the memo is dull or seems to have nothing to do with us, we'll do the same. The way to grab the reader's attention is to have something to say and to say it clearly.

The format of a letter also affects the reader. Most readers are turned off when they see huge paragraphs and long sentences. In Chapter 8, I'll talk about how to use format to invite the reader into the letter.

Watch Out!

The average manager gets a total of 60 pieces of internal and outside mail per week—not including electronic mail (e-mail). You have about 15 seconds to get your message across to her before she loses interest.

Make a Recommendation or Ask for Action

The reader of a memo wants the answer to one question: What am I supposed to do because of this piece of paper? So very early in the memo, often in the first sentence, you must answer that question.

The following openings give some examples of how to do this:

➤ "Many of our employees can no longer find spaces in the company parking lot. This memo presents a solution for your approval."

➤ "This memo requests your approval of $5,000 in expenses to test a direct mail campaign for our new product line."

➤ "I have been interested in working for ABC Industries for some time and would like to meet with you to discuss how I could help your company meet its goals."

With an approach like this, the reader knows right away what you're writing about and why. In fact, you inform the reader about your subject and grab his attention at the same time. Isn't that efficient?

Support Your Position

It's not enough to make a recommendation or request an action. You have to say why it makes sense. You can usually accomplish this with far fewer words than you might think, often in one paragraph or several bullets (•).

When you make a recommendation or request an action, you should also do one or more of the following:

➤ Tell the reader briefly what research or "homework" you did before making this recommendation or request.

➤ Mention an alternative or two and tell why your recommendation is best.

➤ Show the reader the positive impact of your recommendation or request; that is, what's in it for him or for the organization.

➤ Offer the reader any help that you can.

By supporting your position, you stand a better chance of getting the reader to buy in to your request. If you don't mention reasons for your position or benefits for the reader, you will either raise questions or objections, or be ignored.

Mention Next Steps and Deadlines

Be specific about next steps and deadlines. Again, put yourself in the reader's position. How do *you* direct your attention and effort on the job? How do *you* set priorities?

Most of us decide what to do on the basis of urgency. So if you tell the reader what you will do to follow up on your recommendation or request and when you will do it, you create a sense of urgency. Follow-up steps—and deadlines—drive things forward.

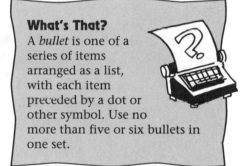

What's That?
A *bullet* is one of a series of items arranged as a list, with each item preceded by a dot or other symbol. Use no more than five or six bullets in one set.

Trick of the Trade
You can call a deadline a deadline if you are writing to a subordinate. But most bosses and peers don't like the term "deadline" from a subordinate or co-worker. In those cases, use the term "time frame."

For example, you can close your letter or memo by saying:

➤ "I'll phone you by the end of next week to get your reaction to this proposal."

➤ "To do the mailing by our target date, Jim and I need your approval by the tenth. If I haven't heard from you by the eighth, I'll call you."

➤ "I realize you're busy, so I'll call next Thursday afternoon to arrange a meeting at your convenience."

Trick of the Trade
Mentioning specific follow-up steps and time frames may get you a definite refusal. That's not all bad. A refusal signals that you should change your approach, ask someone else, or move on to something else.

At the least, these kinds of closings open the way for you to follow up. This is key to getting results. Often one memo will not do the trick because people are busy and overworked. Many dislike change and drag their feet. So if you politely tell the reader how and when you will follow up, you pave the way for getting results.

Strive for Greatness

These "Characteristics of Greatness" apply to almost all business letters and memos. This book will cover various business letters for various purposes in various formats. Most (but not all) of them have one thing in common: the goal of getting someone to approve your recommendation or take the requested action.

This will happen only if the reader reads your memo, understands what you want, sees the reason for your request, and feels a sense of urgency about it. A great memo does all of these things. And your memos can be great.

The Importance of Written Communication Skills

Since a reader can forward a letter to someone else or file it for future reference, you really don't know who will see it. That piece of paper becomes a permanent reflection on you and your ability to think clearly, express yourself professionally, and get things done.

If your memos are poor, the people playing a role in your success or failure will know it. That's why excellent written communication skills top the list of qualifications for success in business year after year.

What People Mean by "Communication Skills"

What does the term "communication skills" mean to you? Do you think of some silver-tongued devil who can talk anyone into anything? Do you think it's about the size of your vocabulary—the more words you know, especially big words, the better? Does it seem to be about impressing people with your brains and schooling?

Some people do think that this is what it's all about, but they're wrong. Instead, good communication:

➤ Puts mutual interests first

➤ Makes the message clear

➤ Shows sensitivity to others' feelings

Let's examine these issues one at a time in the following sections.

Put Mutual Interests First

If you write to puff yourself up rather than to move the business forward, people will know it. They will see that your agenda is yourself, your position, and your interests. However, business is based upon mutual interests. To write a compelling memo, you must identify mutual goals. This doesn't mean your goals come last. It means that everyone's goals have equal importance, or you can't do business.

Let's take an example that at first seems one-sided—a collection letter. Your goal is simple: You want your money. You sold something on credit, and the customer hasn't paid you as agreed. But even here, the reader has goals that mesh with yours: maintaining their cash flow, credit rating, business reputation, peace of mind, freedom from legal action, and (probably) sense of honesty. By mentioning some of these in your collection letters, you create shared goals.

To get results, to get agreement, to get people to take action, you have to get them to see what's in it for them. Whether you're writing a sales letter, a policy announcement, or a deal memo, you have to keep *mutual* interests front and center. Good communicators show that they understand the other person's goals.

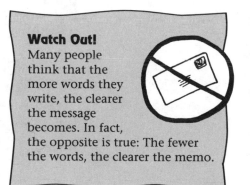

What's That?
A *collection letter* is a written request to a customer to pay a past-due bill by a certain time; it's also called a "dunning letter."

Make the Message Clear

A lot of business writing lacks clarity, for several reasons. Sometimes a muddled memo reflects the writer's muddled thinking. Many writers in business try to impress the reader rather than express an idea. Some writers bury their main point somewhere in the fifth paragraph. Will the reader get that far? Doubtful.

If you want to write business letters and memos that get results, first decide what you want the reader to think or do and then say that, as clearly as you can and as early as you can in the document. Then support what you say with a few key facts.

Watch Out!
Many people think that the more words they write, the clearer the message becomes. In fact, the opposite is true: The fewer the words, the clearer the memo.

Show Sensitivity to Others' Feelings

In our daily dealings, too many of us display insensitivity to others' feelings. If your letters come across as arrogant, angry, flippant, or uncaring, you will not only fail to get results, you'll make enemies along the way.

Professionalism, not to mention good manners, demands that you conduct yourself with an awareness of others' views and feelings. This holds particularly true in business writing.

Displays of anger or inappropriate humor on paper have scuttled many a career. A sarcastic tone, even for laughs, has no place in a business letter (although some bosses seem to get away with it). Comments that might sound witty if delivered in person with a certain tone of voice or facial expression, often come across as demeaning or immature on paper. Worse, you're not around to see the reader's reaction and to apologize.

Sensitivity to others is the positive side of "politics" in business. The negative side is conforming to policies you feel are wrong, flattering people to gain favor, playing the yes-man (or -woman), and other forms of "apple polishing." While some people still employ such tactics, these forms of politics are now valued far less than the ability to get things done. Good communication helps you to get things done.

The Reader Is King

This all adds up to one thing: In business writing, the reader is king, just as the customer is king in any business. Think of your readers as your customers.

If your readers are going to buy in to your ideas and help you to get the results you want, you have to focus on them, on *their* goals and needs, and on *their* feelings, about what you're proposing. Even if you're the CEO, you can't order people to be cooperative. You have to win their cooperation. That's what you can achieve with a truly great business letter or memo.

The Least You Need to Know

➤ A great letter or memo grabs the reader's attention, makes a recommendation or asks for action, supports your position, and mentions next steps and deadlines.

➤ Good business communication calls for a focus on mutual interests, clarity, and sensitivity to others' feelings.

➤ To get results, you have to show people what's in it for them or for the organization.

➤ Business letters and memos move business—and careers—forward.

Chapter 2

What's This Supposed to Mean?!

In This Chapter

➤ Common problems in business writing

➤ What you can do to solve your writing problems

➤ A self-analysis of your writing difficulties

Many people find writing business letters and memos difficult. To understand this better, in this chapter we'll look at common business writing problems.

First, however, you should understand that anyone can have trouble now and then with a specific letter or a certain type of memo. For example, nobody enjoys writing letters of reprimand or rejection (except really mean people—not people like us!). Many people are shy about writing letters in which they have to request an action. Perhaps they fear they will be rejected or they don't believe they have the authority to make the request.

When you have trouble with a specific document, you should review the chapter on that kind of letter or memo. You'll find the models and outlines useful as "thought-starters" and blueprints for your letter. Each chapter in Part 4 also includes advice that can help you understand your role as a business person in that writing situation.

Few of us in business can avoid writing. But there is no real reason to avoid it, once you confront any general problems you have with writing.

> **Trick of the Trade**
> Writing about your writing problem can do away with the problem. If you hate to write or can't get started, write about that for 20 minutes every day for a few days. Often the problem will disappear as you discover the reasons for it and find that writing won't kill you.

What's Your Problem and What Can You Do?

Here are the most common problems I've heard from people in my years as an editor and corporate writing consultant.

Problem: "I Hate to Write"

Some people make "I hate to write" their mantra. After years of repeating this, they really do hate writing.

What Can You Do?

If you say this to yourself, and you have to write on the job, stop saying it.

Also ask yourself this: Do you hate to talk? If you think of writing as talking on paper—and this book will show you how to do that—you stop hating it. But first, stop repeating that phrase to yourself.

It may also be useful to think about what you specifically dislike about writing:

➤ Is it because it's not usually a social activity but rather one you do alone? If so, be sure that you get input from others on a writing task whenever you can.

> **What's That?**
> *Help screens* show how to do the more complex operations in a software package. Usually, you can access "Help" by using the "Search" function available in most word processing software to locate the topic with which you need help. Another way to get help is to choose the "Help" command when you are doing an operation, and the "Help" prompt will come up.

➤ Is it working with words? If you dislike working with words, you definitely must make every effort to write the way you would talk. (I discuss how in Chapter 6.)

➤ Do you dislike computers? Face it: You need computer skills in today's workplace. You can get training. With the tutorials and help screens in today's word processing software, you can learn to write a good memo without spending hours at the computer. *Tutorials* are interactive lessons that show you the basic functions of a software package. You can complete most tutorials in less than an hour, often in less than 30 minutes. Also, you can always do your first draft with pen and paper.

➤ Does deadline pressure drive you nuts? You'll benefit from managing your writing time more efficiently, as you'll see in Chapter 4.

My goal is not to get you to love writing (although that'd be nice), but rather to minimize your pain if you dislike writing but have to do it.

Problem: "I Was Never Good in English"

Many people's writing troubles began in school, which is reasonable. What kid wants a big book report or a huge paper on Brazil hanging over his head for five weeks? And if you didn't get good grades on these projects, it hurt.

Also, a lot of people have been traumatized by teachers who marked them off for word usage, spelling, and punctuation—even when they knew the subject matter. This doesn't make them feel good about writing and can create a life-long lack of confidence.

What Can You Do?

Realize that if you weren't good in English it doesn't have to ruin your business writing. For one thing, many of the rules you learned in school can be bent, even broken, with no loss of power, sometimes with a gain. Business writing doesn't have to follow every point that the well-meaning Miss Grundys of the world tried to drill into us.

Also, practice helps a lot. So can a dictionary and a writing guide like this one.

> **Trick of the Trade**
> If English is your second language, you face a special situation. Spend extra time planning what you will write, and keep your sentences and paragraphs short. In fact, this is good advice for most business writers.

Problem: "I Have No Time"

Like anything else, writing takes time. I often wonder whether people realize that in many jobs writing is as important as meetings and budgets. We make time for important things.

Not having time can come from waiting too long to get started. If you have trouble with writing, you may procrastinate on writing projects, even short memos. (Writing can, however, go much more quickly for you. Taking the three-step approach you will learn in Chapter 4 will make writing easier and faster for you.)

What Can You Do?

If it's part of your job, make writing a priority, because it gets things done. If you are genuinely pressed for time (aren't we all?), there are ways to make time to write.

➤ Carve out blocks of time for writing. Schedule it the way you would a meeting or a sales call. These blocks can be as short as half an hour. Most people feel they need hours to write, which is one reason they never find the time.

➤ If you can close your office door, or at least tell people not to disturb you and let voice-mail answer the phone, do it.

➤ Break up the writing of long, important memos into sub-tasks. For example, gather information in one step, do an outline in another sitting, write a first draft in another, then edit the draft in a final step.

➤ If all else fails, use time before or after hours for writing. (Yes, I'm serious.) Many people do this because they're on the firing line all day. If there's just no other way, it's worth it until you get to where you can easily pump out memos.

Problem: "I Have No 'Style'"

Many people feel that they need to sound like a cross between William Shakespeare and Jackie Collins when they write a memo. They feel they're supposed to sound smart or lofty or commanding or like someone they aren't.

What Can You Do?

Stop worrying. In business, it is *your* personal style as a professional doing your job that is supposed to come through on paper. I'll talk more about this in Chapter 11. This problem goes away if you think less about your style and more about your subject.

Problem: "I Don't Write Well and Others Do It Better"

Many people compare their writing to others', and it doesn't do them any good.

What Can You Do?

You may not be the best judge of your writing skills. I've met many people who do not write nearly as badly as they believed they did. Anyway, you don't have to be A Great Writer to write a great business letter. You merely have to make sure that you include the Characteristics of Greatness.

Watch Out!
Don't avoid or ignore criticism of your writing. Many people do just that because it can be hard to listen to. But criticism from people who know good writing can be your most valuable tool for improving.

When you see others write a memo better than you think you could, look closely at the memo. Analyze it. See how they do it. What kind of an opening do they use? How do they ask for action or help? How do they use specifics and examples to support their point? How do they leave the door open for follow-up?

Don't be shy about going to writers you think do a good job, complimenting them, and asking for pointers. Most people are happy to share what they know and to talk about something they do well.

Assessing Your Business Writing Skills

Now it's time for you to get a better idea of your business writing ability, particularly on letters and memos. Please answer the following questions as honestly as you can:

		Often	Sometimes	Never
1.	When I have a memo to write I get on with it instead of putting it off.	❏	❏	❏
2.	I enjoy writing letters and memos.	❏	❏	❏
3.	I write letters and memos quickly and productively.	❏	❏	❏
4.	Before writing a letter or memo, I make an outline.	❏	❏	❏
5.	I go back and edit my letters and memos.	❏	❏	❏
6.	I have been complimented on my letters and memos.	❏	❏	❏
7.	My letters and memos get results; people respond well to them.	❏	❏	❏
8.	What I write is clear to readers.	❏	❏	❏
9.	I have been given special writing tasks on the job.	❏	❏	❏
10.	On the job, I've been asked to write for the signature of another.	❏	❏	❏

Give yourself a two for each "Often," a one for each "Sometimes," and a zero for each "Never." If you scored 12 or over, you are probably at least an average business writer. If you scored 11 or less, you need to work on several aspects of your business writing.

The first five questions have to do with how you handle the writing process. Low scores here mean that you may simply lack the information you need about how to go about it. Or perhaps you don't go about it the way you know you should.

Questions six through ten focus on the results you are getting with your business writing, with the way it comes across to others. Low scores here mean that regardless of how you are going about it, your business writing could be better.

Where We Go from Here

At this point, the key thing is to relax and know that you are not alone. Most people (including me) have trouble with specific business writing tasks from time to time. Other people find almost all writing difficult.

Wherever you fit in, please understand that business writing is a skill, not an art, and that doing it well requires a bit of work as opposed to a lot of talent.

The Least You Need to Know

➤ Most people have problems with business writing from time to time.

➤ Even long-standing writing problems can be corrected quickly with the right information and some practice.

➤ One of the most common problems, finding time to write, can be overcome by scheduling the task, arranging for privacy, and doing the writing over several sittings.

➤ When you see a memo that works, try to figure out why.

➤ Ask for help and constructive criticism; if someone on the job writes better than you do, he or she may be willing to help you.

The Right Tool for the Writing Situation

In This Chapter

➤ The differences among types of business communications

➤ Ways to inform the reader and get action

➤ Choosing the right written communication

Most people think that the way to write is to just start writing. But throughout this book, I'll stress that it really pays to *think* before you write. Think about your reader, your message, and the best tool for getting your point across.

This chapter will look at the major forms of written business communications and their uses.

What's the Difference Between Letters and Memos?

Is there a difference between letters and memos? Are there other business communications you should know about? The answer to both questions is "yes."

The difference between a letter and a memo is mainly form, but the style is also a factor.

Letters: Professional, Yet Personal

A letter is typically set up on letterhead, with a date, an inside address, and a salutation, then the body of the letter, and finally the closing, signature, and the name and title lines.

What's That?
Letterhead is stationery that has been preprinted with an individual's or organization's logo, name, address, telephone number, and often, fax number, e-mail address, and even the URL (universal resource locator, or "address") for the individual's or organization's site on the World Wide Web.

What's That?
Clip art is a pre-drawn graphic or piece of artwork loaded into a word processing package or available on a CD-ROM or on a database accessible on the Internet. Often the graphic or artwork is in color. (Of course, you need a color printer to get that onto paper.)

If you own a small business or are a freelancer, you can set up your own letterhead with word processing software. While this will not look as good as letterhead done by a printer (especially done in color by a printer), it will be acceptable.

A letter conveys a more personal touch than a memo. Although the language in a letter and a memo can be equally personal, a letter lends itself to a less official, more informal style of communication. You should usually use a letter when you write to someone outside your organization.

The reader will typically see a letter as more personal and as something directed only toward him or her. Thus a letter is usually the best form to use when you are addressing only one person or you want to create that impression, for example in a direct-mail campaign.

Sample 1 shows an example of a letter on "homemade" letterhead. Good word processing software offers a wide variety of fonts (styles of type) in a range of sizes, as well as a library of "clip art" that you can use in this way.

You can incorporate graphics and artwork into your business documents for use in letterhead, or occasionally to add visual interest—but be tasteful and don't overdo it. We'll discuss this more in Chapters 8 and 27.

Sample 1 on the following page has each of the four "Characteristics of Greatness" discussed in Chapter 1.

The Coffee Klatch

901 Washington St.
Dumont, NJ 07628

September 5, 1997

Mr. Ralph Jones
Director—Career Development Office
Dumont Community College
345 Deer Park Lane
Dumont, NJ 07628

> A subject line tells the reader what this letter is about right away.

Subject: Request for Job Bank Listing

Dear Mr. Jones:

We are a local coffee-shop chain with five units in the Dumont area. I am writing to you because we are often seeking responsible young men and women to work part-time, and we would like to list open positions in your job bank.

Our rapid growth means that your students would have a good chance of finding employment with us. Our standards of service and policy of job rotation give young people a chance to learn how a business operates. Students also develop good work habits and can move to positions of greater responsibility, such as shift leader and assistant manager. We offer flexible hours and a starting salary of $6.50 an hour, with annual raise reviews.

I would be happy to meet with you at your convenience at your office or at one of our units.

I'll call you early next week to learn how the job bank works and to see if you would be interested in listing openings at The Coffee Klatch. Thank you for your consideration.

Sincerely,

Lou Brown

Lou Brown

President

Sample 1: "Homemade" Letterhead.

Memos: A Bit More Official

A memo (short for memorandum) is typically set up in a special format, which may either be generic or specific to the organization. A generic format is usually pulled from a word processing software's library of templates, or just typed on a word processor by the writer.

The appearance of a memo is more official than that of a letter. The language you use in a memo can be just as personal as in a letter, but a memo lends itself to a more formal tone. (We'll discuss language and tone in Chapter 11.)

Sample 2 in the following section shows a typical memo.

Two lines on the header of Sample 2 may need explanation:

The "Re" line ("Re" is pronounced "ree," short for "regarding") lets the reader know right off what the memo is about. Instead of "Re," the word "Subject" is often used. Looking back to Sample 1, you'll see that the same device can be used in a letter to let the reader know right away what the letter is about. A "Re" or "Subject" line also helps the reader file the document.

Don't settle for a bland subject line that tells the reader very little. Be as specific as you can without getting wordy (more than one line is too much). In Sample 2, the line "Request for a Meeting to Discuss Expense Controls" tells the reader much more than a line like "Expense Controls" or "Meeting Request."

The "cc" line tells the recipient who else you are sending the memo to. The term "cc" (often written in capital letters) is the abbreviation for "carbon copy." This is a holdover from the days when people used carbon paper to make copies when typing the original. A "cc" can also be placed at the end of a letter or memo instead of before.

Another device you can use when you have more than four or five readers to be "cc'd" on a memo is the *distribution list*. This is a list of people who will receive their own copy of the memo. It usually appears at the bottom of a one-page memo or on the last page of a longer memo, and usually contains the first initial and last name of each person on the distribution. Sample 3 in the following section shows a distribution list following Sue McFarland's memo.

Watch Out!
On a memo there is no real space for a signature, as there is on a letter. This means that anyone could type a memo in anyone else's name. This dishonesty occurs very rarely, but to be safe, many people sign their initials—or sometimes their first initial and last name or first name and last initial—near their typewritten name on the "From" line. This is a good habit to get into.

Using the "CC" to Get Action

The "cc" can be a powerful tool in getting action from your reader, but you must use it carefully.

For example, consider Sample 2. If P. Lowy, who was cc'd on the memo, is Jack Entrup's boss, Sue McFarland's strategy was to let Jack know that his boss (Lowy) knows that she is requesting this meeting. This puts pressure on Jack. Depending on the personalities involved, Jack may take Sue's move either as a threat or as just keeping Lowy up-to-date.

Now consider the version of this memo shown in Sample 3. Here Sue has a distribution list of seven people. Whatever the personalities, it's safe to assume that Jack will not appreciate this move on Sue's part: Now seven people know that Jack's expenses are running over budget. The memo makes Jack look bad to a lot of people. Sue may be at her wit's end with Jack or she may have gone too far here, or both.

Trick of the Trade
It is wise to keep a hard copy of any letter or memo that you think you'll have to refer to in the future. Don't rely on your computer or disks as your only filing system. Set up a filing system that works for you and use it for important letters and memos. You want to be able to lay your hands on important documents quickly.

A salutation (Dear So-and-So) should never go on a memo. This is another reason that memos are less personal and more formal.

Since memos have no inside address and have a more formal look, they are mainly used inside rather than outside an organization. I'm not saying that you would always use a memo internally and always use a letter outside, but that is the way to go in most cases.

Memos to the File: A Record-Keeping Tool

A memo to the file is a memo that you write to yourself to record a conversation or event for yourself and for others, such as those who will fill your position after you.

This memo is a particularly good method for keeping a record of problems. Typical uses would be to create a written record of a verbal reprimand or to record promises from a supplier. Such a memo can be very informal, as shown in Sample 4.

A memo to the file can go into a folder that you keep for such memos or into the file that your company maintains on a supplier or employee. It serves as a record, a reminder, and a piece of evidence.

Memorandum

Date: September 5, 1997

To: Jack Entrup

From: Sue McFarland *S.M.*

Re: Request for a Meeting to Discuss Expense Controls

cc: P. Lowy

> Sue gets Jack's attention by "cc-ing" (sending a copy of her letter) to Jack's boss.

Since expenses in your department are running about 16 percent over budget, I would like to meet with you to discuss ways in which we can get them back under control.

The discussions we have had up to this point have been informative, but not terribly effective. I realize that your sales are also running above budget, and that is good news. But your sales are only 8 percent above budget while expenses are ahead by double that.

I'm sure you'll agree that we have to address this situation sooner rather than later. The fourth quarter will make or break our division's performance for the year.

I'll call you on Friday to arrange a meeting for early next week.

Sample 2: Typical Memo.

Memorandum

Date: September 5, 1997

To: Jack Entrup

From: Sue McFarland *S.M.*

Re: Request for a Meeting to Discuss Expense Controls

cc: Distribution

Since expenses in your department are running about 16 percent over budget, I would like to meet with you and Peter to discuss ways in which we can get them back under control.

I'll call you on Friday to arrange a meeting for early next week.

Distribution:

P. Lowy

C. Probyn

W. Carter

D. Wyss

R. Brinner

K. Mulvaney

M. Montgomery

> A distribution list lets you "cc" more than two or three people.

Sample 3: Memo with Distribution List.

Memo to the File (by Vivian Singer) *VS*

September 15, 1997

The repairman from Acme Copier Sales visited us again today and again claims to have fixed the copier in the east hallway. This is the third time in two weeks they have had to repair this machine.

I told the repairman, Fred Stybel, that next time we will demand a replacement machine. He told me (in a friendly way) that I would "have to take that up with the office."

I called Mandy Kemp at Acme (212-555-0800) and told her of our situation. I mentioned that it was unacceptable and that we would demand a new machine if this occurred again. I stated that this many repairs is not OK for a machine that is only four months old and is used well below the usage it is rated for.

Mandy said that she would have to deal with this situation if and when it happens because she believes that the machine is now fixed for good.

We will see.

Sample 4: Memo to the File.

> Always mention the next expected step when you're making a record of a problem.

Handwritten Notes: Very Personal, Very Proper

The handwritten note is becoming a thing of the past, which is too bad. A handwritten note is the ultimate personal touch. Until recently, notes were *the* networking tool. George Bush and Jackie Kennedy were both famous for sending handwritten notes to friends and contacts.

Trick of the Trade
For notes, you can use note cards, blank greeting cards (less formal and usually much less classy) or, my preference, stationery. You can find special notepaper with matching envelopes at fine stationery stores.

Although today's informality and busy pace—plus telephones and all-purpose greeting cards—have cut into the use of notes, don't discount them. They may seem a bit formal, but they still strike the right—well, *note*—on many occasions.

Handwritten notes typically express congratulations (on a promotion, for example), or thanks (for example, for a luncheon or dinner). They can also be used to keep in touch or to announce personal or professional news.

Although they are not as widely used as in the past, nothing should stop you from writing a note if you want to. Just be personal and write from your feelings—but don't gush.

September 21, 1997

Dear Jean,

Thank you for the wonderful dinner this past Saturday. Your years of living in Italy have certainly paid off if we can go by the lasagna you served. Steve and I truly enjoyed the evening and will remember it for years to come.

It's great to meet such nice people when you're new to a city. Thanks so much.

Best wishes,

Judy

> A note like this takes minutes to write, but can be remembered for years.

Handwritten Note.

E-Mail: Fast, but Loose

Electronic mail (e-mail) has become so prevalent that an entire chapter of this book—Chapter 28—has been devoted to the subject. For now, know that e-mail messages are less formal, less private, and more perishable than letters and memos. But they do get your message out fast, especially if you need to reach a lot of readers quickly.

The reasons for writing letters and memos are different from those for writing e-mail messages, as you'll see in later chapters.

Watch Out!

E-mail is not a secure, confidential means of communicating. Many companies admit that they routinely monitor employees' e-mail. It's quite possible that companies that do not admit it are also monitoring e-mail.

Remember, too, that "hackers" can intercept e-mail, or it can be lost through human or electronic error. The motto is, "Don't put it on e-mail unless you don't care who sees it."

When to Write

Writing, the phone, e-mail, and face-to-face meetings are all here to stay. So when should you write?

In general, use writing when:

➤ You need to be absolutely clear.

➤ You want to leave a "paper trail."

➤ You need to reach more than one person but don't need a meeting (even a conference call limits you to two or three other people).

➤ You have the time to write the piece and have it delivered.

When to Use a Letter and When to Use a Memo

Use a letter when you:

➤ Write to someone outside of your organization.

➤ Need to reach only a few people with the original and cc's (exception: direct mail).

➤ Want a personal touch, whether you know the reader or not.

Use a memo when you:

➤ Write to someone inside your company.

➤ Need to reach many people with copies of the document.

➤ Want a more formal, official look and style.

The Least You Need to Know

➤ Writing provides a way to reach multiple readers with a clear message, and it creates a record.

➤ Letters tend to be more personal and geared toward communications outside the organization, while memos are more formal and geared toward internal communications.

➤ A memo to the file provides evidence of a verbal conversation.

➤ The "cc" can help you get action, but be sure to use it with sensitivity toward the people involved.

➤ The choice of what to write and what form to use always depends on your message and your audience.

Part 2

Writing: It's Easier Than You Think (So Please Relax)

Do you enjoy writing? Does writing "flow" for you? Have you ever experienced the creative energy of having your ideas and words moving effortlessly from your mind to the page? Do you feel that you write well and that others respect your written communication skills?

Or is writing a chore for you? Is it something that you try to avoid? Does the thought of having to write a letter or memo turn you off? Do you get the sense that people would rather not read what you write?

The way you answer these questions may have something to do with your approach to the writing process. If you find yourself muddling through, struggling over every other word, trying to puzzle out what you're really trying to say when you write, the problem may be the way you go about writing.

Writing shouldn't be a hassle—if you know how to go about it.

Chapter 4

Three Easy Steps to Eloquence

In This Chapter

➤ How the writing process really works

➤ The three steps to good writing

➤ How to budget your writing time

Writing consists of three separate steps. Master this principle and you're already way ahead of the pack! The three steps are:

1. Planning

2. Drafting

3. Editing

Notice I said "separate" steps. It's important to do these steps in sequence, beginning with a plan or an outline, then coming up with a draft based on that plan or outline, and finally editing that draft.

It's OK to do the three steps all in one sitting, but it is *not* OK to combine them into one step (also known as "muddling through"). And don't try to omit the planning or editing step! That's what a lot of business writers do, and it's where most of their problems begin.

Let's take a look at each of these steps—separately.

Step One: Plan (Decide What to Say)

By a plan, I mean anything from a formal outline like the ones you were taught to do in school—you remember, with the Roman numerals and the letters of the alphabet and so on—to a set of bulleted points on a cocktail napkin (not recommended, but often used).

Your plan does not have to be elaborate. This isn't school, so you aren't going to have to show your outline to anyone. You do it only to get your thoughts down on paper in some logical order *before* you begin writing your actual letter or memo.

How Planning Helps You

If you have trouble getting started with your writing, coming up with a plan first helps a lot, because in the plan you don't have to worry about your writing and how good or bad it is or about grammar or spelling. You are just jotting down the points you will cover.

A plan also helps jump-start the flow of your ideas and helps you get all your points together before you start to write. You can see from your outline whether you have covered all the points you need to cover. Your outline will let you know whether you have to talk with someone or do some research before you write.

A plan simply represents preparation. It's a matter of being organized and professional in your approach. You wouldn't want a builder to start constructing a house for you without a blueprint, would you? It makes almost as little sense to begin writing without some kind of an outline.

Step Two: Draft (Say It)

Many people think that writing consists of just one step: drafting. People who write without a plan often find writing difficult, slow, and unenjoyable. But when you work from a plan, you can write very quickly. In fact, you *should* write the draft very quickly.

If you write quickly, from a plan, you have a good chance of coming up with something fresh. For many people there is something about writing fast, and the demand that makes on your brain, that boosts creativity.

Here's a key point: Write your draft without editing it. Most people try to edit the draft as they write it. They go back and make changes, and then they change it again. They fiddle around with the wording and even the punctuation. They put the comma in. They take the comma out. Instead, they should be focusing on content.

The quickest, most enjoyable (or, anyway, the least troublesome) way to write a letter or memo is to:

1. Have a plan to follow before you write.

2. Write without editing until you have a complete draft.

Just write it. Don't worry about grammar or spelling or punctuation. Don't judge how it looks or sounds while you're still writing it. Wait until you have something to edit before you start to edit.

Step Three: Edit (Improve the Way You Said It)

When you have a complete draft, pull out your red pen and get to work. During the editing process, you should fine-tune the wording, correct any grammar and spelling errors, and correct or insert punctuation.

You can even pretend to be a real editor, editing the work of someone else, if you like. Some people find this useful because it helps them look objectively at the piece.

The Benefits of Three Steps

This three-step process will give you four great benefits:

➤ Writing will become easier for you.

➤ Your writing style will improve.

➤ The content of your letters and memos will improve.

➤ Writing will become faster for you.

First, you'll find that writing becomes easier. Planning, drafting, and editing are three very different kinds of tasks, each one necessary for good writing. When you try to omit steps or do all three at once, you make writing more difficult.

Second, the style of your writing will improve as your eye improves. When you make editing a separate step at the back-end of the process, you can coolly assess your writing style and make improvements. You are also far more likely to catch typos and grammatical errors using this method.

Third, planning ensures that the content of your document will be complete and organized. Bosses and readers often find that writers leave an important point (or two) out of letters and memos. They forget to include basic information, like the time or place of a meeting or the price of the equipment they are recommending.

What's That?
Typo is short for typographical error. A typo can be a spelling error, misplaced or incorrect punctuation, or just about any small thing in the document that got there by mistake.

Watch Out!
The spell-checking programs in today's word processing software will catch most spelling errors. However, spell-checks will not catch errors that are actually words ("form" when you meant "from"); nor do they flag punctuation errors.

Trick of the Trade
When you organize your information in a separate step—for example, by covering "The Five W's and an H": who, what, when, where, why, and how—you improve your chances of seeing what's missing.

Organized letters and memos are a natural by-product of doing a plan and an edit. In planning, you gather your material and figure out beforehand the order in which you'll present it. In editing, you catch any omission or repetition, or anything that's not in the right order.

Finally, writing becomes faster because you have an outline that tells you what to write and when to write it. Writing becomes an automatic response to having the plan in front of you and having to get the memo done.

Holding off on editing until the draft is finished also speeds up the process and helps you overcome that old devil, writer's block. That's the feeling even professional writers get sometimes that they just cannot write. The best cure for writer's block is to use the three-step approach.

Run Around the Block

As you probably know, your brain has two sides. The left side (or left brain) takes care of the rational, analytical, and judgmental functions your mind performs. This side of your brain is detail-oriented, objective, and step-by-step in its approach.

The right hemisphere takes care of intuitive, creative functions. The right side is oriented toward the big picture rather than details, is subjective rather than objective, and is simultaneous rather than step-by-step in its approach.

Editing requires a rational, analytical, judgmental mind set. The problems that many people have with writing—they write slowly, they think it's no good, they think others do it better, and so on—often stem from editing while they write.

They write a sentence, look at it, and start crossing it out. They agonize over every word. They keep telling themselves that they don't write well. No wonder they hate to write! They are combining two tasks that are so fundamentally different that they actually draw on separate parts of the brain.

Writer's block, mentioned above, is usually caused by excessive self-criticism. When television or the movies want to portray a frustrated writer, they usually show him sitting in front of a typewriter, typing a few lines, reading them over, yanking out the page, crumpling it up, tossing it toward the wastebasket, and missing. Time passes and those balls of paper are now carpeting the floor. That writer has failed to separate the editing function from the drafting function. (On top of that, he's probably trying to write without a plan.)

Overall, there is no surer way to improve your writing than to adopt the plan-draft-edit approach. But some people resist this approach.

Overcoming Resistance to the Three-Step Process

Having spent some years as a writing instructor, I realize that most people don't like to plan. They would rather dive right in and start writing—and edit as they write.

When people resist the three-step approach, they usually say one of two things:

"I don't have time to plan."

or:

"I like to get as close as possible to final form on my first shot."

Let's take that first statement. It doesn't hold up. The time you save by not planning will be the time you waste by muddling through. Planning makes writing go faster.

If you're like most people who adopt the three-step process, you'll find that you do spend more time planning than you did before. But you'll also find that you save even more time by writing the draft much more quickly than you could before. And you can do that because you not only have a plan, but you have stopped editing as you write.

The second statement, about getting as close as possible to final form on the first shot, is understandable. The computer encourages such thinking because it looks like final form on the screen. But while it may look like final form, it is anything but final.

Typically, people who want to rush right to the final form aren't writing very well. Getting it done and getting it done right can be two very different things. These writers usually spend a lot of time editing as they write, often without realizing how much time goes into that editing. Had that time gone into planning, the draft would have gone more quickly and the final product would have been better.

Trick of the Trade
Over time you'll find yourself spending less time editing as the quality of your writing gradually improves. Trust me, it happens.

Budgeting Your Writing Time

I asked people in the hundreds of writing workshops I led to tell me how they allocated their writing time across the three steps.

I usually heard things like, "0 percent planning, 100 percent drafting, and 0 percent editing;" or "10 percent planning, 80 percent drafting, and 10 percent ed iting." A couple even said, "100 percent on planning and drafting and edit-ing—all at once."

Break It Into Thirds

I'm here to ask you to allocate about one-third of your writing time to each of the three steps. This means you should spend about *one-third on planning, one-third on drafting,* and *one-third on editing.*

For most people, this will mean more planning and more editing (separate from the drafting) and a lot less time writing the draft.

Even if you have only one hour to spend on a writing task, you should budget your writing time roughly into thirds. When I worked in big companies (and sometimes even now), I often had to get letters or press releases out quickly, sometimes in just an hour. In those cases I would spend about 20 minutes getting my information organized, usually as a list of points to cover. A point could be one word, several words, or a full sentence. Then I would review the points, maybe add a few or cross out a few, then number them and put them in order. My plan was complete.

Then I would spend about 15 or 20 minutes writing a fast draft. After I had a complete draft, I would spend the remaining time—20 to 25 minutes—editing the piece.

I found this much better then thrashing around for an hour, trying to get by without a plan or trying to draft and edit at the same time.

As Easy as One-Two-Three

Millions of writers have found the plan-draft-edit approach to be the single best tool for making writing easier and more enjoyable. And that includes me. These three steps free your mind to do what it does best at each phase.

Remember:

1. Step One: Plan (Decide What to Say)

2. Step Two: Draft (Say It)

3. Step Three: Edit (Improve the Way You Said It)

The Least You Need to Know

➤ Business writing is a skill you can learn, not an inborn talent.

➤ Writing consists of three separate tasks: planning, drafting, and editing.

➤ Perform these three steps separately, even if you do them all in one sitting.

➤ Budget your time on a given writing task as follows: one-third planning, one-third drafting, and one-third editing.

Chapter 5

Step One—Know Where You're Going and Who You're Taking with You

In This Chapter

➤ Defining your message

➤ Understanding your reader

➤ Getting started on the writing process

➤ Creating a useful plan quickly

Too many letters and memos use too many words to say too little. Common reasons for this include:

➤ Being unclear about the point of your letter or memo

➤ Trying to make too many points in one document

➤ Blurring your message because you think readers will find it unpleasant

➤ Wordy, unclear writing

I won't worry about that last point here; it's covered in Chapter 7. This chapter deals with the first three points, because a good plan should address them.

An Exercise in Pointlessness

For your memo to make a point, you have to have a point. Please read Sample 1, a memo from a subordinate to his boss, and decide what it is about.

To: Susan Larabee, Director of Marketing

From: Cliff Richards, Manager of Customer Service

Date: October 11, 1997

Re: Office Space

> This memo throws too much at the reader too quickly.

Given that we have added five new people to our staff in the last quarter, some issues have come up about office space. Gene Michaels, a grade 17, was hired in August and was put in a cubicle. During the interview process, he had asked for a windowed office because he needs light in the winter time. He says that he was told by Jeff Gleason in Human Resources that he could be considered for one. But his grade is too low for him to rate an office, certainly one with a window. I think this could be a problem.

At the request of Facilities Management we doubled up Maria, who also joined us in August, with Cynthia in Cynthia's office. Cynthia isn't too happy about this. Shouldn't Maria be in a cubicle? We would have to add one and since Facilities says you really can't add just one, we would have to add two. Maria is a grade 17 also.

Everett, who just joined us last week, is in the windowless office just to the right of the entrance to the department. He says there is a burning, electrical smell in there sometimes. Charlie in Facilities Management thinks it's Everett's imagination. In general, I don't think Facilities has been very responsive to our office space problems.

Also, there is our relationship with the sales force. They seem to think that Customer Service is their private staff instead of Customer Service. They have us doing a lot of work that their people should be doing.

Sample 1: A Poorly Organized Memo.

What's the Problem?

People write memos like this all the time. We can only wish the reader (and for that matter, the writer) luck. What's the purpose of this memo?

It is clearly not a recommendation. There are a couple of questions in the memo, but no clearly stated request. And if the purpose is to inform the reader (that's my guess), it should not be posing questions in the way that it does.

On top of this, the final paragraph has nothing to do with office space. This reflects the overall lack of focus in the memo.

Trick of the Trade

You may find it useful to think of your letter or memo as a product. A product is a reflection on the person or company that made it. A product also has requirements: It has to serve its purpose, it has to be of good quality, and it has to sell. In business writing, if the "customer" ignores the product, you have failed.

A memo like Cliff's tells the reader that the writer is confused, frustrated, and not on top of things. This is not exactly the image any of us wants to project.

This kind of memo is caused by poor planning, or no planning. The writer *seems* to have a point, but we don't know what it is. Unfocused memos like this just throw a lot of facts at the reader. Presumably, the reader is supposed to figure it all out.

It's your job as the writer to figure it all out—and then present it to the reader. Cliff's memo displays a common fault: He appears to be trying to figure it all out on paper, in the memo.

That doesn't make a good memo. Cliff needs to figure it all out and *then* present the result to Susan—as a request or recommendation or as information. The best response that Cliff can hope for with this memo is a call from Susan asking what the heck is going on in his department.

To Make a Point, You Must Have a Point

In his office-space memo, Cliff should have decided up front, before writing, what main point he wanted to make to Susan. His point could have been to make Susan aware of office space problems, or perhaps Cliff could have recommended a solution. That recommendation for action would be his point. Maybe he should be requesting a meeting between him, Susan, and someone in Facilities Management. If so, that should be his point.

Watch Out!
In general, don't use memos to make your problem your boss's problem—or anyone else's. Use your memos to request action or to recommend solutions.

Whatever his point is, he should not be blurring it either because he hates to deliver bad news or because he can't get organized. Rather, he should decide on his point, present it, and support it with an organized presentation of facts and opinion.

Sample 2 on the following page shows a better way Cliff could have presented this entire issue.

To: Susan Larabee, Director of Marketing

From: Cliff Richards, Manager of Customer Service

Date: October 11, 1997

Re: The Need for Additional Office Space

(This revised memo does a good job of "setting up" the writer's problem.)

Given that we have added five new people to our staff in the last quarter, we're now very short of office space. I am writing to recommend that you and I meet with Facilities Management to work out a solution, or at least to improve the situation.

Here are the key issues along with the approach I'd like to take on each one: *(Cliff makes good use of bullets.)*

➤ Gene Michaels was hired as a grade 17 in August. He was assigned to a cubicle, but wants a windowed office because he needs light in the winter. He says Jeff Gleason in HR told him when he interviewed with us that he could be considered for an office. Jeff did say this, but adds that he never promised Gene an office. I'd like to find a way to get Gene enough light without giving him an office.

➤ Maria joined us in August as a grade 17 and should be in a cubicle. Instead, we have her doubled up with Cynthia in Cynthia's office. I want to talk with Facilities about adding a cubicle for Maria.

➤ Finally, Everett, who just joined us last week, says there is an electrical, burning smell in his office. Charlie in Facilities think it's his imagination, but I smell it in there too. I'd like a more thorough investigation by Facilities.

I'm prepared to meet with Facilities alone on this, but I feel your backup would help me get these issues resolved faster. Please let me know if I can set up this meeting with Facilities and if you could attend it. Can we talk after you've reviewed this memo?

Sample 2: A Well-Organized Memo.

Except for the recommendation to meet with Facilities Management, the content is similar, but the approach is quite different.

➤ The second memo is organized and focused. It has a point, states that point, and supports that point. Also, notice there is no mention of the sales force issue, which doesn't belong in this memo.

➤ It considers the reader's needs. The reader wants to know what is being requested or recommended. That is now clear.

➤ The writer did some research up front (verifying what Jeff told Gene, finding that there is an odor in Everett's office) and mentions that to Susan. In planning you must anticipate the reader's questions ("Is there a smell in there or not?") and answer them.

The entire approach in this second memo is one of being on top of things. Cliff did some research, laid out the problems, presented solutions, and asked for help.

Reader Analysis

To write a memo like the second one, you have to consider the reader and her needs. You must meet the reader's needs in order to get yours met. After you have your point defined in your mind, ask yourself:

➤ Who is my reader?

➤ What does the reader know—and need to know—about the subject?

➤ What do I want the reader to do?

Consider the position of the reader. Do you report to the reader? Does the reader know you? Trust you? Is the reader basically interested in your point, or not? Will he be supportive of your potential solution, or not?

The answers to these question will help you know what to say in your memo.

How Can I Help the Reader?

If the reader knows you and cares about the subject and will be supportive of your point, you have a relatively straightforward task.

If you don't know the reader or she might not be supportive, you have work to do. You must establish your credibility on paper. You must show the reader what is in it for her, or how the greater good would be served. You must give the reader enough information to go on.

How to Establish Credibility

Here are two of highest compliments you will hear in business:

➤ "You really do your homework."

➤ "You're very organized."

When you hear these it means that you're on top of the situation, rather than the situation being on top of you. It means that others like the way you handle yourself on paper. Until you are a famous CEO, "doing your homework" and "being organized" represent the surest ways to establish your credibility.

Do Your Homework

"Doing your homework" means that you research a situation before you write about it. This may mean making some phone calls or meeting with people. It may mean a visit to a library or a search of articles in an online database. It may mean a research project—for example, a survey of suppliers, customers, or employees. Or it may simply mean reading some files to get yourself updated on "the story so far."

Unless you know all about the topic, research is the first step in planning. In fact, even if you do know all about the topic, having more information can raise your credibility. If you have research to back up what you say—if customers say it, if suppliers say it, if the *Wall Street Journal* says it—your credibility increases. And you have "done your homework."

Trick of the Trade

One of the best ways to gather information to support your point in a memo is to conduct some quick and dirty research. Four or five phone calls or e-mail messages to fellow employees, customers, or even suppliers will usually yield opinions, examples, or areas of concern that would be impossible for you to get any other way.

When you do quick and dirty research on the phone, write out the questions you will ask beforehand. Keep it to a brief explanation of why you're calling, plus three to five questions on the subject. Write down the answers in the respondent's words. A quote or two from another source often makes a memo memorable.

A word of caution: Make sure you have the authority to make these calls. For example, in many companies salespeople get very upset when their accounts are called without their knowing about it. If in doubt, get clearance to make these kinds of calls.

Getting Ideas and Getting Them Organized

After you've got your point, analyzed your reader, and done any necessary research, planning a letter or memo takes two final steps:

1. Generating ideas for your letter or memo

2. Organizing your ideas into an outline

Generating Ideas

As a business writer, you will often be writing in order to motivate others to follow your suggestions, implement your plans, and support your positions. This means that writing a memo often takes more than simply having a point, knowing your reader, and doing some research. It means that you may have to dig more deeply and, using your message and research as raw material, come up with a creative approach to the situation.

Today, it often takes true creativity to excel in business. Devising new strategies, solving old problems, and meeting competitive challenges require fresh thinking. Therefore, when your writing deals with strategic issues, thorny problems, or competitive challenges, you should take another step before the actual writing in order to generate ideas that reinforce your message and move the business forward. Those kinds of ideas are what you ideally want to present to the reader.

How do you get these kinds of ideas?

Although ideas can hit you any time—as you shower, on your commute, while you exercise—there is a technique for generating ideas. There is a way to prompt your mind to come up with ideas. The technique is called *brainstorming*, and it can be a very useful tool in business writing.

The Brainstorming Technique

Brainstorming is traditionally a group exercise for generating ideas, but you can get good results doing it alone. In a brainstorming session, a group—usually four to eight people—spends as little as ten minutes or as long as an hour coming up with as many ideas as they can on a topic. Typical examples of a topic for brainstorming include:

➤ How can we grow faster?

➤ What is the best way to introduce our new product?

➤ How can we attract better job applicants?

➤ How can we increase productivity?

Brainstorming works best if you limit the session to one topic and push as hard as you can on that topic. Almost any open-ended question—that is, one you cannot answer "yes" or "no" to—can work as a topic. Also, you don't have to use a question. For example, the topic could be "ways of addressing our office space problems."

There are only two rules in a brainstorming session:

1. Everyone should mention any idea that comes into his head.

2. No one is allowed to criticize another's idea.

Both of these rules help the creative, right side of your mind bypass the judgmental, left side of your brain. Being judgmental kills creativity. Brainstorming overcomes judgment, and also produces a lot of ideas because one idea will generate another idea the way one firecracker in a string sets off the next, and so on.

In brainstorming the goal is quantity of ideas, not quality. The more ideas you come up with, the more chance you have of coming up with some that are truly new and creative, or with a breakthrough idea.

What's That?
A *breakthrough idea* represents a totally new way of looking at a situation. It's a new solution or point of view.

Creating a Brainstorm

Although brainstorming began as a group exercise, I suggest you try it by yourself when you plan a letter or memo.

After you've defined your topic and have done any necessary research, ask yourself a question and write down as many ideas as you can. Do this as quickly as you can. The faster you go, the better your chances of bypassing that judgmental left brain.

Here's an exercise that will show you how this works.

Try It Now!

Pick a topic from your own work life. For example, you may have to write a memo or put a request in writing. Or you can chose a new topic such as "Why I should be promoted" or "Why I should receive a raise."

If you're not employed, your topic could be "Why I should be hired as a So-and-So at Such-and-Such Company."

If you have your own business, your topic could be "Why should new customers do business with me?" Once you have a topic, follow these instructions:

Allow yourself 10 to 15 minutes for this exercise, and

➤ Write your topic at the top of a page or computer screen.

➤ Jot down or type as many ideas as you can on the topic; also jot down those that seem unrelated.

➤ Use up the entire time, even if you feel you're running out of ideas.

You should use all 15 minutes, because in the first few minutes you'll tend to come up with standard ideas. Then, after you "hit a wall," you may get a burst of genuine creativity.

Again, don't judge any idea. Write them all down. Writing down any idea that you get signals your brain (both sides of it!) that you are open to ideas.

Question Yourself

Another way of generating ideas is to ask yourself a series of questions, then answer them. The "Five W's and an H" traditionally used by professional journalists is one ready-made set of questions you can use: *Who? What? When? Where? Why? How?* Always ask "How?" in a business situation: "How long will this take? How much money should we budget for this?"

You can also create your own questions. Try asking yourself the questions your reader might ask. For instance:

➤ Is this costing us money?

➤ Are customers or employees being affected?

➤ Are there legal issues involved?

➤ What's been tried to solve the problem?

➤ What outside resources can we tap?

Getting Organized

After you have your ideas, it's time to judge them and get them organized into an outline. Follow these steps:

1. See which ideas you can omit and which ones go together. If you have a lot of ideas, start with a fresh page for this step. If you have just a few ideas, you can group them by number or symbol. For example, put a "1" next to the ideas that go together, a "2" next to those for the next group, and so on; or use one asterisk, two asterisks, and so on.

2. Write headings for the groups of ideas that describe the sets of ideas. You don't have to use the headings, or all of the ideas, in the final memo, so if you're in doubt, leave the idea in. In this step you are creating the outline.

3. Look over the outline with an eye toward the sequence of the ideas. Are the common ideas grouped together? Do the thoughts flow logically? Can anything be eliminated? What effect will the sequence—the order in which you present the ideas—have on the reader?

Your outline should look something like the one on the following page.

Topic: How Do We Solve Our Office Space Problems?

Opening: Introduce topic

➤ Describe problem

➤ Mention how serious

First Problem:

➤ Describe problem

➤ Add to description

➤ Who is affected

➤ Costs and effects

Second Problem:

➤ Describe problem

➤ Add to description

➤ Who is affected

➤ Costs and effects

Third Problem:

➤ Describe problem

➤ Add to description

➤ Who is affected

➤ Costs and effects

Closing:

➤ Ask for action

➤ Mention follow-up

➤ Mention time frame

Sequencing: First the Good News, then the Bad News

Have you noticed that letters with bad news rarely begin with the bad news? For example, early-stage collection letters usually start out by noting that, "You have been a valued customer for years, and we want to continue that relationship."

Meanwhile, letters with good news—or at least what the sender wants you to think is good news—tend to let you know that right off. For example, "Congratulations, you have won a free test drive of the new Roadblaster Dream Machine!"

What's at work here?

Frankly, what's at work is management of the reader. Nobody likes bad news. So if the reader would see the point of your memo as bad news ("We will be doing away with casual Fridays from now on") you should sequence the message so that the bad news comes later. Build up to it and help the reader understand the situation in context, but don't blur the message or take forever to get to the point.

If you have good news ("We are on our way to record profits this year and every employee will share in this success") you should lead off with it. That way, you grab the reader's attention.

I'll explore sequencing more in Part 4 when I turn to specific types of letters and memos.

Plan Your Work and Work Your Plan

A builder needs a blueprint and a writer needs an outline. The steps in planning are:

1. Define the major point or message of your letter or memo.

2. Do any necessary research.

3. Analyze your audience.

4. Generate ideas with brainstorming or another technique.

5. Organize and sequence your ideas into an outline.

The Least You Need to Know

➤ You need a plan if you're going to write clear, focused letters and memos.

➤ To make a point, you have to *have* a point, so first decide what your major point will be.

➤ Analyze your readers: What is your relationship? What do they know about the topic? Will they resist your message?

➤ Brainstorming can help you get lots of ideas quickly.

➤ Questioning yourself can help you generate useful ideas, particularly if you take the reader's point of view.

➤ The sequence of the ideas in your memo will affect the reader. Remember, you want the reader to read and keep reading, and to take the recommended action.

Chapter 6

Step Two—Get Those Fingers Moving

In This Chapter

➤ How to make a draft out of your plan

➤ How to sound like yourself

➤ Putting the reader in the picture

➤ The secret to writing quickly

How do you use your outline? If you can't read a blueprint, you can't build a house. This chapter will look at how to use the plan you create in step one of the writing process.

This chapter is about what most of us think of as writing: putting our thoughts into sentences and paragraphs. If you have ever had trouble doing that, you'll notice a big difference when you follow a plan.

How Do I Follow a Plan?

Once you have a plan, you have answered some major questions:

➤ What's my point?

➤ Who is my reader?

➤ What am I going to write about?

➤ In what order am I going to write about it?

What's That?
A *topic sentence* is the first sentence of a paragraph. It tells the reader what the paragraph is about.

So...start writing!

That's right, start writing? But "How?" you ask.

Here's how: Take the first point on your outline and write that idea down in a sentence. That sentence is the topic sentence of your first paragraph. Develop the idea in that paragraph. Then move onto the next idea in the next paragraph.

One Idea Per Paragraph

For topic sentences to work, you must write about only one idea per paragraph. Think of the paragraph as the building block of the document.

Many writers create problems for themselves (and their readers) by trying to get one sentence, one paragraph, or one document to do too much. So they write long sentences that no one can understand. They write long paragraphs with too many different ideas. And they try to make three, four, or more big points in one memo. You're lucky if the reader can absorb one big point per memo.

The Topic of Topic Sentences

Sample 1 on the following page, a letter asking for a job interview, shows how topic sentences work.

Notice that the first and last paragraphs are only one sentence long. I put those in on purpose because I've met many people who believe that you can't write a one-sentence paragraph. You can. They are not at all improper, and they can be very effective.

Now let's look at the three middle paragraphs. Each of these paragraphs has only one topic, and that topic is stated in the topic sentence.

➤ The topic of the second paragraph is the reason for Lee's interest in working for Rincon.

➤ The topic of the third paragraph is Lee's sporting-goods sales experience.

➤ The topic of the fourth paragraph is Lee's interest in interviewing with Mr. Conway for a sales position.

Kevin Conway
President
Rincon Surfboards
999 Ocean Way
Redondo Beach, CA 09887

Strong topic sentences help you—
and the reader—to stay focused.

Dear Mr. Conway:

I am writing to tell you of my desire to work as a salesperson for Rincon Surfboards.

My interest in working with Rincon grew out of my experiences with your product. I am a three-time champion of the South Atlantic division of the International Surfriders Association. I rode a Rincon to each of those championships. I also won the Waimea Invitational in 1995 on a Rincon. I've tried other boards, but they don't ride like my Rincons (I own three of your boards).

More important, I offer a record of success in sporting-goods sales. As the enclosed resume shows you, I have successfully sold light boats and windsurfing gear to distributors throughout the South Atlantic region. Over the past three years, I have met or beat my sales targets in all but one month, and that was when Hurricane Icabod hit the Carolinas.

I'd like to set up a meeting soon to interview with you for a sales position. I'll be in Southern California for the first two weeks of next month and would like to meet with you during my visit. Knowing that you're busy, I won't waste your time. As a surfing enthusiast, a believer in Rincon boards, and a successful salesperson, I feel I have a lot to offer your company.

I will call you next week to see about arranging a meeting, and I thank you for your consideration.

Sincerely,

Lee Shaw

Lee Shaw

Sample 1: A Letter Asking for a Job Interview.

What's So Terrific About Topic Sentences?

Topic sentences keep you on track while you're writing and they keep readers on track while they're reading. They keep you on track because if you limit each paragraph to one topic, you know what to put in and what to leave out of that paragraph. The reader stays on track because the ideas are logically presented.

As you write each paragraph, write down a topic sentence, then write sentences that develop that topic. These sentences will usually build on the ideas in your plan, but it's also OK to add new ideas.

Building Paragraphs, Sentence by Sentence

Before you know it, you're writing. You may have heard the old joke, "How do you eat an elephant?" Answer: "One bite at a time." You write a letter or memo (or a book) one sentence at a time. (OK, actually it's one *word* at a time, but let's keep this manageable.)

How do you write all these sentences? I suggest that you write them the way you would say them: Write the way you would talk. This means that you shouldn't think about how it sounds but rather think about what you're saying. Just say it. On paper. Look at the point in your plan, and write about it the way you would talk about it.

Think of writing as talking on paper. This is especially important if you have trouble writing. In business writing the goal is to express your ideas clearly and concisely while sounding like yourself. You do it on the phone every day. There isn't one reason that you can't do it on paper—provided you think of writing as talking on paper.

Right now, I am not physically in the room with you and the ideas I'm expressing were put on paper months or years ago, but I am still talking to you. That is the mind set that I've developed as a professional writer. That is the mind set that you should develop. If you can talk, you can write great business letters and memos.

Keep Writing

Remember the rule: Don't edit as you draft. Editing as you draft will slow you down—maybe to a standstill. You don't want a case of writer's block, do you? Then keep writing.

What if, as you are writing, you think of a better way to say something? What if you think of a better word? Shouldn't you go back and make the change right then and there?

No! Just keep writing. And before you know it, you'll have a finished draft. Believe me, if the change is worth making—and, very often, it is—you'll remember what the change was when you go to edit the piece when it's finished.

A Few Words on Sentence Length

While you shouldn't worry about it at this point, I'll say a brief word here about sentence length. After all, the draft stage is when you have to write complete sentences.

Many memos lack clarity because the sentences are just too long. When a sentence is too long, it's tough for the writer to control and hard for the reader to understand. I'm not saying that all of your sentences should be short. You want variety and your reader does too, so aim for a mix of long and short sentences in most paragraphs.

Trick of the Trade

Here's a tip I've found useful: Use longer sentences to convey information and to set readers up with the background they'll need in order to understand your point. Use shorter sentences to make the point. For example:

"During the past three years, we've tried many ways of selling the Supremo Widget, including direct mail, telemarketing, in-person calls, trade shows, and independent distributors. Nothing has worked. We simply can't sell it."

"What could be clearer? The product is a loser."

How Long Is Too Long?

There are some general guidelines on sentence length. Your *average* sentence should be in the range of 15 to 20 words. Your *maximum* sentence length should be about 30 words.

Notice that I'm not saying that all of your sentences should be 15 to 20 words. The average for all the sentences in a given letter or memo should be in that range. Nor am I saying that you should never write a sentence longer than 30 words. But if you do, be careful. A sentence that long is hard for you and the reader to keep track of, and it will raise your average. Then you have to balance things out with shorter sentences.

By the way, the reader won't notice the length of your sentences if you handle sentence length well. If you don't handle it well, bad things happen.

What happens? Short sentences sound choppy. Choppy writing irritates readers. They see it. They hear it. They become aware of it. It draws their attention to the writing. Then they lose track of the ideas. You'd be irritated if I kept writing like this. Right? I'll stop. Honest.

On the other hand, long sentences tend to wear your readers out as they try in vain to follow your train of thought and the development of your ideas and the

49

content of your message way back from the beginning of the sentence, trying to see it through to the end without any kind of a break for them to catch their breath. If you put enough long sentences together, you will probably not irritate your readers, but you will put them to sleep, provided they keep reading, which most of them will not be able to do with their eyes closed.

Variety. That's what you want in sentence length.

What About Paragraph Length?

The basic rule for length—variety—is also true for paragraphs. Too many short ones create a choppy effect and make your memos look like pages of bulleted points. On the other hand, too many long paragraphs scare readers off with huge blocks of text. It looks like too much to read.

Paragraph Length Guidelines

In a typed letter or memo, you generally want paragraphs from a line or two long up to a maximum of about six lines or so. If you write a paragraph of more than six lines, you run two risks:

➤ The reader may get lost or bored with all that text.

➤ You may create a paragraph with more than one topic.

Notice that bullets, which you see used throughout this book, are a good way to make several points neatly. (I'll discuss them in Chapter 8.)

Remember, these are *guidelines*. I'm not saying that you should never write a paragraph longer than six typed lines. I'm saying that if you do, you should be very careful to keep the material under control.

Putting the Reader in the Picture

Readers of business letters and memos are always asking themselves, "What has this got to do with me? What, if anything, am I supposed to do because of this piece of paper?"

To engage the reader, put him or her in the picture. Essentially, there are two ways to do this:

1. Tell the reader what the material has to do with him or her.

2. Address the reader directly by using the words "you" and "your."

In Chapter 5, I discussed telling the reader what the material has to do with him. This means you have to tell the reader what you're requesting of him or recommending he do. If you are just conveying information, tell him that.

Focusing on the reader when you analyze your audience with questions like "What does my reader know?" helps you place the material in the reader's frame of reference.

Say "You"

Using the words "you," "I," "your," "mine," "we," and "ours" is also key in creating the personal style of writing preferred in business today. And the chief words here are "you" and "your."

Look back at Lee Shaw's letter requesting the surfboard sales job. She uses the word "you" right in the first sentence: "I am writing to tell you of my desire…" She goes on to say, "I'd like to set up a meeting soon to interview with you for a sales position…" and so on. Lee's closing sentence mentions "you" twice and "your" once.

People respond to this because it sounds to their inner ear as if you are talking to them. This is "writing the way you would talk." It's not a way of tricking the reader, but a way of placing the reader front-and-center. You are addressing the reader; why not address him or her directly?

The notion of being indirect or constantly using the "editorial we" is outmoded. There is nothing wrong with using this, but don't overuse it and don't be afraid to say "I," which is more personal and usually sounds more convincing. It is also somewhat outmoded to use the word "one"—as in "If one were to understand the situation, surely one would support me."

> **What's That?**
> The *editorial we* refers to use of the word "we" even when you are really one person doing the writing.

You'll find the "you approach" is used all the time in direct mail for one simple reason: It works.

"Well, Jim…"

Using the reader's name in the body of the letter is generally not a great idea. This is often done in direct mail (for example, "Like most writers, Mr. Gorman, you need to stay informed. That's why we're bringing you this special offer."). I'm not impressed with the personal touch of my name inserted by computer into direct-mail pieces. However, this must be working, because direct-mail houses regularly test copy strategies and drop the ones that don't pull in orders.

I feel that in a business letter or memo, direct use of the reader's name is not useful unless you know the person well and it is part of your style. ("Jim, I know your people are already going flat-out, but our growth depends on your help.") Otherwise, it can sound forced or phony.

The key is to think about the reader and "talk" to him or her. Tell that other human being, person to person, what's on your mind.

The Secret to Writing Quickly

Let's get back to the issue of writing quickly. This is about personal productivity, which is key to your success. Today, we don't have the luxury of taking hours and hours to turn out a "perfect" one- or two-page memo. You may have less than an hour.

Again, think about how you budget your writing time. Spend a good third of the time you have allotted for the writing task to come up with a plan. Get the plan squared away. Then do the draft—without editing it as you write it.

Doing the draft on the basis of the plan works not just because you have a plan to follow, but because doing the plan sets the material up in your mind as well as on paper. The act of planning signals your brain that a writing task is ahead, and your brain begins preparing for the task. So you are set up to write quickly.

In the end, the ability to write really fast comes down to experience. I can show you techniques, like planning and holding off on editing, but only you can supply the experience.

If you follow the three-step process in your business writing, you'll find that in several weeks you'll be writing faster. Your writing skills are like a set of muscles: The more you use them, the stronger they become.

The Least You Need to Know

➤ To follow your plan, take an idea from your outline and write it down as a topic sentence. Then develop the idea in a paragraph, describing that idea and building on it sentence by sentence.

➤ Keep each paragraph to one idea.

➤ In a draft, you can write sentences of any length. But get in the habit of keeping your average sentence length to about 15 to 20 words and your maximum to about 30 words.

➤ A paragraph can be as short as one line, even less. In a letter or memo, keep the longest paragraphs to about six lines of type.

➤ Use "you" to put the reader in the picture. This means using the words "you," "your," and "yours," as well as "I," "my," "we," and "ours."

➤ Get in the habit of "talking to the reader."

Chapter 7

Step Three—
Fast Fixes and
Quick Repairs

> ### In This Chapter
>
> ➤ What to do first
>
> ➤ How to identify problems in a letter or memo
>
> ➤ Fixing what needs fixing, quickly

Congratulations! You have a draft. But now what? What kind of shape is it in? Will it take forever to get the letter or memo into final form?

No, it won't. Not with the fast fixes you'll learn in this chapter.

Leave It Alone

The first thing that you should do to a letter or memo you've written is nothing. That's right, nothing. Leave it alone. Get some distance on it. Don't look at it or even think about it for a while.

How long "a while" is depends on the letter and its length and importance. It also depends on how you work and how long you have to get it out the door. If the memo is long and important, it would be good to give it more, rather than less, time to sit. For a short, routine letter or memo, you can get enough distance if you simply turn to another activity for a few minutes—make phone calls, visit a coworker, or go for a walk. Leaving a letter or memo, particularly a long one, alone overnight is best, because the next morning you can see it with really fresh eyes.

The amount of distance you need also depends on how quickly you can shift mental gears. However, unless you get some distance, you stand a good chance of missing the things you are supposed to see and fix.

Watch Out!

If you ever write a letter or memo while you are angry or frustrated, definitely get overnight distance on it. In fact, a couple of days' distance and a chat with someone about it may be in order. Many a career has been scuttled because someone put on paper and sent out what they should not even have said.

Once you've written and sent your letter, it's too late. On the printed page, cool reasoning from a set of facts will get you much further than anger or sarcasm. Also, be careful about what documents you leave lying around where others can see them.

Whether you have five minutes or several days, get distance before you edit. Otherwise, what you've written will tend to sound OK to you. Why wouldn't it? After all, it's the product of your own mind, and that's the mind you're going to use to do the editing.

So first, give your draft a rest.

Finding What Needs Fixing

As you edit a letter or memo, what should you be looking for? The major enemies to beware of are:

Trick of the Trade
The better your plan and the more carefully you follow it, the better your draft will be.

➤ Poor organization of the material

➤ Vagueness and lack of clarity

➤ Wordiness and gobbledygook

With these three things in mind, please take a look at Sample 1 on the following page.

To: Mary Camden, Chief Operating Officer

From: Stan Spencer, Vice President—Sales & Marketing

Date: October 15, 1997

Subject: Our Year-to-Date Sales

I feel that I must bring to your attention the fact that our level of sales for this year is falling well below our objective for the year. This memo will convey the dimensions of the problems and issues that we face and some recommendations for improving the situation.

Our employee turnover in the sales area has been out of whack. Out of six regional managers, two are new this year and two others have less than three years of experience with our company. This might be OK in the software business, but it is not in consumer-packaged goods. On top of that, we have three openings in the sales ranks that have gone unfilled for the better part of the year. These problems seem to all be due to the fact that we have had a new compensation package for salespeople since the start of the year. Since then we have had trouble keeping and attracting talented salespeople.

Then there is the productivity of the remaining sales staff. The new sales call reporting system, which is based on laptop computers, is not giving us the kind of performance we expected to get. A number of salespeople have said they want to stop using the system because they spend more time fooling with the computer and the call reporting system than they do making sales calls. This is bad for morale, to say the least.

This year we are not going to be able to meet our sales targets and the company may as well admit this now instead of later when we can't do anything at all. We also have to get our new salespeople up to speed and we may as well forget about the new call system unless we can improve the user-friendliness of the system. The compensation system is a mess and can only be fixed if we go back to something like the old system that we gave up due to the fact that the commissions got to be so high. At least people were selling then though. I'll keep you updated. Meanwhile, I thought these problems should be brought to your attention.

Sample 1: A Draft Requiring a Thorough Edit.

A memo like this makes the writer sound like he is not on top of things, because it runs on and on.

Now, there's nothing wrong with this if it's a draft. You can do what you want in a draft. But writing like this needs a thorough edit. Unfortunately, writing like this often goes out to readers without one.

He Used a Plan—What Happened?

Stan did use a plan that looked like this:

Paragraph 1. Tell Mary why I'm writing

Sales are below objectives

Make her aware of problems and recommendations

Paragraph 2. Turnover in sales department

Specifics about people

Cause: New compensation system

Paragraph 3. Sales call reporting system hurting productivity and morale

Salespeople don't like it

Paragraph 4. Recommendations

Get salespeople up to speed

Forget new call system unless…

Get back to old compensation system

Stan pretty much followed his plan, but now he has to edit this draft, first by looking for the three things I mentioned that usually need fixing:

➤ Poor organization of the material

➤ Vagueness and lack of clarity

➤ Wordiness and gobbledygook

Fixing Poor Organization

Overall, the memo is not too badly organized, since Stan had a plan. But it could be better. For example, the third paragraph opens with a topic sentence about productivity, when it is actually about the laptop-based call reporting system. It's true that productivity is a related issue, but Stan should mention the system in the topic sentence. ("The new laptop-based call reporting system has cut salesforce productivity.")

When you find poor organization of the material in your letter or memo, do three things:

Review your outline: Did you follow it? If you did, was the sequence correct? Don't go back and fix the outline and start over unless your memo is hopeless and you can see no other fix.

Check your topic sentences: Did you use topic sentences? Could they be improved? (That's Stan's problem in the third paragraph.)

Omit material unrelated to the message: Is each sentence in each paragraph related to the topic sentence? What can you omit without sacrificing clarity?

Fixing Vagueness and Lack of Clarity

Vagueness and lack of clarity often result from a poor choice of words, poor organization, or saying too little about the subject.

Stan's memo certainly includes vague language. For example, the slang phrase "out of whack" tells the reader little. "Out of whack" just means "bad." In this case "quite high" would be more precise.

You'll find more vague language in the last paragraph. Look at the phrase, "up to speed," another example of slang. Does Stan mean fully trained? Does he mean more productive? Does he mean selling enough to make budget?

We will discuss language and slang in Chapter 11. For now, know that precise Standard English words convey more meaning—and sound more professional—than slang. The term *Standard English* refers to the established, uniform, most widely accepted form of the language. This includes the accepted standards of spelling, punctuation, and word definition.

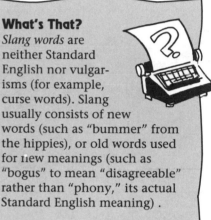

What's That?
Slang words are neither Standard English nor vulgarisms (for example, curse words). Slang usually consists of new words (such as "bummer" from the hippies), or old words used for new meanings (such as "bogus" to mean "disagreeable" rather than "phony," its actual Standard English meaning) .

Fixing Wordiness

Fixing wordiness, a process called *streamlining*, represents the essential skill in editing. Even well-organized writing in proper English will be unclear and tough to read if it is too wordy or riddled with gobbledygook.

The fastest way to streamline a draft is to shorten just about everything. Take long paragraphs and make them shorter or break them into two or even three paragraphs. Break long sentences into shorter ones; replace long words with shorter ones. Get rid of every word that you can without losing clarity or changing the meaning.

What's That?
Gobbledygook is stuffy, pretentious writing. This often results from the writer trying to sound formal or official.

Take a look at the simple job of streamlining I did on the following page. Compare the marked-up version of Stan Spencer's letter with the final version of these two paragraphs. The underscored text is new.

Streamlined version of Stan's memo (first two paragraphs):

> ~~I feel that I must bring to your attention the fact that our level of~~ <u>Our</u> sales for this year ~~is~~ <u>are</u> falling well below our objective ~~for the year~~. This memo <u>describes</u> ~~will convey to you~~ the ~~dimensions of the problems and~~ issues ~~that~~ we face and <u>includes</u> ~~some~~ recommendations for improving the situation.
>
> Our employee turnover in ~~the~~ sales ~~area~~ has been <u>quite high</u> ~~of whack~~ for most of this year. Out of six regional managers, two are new this year and two others have less than three years ~~of experience~~ with our company. ~~This might be OK in the software business, but it is not in consumer packaged goods. On top of that, we~~ <u>We also</u> have three openings ~~in the sales ranks~~ that have gone unfilled for <u>most</u> ~~the better part~~ of the year. ~~These problems seem to all be due to the fact that we have had a~~ <u>Our high turnover began when we started the</u> new compensation package for salespeople <u>at</u> ~~since~~ the start of the year. Since then we have had trouble keeping and attracting talented salespeople.

Final version of Stan's first two paragraphs:

> Our sales for this year are falling well below our objective. This memo describes the issues we face and includes recommendations for improving the situation.
>
> Our turnover in sales was quite high for most of this year. Out of six regional managers, two are new this year and two others have less than three years with our company. We also have three openings that have gone unfilled for most of the year, while another three people are new this year. Our high turnover began when we started the new compensation package for salespeople at the start of the year. Since then we have had trouble keeping and attracting talented salespeople.

Once you have addressed the major organizational problems, clarified any vagueness, and omitted wordiness, you can work on style, punctuation, and some fine points—all of which I'll cover in Part 3. There I'll also cover grammar issues in business writing, which get a chapter of their own. The next chapter will look at issues of format.

Put Your Writing on a Diet

Punctuation is covered in Chapter 9, and style in Chapter 11. In this chapter on editing, I'm focusing on getting rid of wordiness because it's the biggest problem in business writing.

Here are three additional techniques for cutting down on wordiness. These too fall under the general heading of streamlining:

➤ Cutting down bothersome phrases

➤ Eliminating redundancy

➤ Compressing modifying statements

Cut Down on Bothersome Phrases

A number of useless, old-fashioned, bothersome phrases have crept into business writing. Omit them or shorten them when they creep into yours:

Bothersome Phrase	Instead Try
due to the fact that	due to, because
a number of	several, some
each and every	each *or* every (but not both)
it has come to our attention	we've noticed (or omit)
it is important to note that	note that
in the event that	if
please feel free to	please
at this point in time	now

Eliminate Redundancy

Redundancy is meaningless repetition—for example, "We drew some round circles." Some redundancy comes from carelessness, some from bad verbal habits. Eliminate it whenever you see it. It's so obvious in the following examples that I don't even have to show you the fixes.

➤ Final conclusion

➤ Brief summary

➤ Present status

➤ Past history

➤ Plans for the future

➤ First and foremost

➤ Possible risks

➤ True facts

Compress Modifying Statements

Watch out for the words "that," "which," "who," and "when," because they rarely show up in a sentence alone. They usually trail several words behind them. Often you can compress them into a single word, a combination word, or a single modifier. Take a look at the following examples.

Before:

In snowy weather, employees who stay late should use the east door when they leave the building.

After:

In snowy weather, employees staying late should leave by the east door.

Before:

Accounts that are under $500, which amount to about 15% of all our accounts, are those on which we lose money.

After:

We lose money on accounts under $500—about 15% of our accounts.

Before:

Competitors who fight us for market share are those who will try hardest to underprice us.

After:

Competitors fighting us for market share will try hardest to underprice us.

Editing the Easy Way

Here are five steps to doing a quick edit on just about any letter or memo.

➤ *Check for organization.* There should be a beginning that mentions the purpose, a middle that logically presents the material, and an ending that provides a true closing (instead of just stopping, like certain foreign films).

➤ *Check for completeness.* Is information missing? If so, can you get hold of it? If you can't, can you get by without it?

➤ *Make long sentences shorter.* Get the average sentence length into the 15- to 20-word range. Limit sentences to 30 words. Include a variety of sentence lengths.

➤ *Make long paragraphs shorter.* Aim for a mix of paragraph lengths, with none longer than six typed lines or so.

➤ *Eliminate all unnecessary words.* Get rid of every word that you can without sacrificing clarity. Omit bothersome phrases and redundancy and compress modifying statements whenever you can.

If you do all of this, you'll have an acceptable final letter or memo. Of course, you want to go beyond acceptable and on to greatness. That's what the rest of this book is about.

The Least You Need to Know

➤ Even if you use a plan, you will need to edit your draft.

➤ The first step in editing is to get some distance on the piece. On long, complex letters and memos, and on anything you write when you are angry or frustrated, try to get overnight distance.

➤ Check for organization and completeness first. There is little sense in editing sentences and words if you still have to rearrange or add material.

➤ Wordiness is a major problem in business writing. Streamline your sentences by eliminating every word you can without changing the meaning or sacrificing clarity.

Chapter 8

What About Format?

Let's say you're sitting at your desk going through the stack of letters and memos in your in-box. You're scanning them, trying to decide what to read, what to get into, what to act upon. You notice that some of these documents turn you off just by their appearance. Just looking at them tells you that you don't want to read them. Others seem to get your attention and pull you in. You're reading them before you know it.

What's at work in these letters and memos? What is it that turns you off or draws you in even before you read a word?

Mostly it's the *format* of the document. That's the subject of this chapter.

Great First Impressions

Please take a look at Samples 1 and 2 on the following pages. Don't read them. Just look at them and see how you react upon first seeing them.

Letter #1

To: Jayne Campbell, Director of Human Resources

From: Scotty Weston, President, Acme Office Equipment

Date: November 12, 1997

Re: Communication Issues

We have to improve the quality of the communications in this company. I would like you to take the lead in this effort in your role as head of Human Resources. Customers regularly complain that they cannot understand the documentation we send out with our products and then that when they call for support, they cannot understand the explanation we give them over the phone. On more than one occasion I have heard complaints that our people seem confused themselves about our products.

Internally, at a recent round of informal breakfasts with employees, the issue of clear communication came up repeatedly. People said that they are not clear about our corporate strategy, about our position in the market, or even about who they report to at times.

We need to take a long look at our needs in this area and then do something. I suggest that we first systematically assess our needs, which might mean taking a survey, and then address those needs, which might mean training. There may also be some simple measures that we can take right away to improve things, such as making sure that the customer support people have been oriented to the products and that they have product samples in front of them as they take calls from customers.

Please give this some thought and present a plan for management's review and approval by the end of the year. While funds are tight as usual, I assure you that we can free up money to address this problem, and that you will have my complete support in correcting this situation.

Sample 1: A Poor Format.

Letter #2

To: Jayne Campbell, Director of Human Resources

From: Scotty Weston, President, Acme Office Equipment

Date: November 12, 1997

Re: **Request for a Plan on Communication Problems**

We have to improve the quality of the communications in this company. I would like you to take the lead in this effort in your role as head of Human Resources.

Background: Who Is Affected?

Both our customers and employees are being affected.

Customers:

Customers *regularly* complain that they cannot understand the documentation we send out with our products. Then, when they call for support, they cannot understand the explanation we give them over the phone. I've heard several complaints that our people seem confused about our products.

Employees:

At a recent round of informal employee breakfasts, the issue of clear communication came up *repeatedly*. People said that they are not clear about our corporate strategy, about our position in the market, or even about who they report to at times.

Potential Solutions: Assessment and Training

We need to take a long look at our needs in this area and then do something. I suggest that we:

> ➤ First assess our needs, which might mean taking a survey.

> ➤ Address those needs, which might mean training.

There may also be some simple measures that we can take right away to improve things. For example, we could make sure that the customer support people have been oriented to the products and have product samples in front of them as they take calls from customers.

Action Requested and Time Frame

Please give this some thought and present a plan for management's review and approval by the end of the year.

Statement of Support

While funds are tight as usual, I assure you that we can free up money to address this problem. Also, you will have my complete support in correcting this situation.

Sample 2: A Good Format.

Which one would you rather read?

Most people would rather read Sample 2. Although I did break up a few sentences that were too long, the main difference between the two memos is in format.

Formatting Tools that Work

What formatting tools have been applied in the second memo? There are several:

➤ *A longer, more specific subject line in boldface type.* That kind of subject line grabs the reader's attention more than the blandly worded one in regular (nonbold) type in the first version.

➤ *A short first paragraph that states the purpose of the memo.* Remember, readers want to know quickly what the memo means to them.

➤ *Headlines in boldface type.* Notice that these headlines are descriptive. Instead of just saying "Background," the heading poses a question. Questions, either as headlines or in the text, tend to engage the reader. (What do you think?)

➤ *Subheads in regular type, underlined.* Subheads are not really necessary in a memo this short, but I wanted you to see how they work. They break up text further and add white space.

➤ *Bullets.* Bullets also break up the text and highlight important material.

➤ *White space.* White space invites the reader into the memo because the document looks as if it will be easier to read—and it will be.

➤ *Italics.* The words "regularly" and "repeatedly" are in italics for emphasis. Scotty wants to get across the seriousness of the problem.

Trick of the Trade

As a rule, stick with 12-point type as your usual font size: It's the generally accepted standard. It's also easy for people to read. (The term "font" refers both to a style of type and a size of type.) Eleven-point type is acceptable at times, but it's harder for many people to read. If your company uses 11-point, use it internally but use 12-point for external communications.

Ten-point type is too small for most people to read comfortably. It also puts far too many words on the page. Anything larger than 12-point looks too large and uses too much space.

Blocks of text turn readers off. It just looks like too much to read. A memo that looks like it's going to take a lot of work to read will lose the battle for reader attention. In contrast, one that looks airy and open, with short sentences, short paragraphs, headlines, bullets, and white space, will probably get immediate attention.

Remember, though: Don't go overboard! Sample 2 is about as far as you should go with format on a memo. Even this level would be a bit too much for a letter.

How Long Is Too Long?

Most people would rather read short memos than long ones. Knowing this, many writers try to keep their letters and memos to one page. For years, several large U.S. companies told employees, "If you can't put it on one page, you don't understand it." (The opposite, unfortunately, is not necessarily true.) This often led to writers using narrow margins, long paragraphs, and small type so they could fit more onto the one page. This, of course, creates the dense, block-of-text look that turns readers off.

You are much better going to two pages and presenting a more inviting, easier-to-read document.

Most business letters and memos should not go beyond two pages. There is no absolute ban on three- or four-page letters or memos, but they should be the exception. Relatively few issues in business demand such a long treatment. Much longer than that and you are really writing a report, which is outside the scope of this book (although the three-step process and many other principles in this book also work well for reports).

If you find yourself always writing three- and four-page letters and memos (or getting a reputation around your organization for writing them), put your writing on a diet. Either you're getting into overkill—writing beyond what you should to cover the issue—or you're in the habit of covering too many issues in one document.

Try to limit a letter or memo to one issue. Covering too many issues in one memo can confuse readers or make you sound unfocused or as if you're complaining. While one issue may have a number of areas, it's best to decide which area is the most important and focus on that. If you have several closely related issues, decide what the overall issue is and address that.

Watch Out!
Don't go wild with format. If you have good word processing software, you may be tempted to use all the fonts and effects—such as italics, underscoring, double underscoring, boldface, and boxes—all at once. Please don't.

Use these effects sparingly. Format and effects should never draw attention to themselves.

What's That?
A *report* is usually a summary, or the summary plus the details, of an investigation, analysis, survey, or other research. The style and the approach to the material is more formal and less personal than that of a letter or memo.

A report can run from three to five pages up to several volumes of more than 100 pages, or any length in between.

How to Shorten Long Memos

After you've done your editing, if your memo is too long (more than three or four pages), you can do one of three things:

➤ Write a short report instead.

➤ Write a separate memo (or two) for the secondary issues.

➤ Use attachments to move material out of the memo itself.

Of these strategies, the first two are self-explanatory, but let's look at ways of using attachments.

Using Attachments

Suppose your memo has financial or technical details that take several paragraphs or a couple of pages to explain. Or you may have background information, such as a page of quotes from survey respondents or the summary of a study or other research. If you included this information, you would have a four- or five-page memo.

In these cases, the best thing is to add an attachment to your letter or memo and simply refer the reader to it. For example, let's say that you have detailed sales projections for the next three years for several sales regions, plus some footnotes, and you don't want all this in the memo. Just add attachments. That's what's been done in the example on the following page.

Then, in the body of the memo, direct the reader to the attachments with a sentence such as, "Please see Attachments A, B, and C for detailed sales projections."

You can also use attachments for text material. Suppose you have a lot of technical details on some equipment you are requesting for your department. You can add an attachment with the title, "Equipment Specifications" or "Technical Note on Equipment Requirements" and put those details there.

An attachment is a great way to show that you have done your homework thoroughly. Those who want or need to study the details can do so; those who do not can ignore them. But everyone will see that you did your homework.

Trick of the Trade

One way to make detailed information available to readers is not to include it in the memo but to add a sentence such as, "If you would like the complete details of this analysis, please call me and I'll send them to you." Readers who want the details can get them; others won't be burdened with the paper. (This also saves wear and tear on your copier!)

Attachment "A"

Sales Projections by District, Eastern Region

(in millions of U.S. dollars, 1998–2000)

	1998	1999	2000
New England *	5.4	6.4	7.8
Mid-Atlantic * *	9.8	11.8	13.0
South Atlantic * * *	7.8	8.2	8.8
TOTAL	23.0	26.4	29.6

ME, VT, NH, MA, RI, CT
* NY, NJ, PA, OH, MD, DE, DC
* * VA, WV, NC, SC, FL, GA, AL, TN, KY

An Attachment to a Memo.

Other Formatting Tools

So far we've covered the basic formatting tools—boldface and italic type, underlining, bullets, and white space. We haven't talked about clip art or the more exotic fonts. My advice is to use these rarely except in your letterhead, as discussed in Chapter 3. In a business context, it's best to stay away from anything "cute," and that includes clip art and fancy type in the body of your document.

Trick of the Trade

The most popular fonts for business letters and memos are Times New Roman and Courier, and for faxes, Arial. Stick with these fonts and you'll be fine.

Charts

In practice, charts are seldom used in the body of a letter or memo, but inserting one or even two can occasionally be useful if they summarize data that supports your point dramatically. Be sure that any chart you present is accurate and properly labeled.

Charts can quickly present a visual story that you would need many words to tell if you were trying to describe the relationship among the numbers in a table. Types of charts include bar charts, pie charts, and line charts.

What's That?

A *chart* or *graph* pictures the relationship between two or more sets of data; for example, sales and time periods, interest rates and loan volume, or prices and profits.

Charts are most commonly used as attachments to memos and reports. If you write reports, you should learn a bit about how to create charts. The most popular spreadsheet programs, Microsoft Excel and Lotus 1-2-3, allow you to create charts in black and white or color from data you insert into the tables in the spreadsheet. Then you simply "cut and paste" the chart into your document in the word processing program.

What's That?
A spreadsheet program consists of columns and rows that form "cells" into which you can place data or text.

It can be quite effective to include a small chart in a memo. Just be sure that it dramatically supports your point. Otherwise, it will look as if you are showing off. The following example shows a properly labeled bar chart.

Quarterly Sales by District
(1997, in millions of U.S. dollars)

Bar Chart.

Boxes and Callouts

Boxes call attention to information. With good word-processing software, you can readily place a box around material to set it off or highlight it. Direct mail pieces or sales letters offer an opportunity to use boxes because you are trying desperately to get and hold attention and to highlight a real "grabber." A *callout* is a bit of text, either boxed or not, that points out or explains a point in the text itself. For example:

> Call Us Now!
>
> If you call our toll-free number (1-800-555-1234) to order your sample within 48 hours, we will include a voucher for a *20% discount* off your first purchase. Please act now!

In fact, the book you have in your hands shows you (I hope) how effective boxes can be when you have to present lots of information of different types.

Form the Good Format Habit

If you think that letters and memos are just words on paper, please realize that those words add up to a visual experience for the reader. That visual experience can be either pleasant or unpleasant, and if it's unpleasant, you will lose readers.

I'll examine many specific formats for letters and memos in Part 4. In this chapter, I've given you basic tools and general guidelines that you can apply to a variety of documents to grab reader attention and support your points.

The Least You Need to Know

➤ Large blocks of text turn readers off. Use formatting tools to create open and airy documents.

➤ The major formatting tools include a specific subject line in boldface type, a short first paragraph stating the memo's purpose, descriptive headlines and subheads, bulleted points, white space, underscoring, and italics.

➤ Unless you decide to write a report instead, you can shorten long memos by dividing them into separate memos, using attachments, or both.

➤ Use formatting tools to support your point and to make things easy for your reader, not just because they are available.

➤ Use these tools sparingly and tastefully or they will draw attention to themselves and lose their effect.

Chapter 9

Where the %&@# Do the Commas Go?

In This Chapter

➤ A quick, straightforward guide to proper punctuation

➤ How to use—and not use—punctuation to make your point

➤ Going beyond the comma and the period to enliven your writing

---

Do you really have to think about all those commas, colons, dots, and dashes?

Fortunately, no. You just have to know a few simple guidelines regarding the major forms of punctuation. If you can handle that (and I *know* you can) you can then go on to use punctuation to boost the power of your message.

What's It All About?

Think of punctuation marks as a set of signs and signals, the kind you see when you're walking or driving down a city street. Punctuation tells you when to pause, when to stop, what's ahead, and where you've been. Picture the chaos on the city streets if there were no signs or signals.

Can you imagine what trying to read would be like if there were no punctuation?

Punctuation helps you as a writer to control the relationships among all those words you're writing. That means it also helps the reader understand what you're saying. Punctuation is essential to clear writing.

What Will People Think?

Consider this: In most organizations, many people know proper punctuation. If you don't, you look bad. If, on the other hand, you know proper punctuation, you and your letters and memos look great.

Incidentally, you don't have to think much about punctuation while you're writing your draft (and not at all while you're planning). In fact, if you find yourself thinking about it while you're writing the draft, try to stop thinking about it during that step.

Now let's take a quick tour of the major punctuation marks and see how to use them. For each type of punctuation, I'll give you a brief comment and then a few guidelines and examples. (I won't bother you with periods and question marks, which you already know about.)

Comma, Comma, Comma

The comma tells the reader to pause. As a writer, you should think of the comma as a tool for joining and separating words within sentences.

1. Use a comma to link two separate ideas that go together.

   Mark is probably the best manager we have, and that's saying a lot.

   Our sales are rising quickly, which means that our profits will soon rise too.

   We installed a new computer, but we haven't seen a productivity increase yet.

2. Use commas to separate extra information from essential information.

   Our company, which was founded in 1901, will soon celebrate its centennial anniversary.

   John McCormick, the president of our company, has hired a team of consultants.

3. Use commas to separate the items in a series.

   Marie, Jacques, Steve, and Diane joined us recently from our Canadian subsidiary.

   Increasing our sales, lowering our costs, or shrinking our business represent our only options.

4. Use a comma (or two) to separate an introductory or qualifying word from the rest of a sentence.

   Ideally, we should see rising exports in the next several years.

   The main issue, however, is how to increase investment in our region.

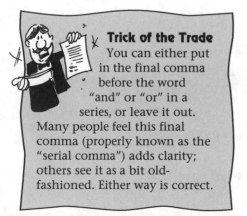

Trick of the Trade
You can either put in the final comma before the word "and" or "or" in a series, or leave it out. Many people feel this final comma (properly known as the "serial comma") adds clarity; others see it as a bit old-fashioned. Either way is correct.

With commas, don't go crazy trying to remember rules. Instead, get a feel for where the commas go by reading your sentences aloud. Then put a comma where you would pause.

You can learn to do a lot of punctuation, not just commas, by ear. Your sense of how your writing sounds tells you a lot, if you let it. The best way to get the rhythm of your writing is by reading it aloud to yourself.

Colons: When Should You Use Them?

The colon indicates a longer pause. It says to the reader, "and here it is" or "here they come."

1. Use a colon before a list.

   We need the following items at the presentation: a projector, a stand, a screen, and a pointer.

2. Use a colon to introduce a major point or conclusion.

   The bottom line is this: We won the battle for market share.

   Only one person could possibly close this deal: Harry Jenkins.

   If the item following the colon is a complete sentence, capitalize the first letter; otherwise, leave it lowercase.

Don't Fear the Semicolon; Instead, Learn to Use It

The semicolon mystifies business writers more than any other form of punctuation; therefore, most try to avoid using it. It's really quite simple.

1. Use a semicolon instead of a conjunction, such as "and" or "or," to link two equally important ideas.

   The company will buy more equipment next year; the new machinery will double our capacity.

   Asian management practices often find their way to North America; North American marketing ideas move quickly to Asia.

2. Use a semicolon before "however," "therefore," "moreover," "in addition," and other transition words and phrases that link two sentences.

   We need to raise prices; however, that is sure to lower our sales.

   Many of our workers want early retirement; given this, the layoff will be fairly painless.

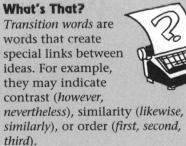

What's That?
Transition words are words that create special links between ideas. For example, they may indicate contrast (*however, nevertheless*), similarity (*likewise, similarly*), or order (*first, second, third*).

The Apostrophe's Uses

Many business writers are needlessly confused by the apostrophe. It's a relatively straightforward form of punctuation.

1. Use the apostrophe in contractions to indicate missing letters.

   I'll get back to you with an answer soon. (I'll = I will)

   The new copier can't handle the volume we were told it would. (can't = cannot)

   Using contractions in business letters and memos is now widely accepted. It adds a personal touch, because it sounds as if you're talking directly to the reader.

Watch Out!

Writers often confuse different words that sound alike. Two common pairs are *its* and *it's* and *your* and *you're*.

"*Its*" is the possessive form of "*it*," as in, "*This company has lost its bearings.*"

"*It's*" is the contraction for "*it is,*" as in, "*It's sure to rain this Saturday.*"

"*Your*" is the possessive form of "*you,*" as in, "*Mark your answers clearly.*"

"*You're*" is the contraction for "*you are,*" as in, "*You're sure to be satisfied with our service.*"

Be very careful with these kinds of words when you're editing.

2. Use the apostrophe to indicate possession.

   Mary's analytical skills have improved during the review period.

   The software's warranty will remain in effect.

Watch Out!

Forming possessives for words that are plural or end in "s" can be tricky.

Correct:

My boss's office was professionally decorated.

Our bosses' offices were professionally decorated.

Incorrect:

My bosses office was professionally decorated.

Our bosses's offices were professionally decorated.

I Say, "Learn How to Use Quotation Marks."

Quotation marks serve three basic functions in business letters and memos.

1. Use quotation marks to indicate something said or written by someone else.

   One survey respondent said, "You guys are miles ahead of the pack."

   According to the New York Times, *personal-computer sales "will rise dramatically next year," and that's our forecast too.*

2. Use quotation marks to clarify a word or term that should stand apart.

   When you click on "Help," a menu will drop down.

   Please send a sample to everyone who chose "Very Interested" in response to question four.

3. Use quotation marks to indicate irony or humor.

   The government's "tax breaks" never put money in our pockets.

   Some employee "socializing" breaks up marriages.

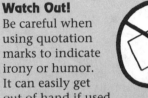

Watch Out!
Be careful when using quotation marks to indicate irony or humor. It can easily get out of hand if used too often. Also, use discretion and common sense. For example, don't refer to your Chief Executive Officer as "Chief Executive Officer."

The Hyphen Is a First-Rate Helper

The hyphen adds clarity by helping readers know what words go together.

1. Use a hyphen to tell readers what words go together, if there is any ambiguity.

   A strong marketing effort must be our first-line defense.

   Fat-burning snacks are selling very well.

2. Use a hyphen in certain combination words when they are modifiers and not when they are nouns or verbs.

   We expect strong fourth-quarter sales. (modifier)

   We expect sales in the fourth quarter to remain strong. (noun)

   Follow-up steps will include more meetings and more memos. (modifier)

   I will follow up with all participants in this project. (verb)

3. Use a hyphen when you break a word at the end of a line of type.

   We've lost customers whenever we've lost sight of the fundamentals in our business.

What's That?
A *noun* is a person, place, or thing. A *modifier* tells us about the person, place, or thing: a tall man (what kind of person), an expensive restaurant (what kind of place), a broken-down car (what kind of thing).

Dashes—How Dashing!

The dash is underused in business letters and memos. While overusing it would be worse, the dash—if used properly—can boost the power of your message. Don't use the dash (—) and the hyphen (-) interchangeably. The dash is longer and is used differently from the hyphen.

1. Use a dash instead of a colon (but not before a list) when you want to emphasize a point.

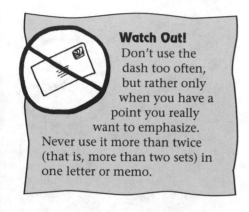

Watch Out!
Don't use the dash too often, but rather only when you have a point you really want to emphasize. Never use it more than twice (that is, more than two sets) in one letter or memo.

Those who opposed our new strategy were correct—we lost business.

We now know what we should have known all along—our price increase won't stick.

2. Use two dashes to set off a point that you want to emphasize within a sentence.

To fight the toughest of government agencies—the IRS—was lunacy.

Homebuyers who want low interest rates—and who doesn't?—will love our new plan.

Parentheses Work Together (and Travel in Pairs)

In my experience, writers either don't use parentheses at all or they use them too often. This punctuation has its uses but shouldn't be overused. If you over-use parentheses, your readers will think you're always qualifying what you say or constantly adding little asides.

Watch Out!
Put the period or other punctuation that goes at the end of a sentence outside the final parenthesis, as in the first example shown in 2, unless the entire sentence is in parentheses, as in the second example.

1. Use parentheses to set off extra material that you want to gently emphasize.

Experienced people (and Karen is one of them) know that you need a plan before you act.

2. Use parentheses to set off directions to the reader.

Our budget calls for a 12% reduction in paper costs (see Attachment "C").

This memo summarizes our strategy for next year. (If you want complete details, please call me at extension 947.)

Wow! The Exclamation Mark

I believe that the exclamation mark (also known as exclamation point) should rarely, if ever, be used in a business letter or memo. Unless handled properly, it seems cute or juvenile or like something out of a gushy article in the company newspaper.

1. Avoid the exclamation mark in most letters and memos. It's better to find the right word or words to create the excitement you're trying to convey with the exclamation mark.

   Instead of: *Our sales have increased by 45% in the past year!*

   Try: *Our sales have bounced up a dramatic 45% this year.*

2. Use the exclamation mark only in special situations. Two situations in which I'd use the exclamation mark would be in memos for certain announcements and in sales letters, and then mainly because readers expect it.

   The holidays are here! That means it's time for our Toys-for-Tots drive.

   You can cut your employee benefits costs by up to 30%!

That's About It (Period)?

Aside from periods and question marks, these nine punctuation marks—commas, colons, semicolons, apostrophes, quotation marks, hyphens, dashes, parentheses, and exclamation marks—are the ones you'll use in business letters and memos.

I strongly suggest that when you edit a letter or memo, you do three passes through it. The first pass should be for meaning and clarity, the second for grammar and usage, and the third for punctuation. It's very difficult to do it all in one pass, even on a one-pager.

Follow these guidelines and you'll stay out of trouble. But keep in mind that these are basic guidelines. For a deeper examination of the rules of punctuation, consult a good grammar or writing style book such as the *Chicago Manual of Style.*

The Least You Need to Know

➤ Punctuation shouldn't be a problem. A few guidelines tell you all you need to know to write great business letters and memos.

➤ As with format, your reader and your message should guide you in punctuation. Don't use punctuation to get cute or to show off. (I do some of that in this book—but this is a book. Use the sample letters and memos in this book as models, not the text!)

➤ Get used to the colon and semicolon; they can help you link ideas without using another word.

➤ Don't overuse any form of punctuation, even commas. Be especially careful not to overuse dashes and parentheses, and use the exclamation mark rarely.

➤ You can quickly get to a point where you can do most punctuation by ear. Train your ear by reading your letters and memos aloud to yourself for a while.

Chapter 10

When They're Looking Over Your Shoulder

In This Chapter

➤ The special challenges in writing for others

➤ How to get it right the first time

➤ How to edit the work of others

If you work for an organization of any size, sooner or later you may find your-self having to write for others. In some cases this will mean writing for one person; for example, your boss may ask you to write a letter to a client for her signature. In other cases it may mean writing for an entire committee; for example, you may have to write a memo summarizing a team project.

These writing situations can be tricky. If you don't have an approach to them, you can spin your wheels through several drafts and still not satisfy anyone. In this chapter you'll learn an approach that works.

Situations When You Write for Others

Management is the art of getting things done through others. Writing happens to be one of the things that others may need to get done through you. Here are some typical examples:

➤ Your boss receives a customer complaint and asks you to write a reply.

➤ Your boss asks you to write a letter confirming your company's attendance at a conference.

➤ Your boss asks you to write a letter declining to make a donation to a charity.

➤ You are on a committee investigating safety issues at your company and must write a letter to various managers requesting their cooperation.

➤ Your company needs a good sales letter to open doors to new clients.

➤ You are asked to rewrite your credit department's collection letters.

Your boss has a right to ask you to write for his or her signature. This happens all the time in business. It's an accepted fact of organizational life. And while many people will try to shirk the writing involved in being on a committee or team, somebody winds up doing it, and you're somebody. In fact, the better a writer you become, the more you'll find yourself writing for others.

In any of these situations, there are more people involved than you and your readers.

Writing for Bosses

Whenever you write for the signature of another, that person has the right to make changes so that the writing will sound the way he or she wants it to sound. Don't be too surprised to find your boss editing your writing, changing your meaning, or even criticizing your work.

You may well ask, "If they want to change it, why don't they just write it themselves?"

Good question. But often they don't. Some bosses lack confidence in their writing. Some write poorly and know it. Many feel that having someone do a draft for them to react to and "fix" is faster than writing their own.

Two things can help:

➤ Realize that doing it "their way" is just part of the process. Don't take it personally. The fact is, editorial comments improve most letters and memos.

➤ Do all you can to understand "their way" sooner, rather than later, at several points in the writing process. That's what this chapter is about.

Writing for a Committee

You may have heard the expression, "A camel is a horse put together by a committee." This often applies to documents that come out of committees. The more people you must satisfy (other than your readers), the harder it gets. So again, you need to do two things:

➤ Realize that you're representing the views of others in this memo, not just your own. This is different from presenting only your view.

➤ Do all you can to learn what others' views are earlier, rather than later, in the process. Again, this chapter will show you how to do this.

Specific Problems in Writing for Others

Here are the major complaints I've heard from people who must write for others:

➤ "I'm working in the dark because she doesn't know what she wants until she sees it."

➤ "If they 'fix' it one more time, it'll be broken forever."

➤ "It sits on his desk for a week before he gets back to me."

➤ "Their edits and comments contradict one another."

➤ "I really don't know who I'm writing for."

Most of these problems can be addressed in the following six-step process.

Six Steps to Writing It Right for Others

Whether you are writing for one person's signature or for a committee of 20, use these six steps to manage the process:

1. Understand the goal and the message.
2. Analyze the audience.
3. Get ideas—and agreement—on paper.
4. Write alone.
5. Get and enter all edits.
6. Get final sign-off.

Here's how you can make these steps work for you.

Understand the Goal and the Message

Whenever someone says to you, "Could you write a letter for my signature on that?" or "Would you please write that up in a memo for us?" be sure you know what "that" is.

Ask two questions:

➤ "What goal are we trying to accomplish with this letter or memo?"

➤ "What do you think is the best approach?" ("What's the best way to say it?")

In asking about the goal, you may find that a letter or memo isn't even necessary. A phone call, e-mail, or a meeting might work better. For example, if the goal is to get input on an issue from several people, the telephone or e-mail might be faster.

If you understand the goal, you'll be able to craft a better message. But be sure to get specific ideas on the message—that is, on how best to say it to achieve the goal—from whoever is asking you to write. Ask questions like:

"What approach would you like us to take in this letter?"

"What do you think the overall tone should be?"

"How do you think this memo should present this?"

"How long do you think the memo should be?"

Questions like these, and any others specific to your situation, will help you understand what direction to take with the message.

Analyze the Audience

As always, the more you know about the reader, the better. At times you can find yourself writing for readers you know very little about. This may be because the person asking you to do the writing knows very little about the reader. (Could that be why they're asking you to do the writing? Hmmm.) Or it may be because the reader is somehow "off limits" to you.

Trick of the Trade
Sometimes you may have to press a bit to get the information you need. If the person asking you to write is not forthcoming, say something like, "Would it be useful for me to talk with someone else (such as the reader)?" or "Charlie, I'm not terribly comfortable writing without knowing a bit more. What background can you give me on this?"

In either case, get as much information as you can about the reader or readers. Take the questions you would ask yourself about your reader if you were writing for yourself and ask them of the person you are writing for:

"Who will the reader be?"

"What does the reader know—and need to know—about the subject?"

"What do we want the reader to do?"

"Does the reader know and trust us?"

"Is the reader likely to be interested and supportive, or not?"

"How can we help the reader?"

As is the case when you are writing for your own signature, the answers to these questions will help you know what to say.

Get Ideas—and Agreement—on Paper

The single biggest mistake that people make when writing for others is to write too much before getting comment. The worst version of this mistake is to go and write the entire memo and then hand it in for comment. Only do this if the memo is very short and you have done a lot of writing for the person who must sign it. Never write an entire piece for a committee.

What should you do instead?

Do an outline and show them that. Telling them verbally about the approach you are going to take and the points you will cover is not enough. They can easily say "yes" and then later look at what you wrote and say, "This isn't what we talked about."

Most people will give more thought to something that you hand them in writing. So start with a quick outline of the points you'll cover, and give it to them for feedback. Don't ask if it "looks good"—it's too easy for them to just say "yes." Instead ask, "What do you think should be added?" or "How could this be improved?" By doing this, you'll get them to focus.

When you're working with a committee or team, circulating an outline before you write the actual piece is essential. Attach a note as in the following example.

To: Distribution

From: John Henry

Re: Memo to Summarize Group Project

Please examine the attached outline for the memo I'll be writing on our recently completed project. This outline shows the points the memo will cover and the order in which it will cover them.

If you have any comments, including items you would like to add or omit or suggestions on the sequence, please let me know as soon as possible or by Friday the 22nd at the latest. If I don't hear from you by then, I'll assume that you approve of this approach.

Thanks in advance for your help on this.

This note is cordial, but it puts the responsibility on each team member to examine the outline and get back to you. This usually saves you from having to chase them for their input. (Even with this approach, you might have to chase certain people.)

You may find that some of the comments that you receive on the outline are in conflict. Try to resolve them in the outline—for example, by including both conflicting points but emphasizing one of them—or get on the phone, perhaps on a three-way call, and resolve the conflict. It's crucial to get the conflict resolved, or better still, to get the team members to resolve it, *before* you begin writing the draft.

> ## Watch Out!
>
> Some people try to get others to resolve their conflicts, and you can meet such people when you are writing for a team: Charlie wants X to be the conclusion and Lou wants Y to be the conclusion. Either person, or both of them, may put you in the position of resolving this difference of opinion.
>
> Getting involved, which can be difficult to avoid, can work either for you or against you. If you're a good "politician" and can keep everyone happy, it can work well. If not—and it's often impossible to keep everyone happy in the face of real differences—you can get caught in the middle and make enemies. As the title of this box says, "Watch Out!"

Write Alone

Just as only one person at a time can drive a car, only one person at a time can write a letter or memo. What we might call "back-seat writing" usually slows things down, at best. At worst, it results in disjointed writing and a lot of suffering.

Writing can be tough enough when done alone. Adding co-writers or commentators, people who are asking you (or telling you) what to write during the actual writing, makes it far tougher.

True co-authors usually let one person write a draft alone. Then the other or others comment on it or rewrite it afterward. If someone wants to be in the room and take part in the actual writing, you can try letting them. But I would advise saying, "How about if I write a draft for your comment? Or maybe you should write the draft. I would really prefer that we not both write the same piece at the same time."

Dealing with others' rewrites can be a chore, but it is easier than having them rewrite your material as you're trying to write it.

Get and Enter All Edits

The first edits to enter are your own edits. Before you hand a letter to someone else for their signature or before you circulate a memo for group review, it should be as good as you can make it. No one wants to edit your work for clarity, grammar, and punctuation. They want to focus on content.

Attach a short memo or note, as in this example:

To: Distribution

From: John Henry

Re: Memo to Summarize Group Project

Here is a draft of the memo to summarize our recently completed project. I've edited it for grammar, spelling, punctuation, and style, but I'm open to comments.

Please pay especially close attention to content. I've incorporated all the points on the original outline. However, we want to be sure that this is what we want to say and the way we want to say it.

Please get your comments to me by Wednesday the 9th. If I don't hear from you by then, I'll assume that you are happy with the memo as it is.

Thanks for your help.

Circulate a letter or memo for comment in one of two ways:

1. Distribute a copy to each person for their comment.

2. Circulate one copy from person to person among the group for their comment.

Each method has its benefits and drawbacks. The first method is fast and gives each person his or her own fresh copy to comment on. However, it leaves you to resolve any conflicting comments. The second method lets each person see and consider previous edits, but it takes longer and may still not resolve all conflicts. Besides, most team members will probably want their own clean copies for review.

Your best bet is to distribute a copy to each member the first time around and try to address all comments in one shot. On many projects, however, this will be impossible. Try to limit the process to two rounds of edits. More than two rounds often creates wear and tear (especially on you) with little added benefit. It may make sense to get comments for the second edit by circulating one copy rather than distributing copies to each person.

To circulate one copy of a memo (rather than distribute multiple copies), you need to attach a *circulation list* to that one copy.

> **Trick of the Trade**
> Type <u>DRAFT</u> across the top of letters and memos that you circulate for comment to remind the reviewers that this is a draft, not the final copy. If anyone becomes hypercritical about something, you can point out that this is a draft and that you'll fix the problem in the final.

What's That?

A circulation list is a list of names attached to a document. Each person on the list reads the document, then checks or crosses off his or her name, and passes the document on to the next person. For example:

Circulation: ~~J. Keith~~

~~S. Jones~~

M. Trankas

H. Kreitzer

Return to: Frank Hoban

Get Final Sign-Off

After you have had one or two rounds of edits, you should have incorporated all comments and changes. At that point, you're ready to request final sign-off. Circulating one copy with a circulation list is definitely a good strategy at this stage. It tells everyone, "Speak now, or forever hold your peace."

When circulating a memo for final approval, if you list the most senior person first and he or she signs off on it, you improve the chances that everyone else will too.

Again, you can attach a note or short memo to the piece itself.

To: Distribution

From: John Henry

Re: Memo to Summarize Group Project

For your approval, here is the final version of the memo summarizing our recently completed project. I believe it does the job, and I enjoyed working on it with you.

Since we want to get the memo distributed as soon as possible, I need your sign-off by Friday the 23rd.

Thanks again for your help.

Notice that this memo asks others for their approval in the form of a sign-off, which they should do by writing their initials near their names on the memo. In my experience, it's good to have actual final sign-off. If something goes wrong with the memo—if it is poorly received or contains a major mistake or omission—you want the responsibility (or should I say blame?) to be shared. If you have actual sign-off, nobody can say he didn't see the final version before it went out.

Six Steps to Sanity

To preserve your sanity when writing for others, use the six steps we've just covered. If you are writing for just one person, such as your boss, you won't need circulation lists and can perhaps do away with the cover note or memo. However, be sure to employ the essential elements of these steps. With a structured approach, writing for others doesn't have to be exhausting.

What's That?
A *cover note* or *cover letter* is a letter (or memo, but people rarely say "cover memo") that accompanies and explains other material.

Editing Someone Else's Work

What about those situations when you are on the other side of the task? What if someone is writing for you? Here are some guidelines:

➤ Be as clear as possible about what you want said and how you want it said.

➤ Tell the writer all that you can about the reader.

➤ Give the writer thoughtful, timely suggestions on the outline and on each draft.

➤ Take your rightful role in resolving any conflicts with other committee members.

➤ Correct any grammar, spelling, and punctuation errors you find, but don't change the wording if it is clear and correct.

Here are the three biggest complaints that business writers have about the editing they receive in business (most of which is not from professional editors):

➤ "They take too long to get back to me with their comments."

➤ "They change the meaning of what I write."

➤ "They make changes for the heck of it or to make it sound as if they wrote it."

Be sure to understand that when someone writes for you or for a group that you're part of, it's not going to sound as if you wrote it. Accept that up front and the task will go more smoothly all around.

The Least You Need to Know

➤ In business, sooner or later you will probably have to write for others.

➤ Since writing for others can be challenging, it helps to follow a process.

➤ The more input you get from others early in the process, the better.

➤ Remember to ask for comments *before* you write the piece. Start with an outline that you can hand around.

➤ Give people deadlines and time frames for getting material back to you with their comments and changes.

Part 3
Taming the Wild and Wooly Memo

If you know how to tame the wild and wooly memo, you'll have the well-tempered memo. The well-tempered memo is smooth and, well, has a way with words. Its writer can adjust its style, making it formal enough for the highest-end audience or informal enough so the gang knows you haven't moved uptown. It never gets too stuffy on the one hand or too breezy on the other. Its tone can be personal or impersonal as the situation requires.

Although it might get a little frisky at times, the well-tempered memo usually dresses itself in proper English and always avoids mistakes in grammar and usage. Its writer knows the common errors and knows how to avoid them. She or he also knows just what to do in moments of confusion.

Of course, the well-tempered memo is always beautifully turned out. It will always be found with correct margins and spacing. It's in the proper form and does nothing to disturb the reader's sense of what's right. In fact, the well-tempered memo is very particular about how it is seen in public.

In three easy chapters, you can learn the secrets of the well-tempered memo. Your readers will thank you—and your memos will repay you.

Chapter 11

Put Your Personality on Paper

In This Chapter

➤ Understanding writing style

➤ Choosing the right style for each letter and memo

➤ How to adjust your writing style

Part 2 showed you how to get your ideas down on paper and into a business letter or memo. This chapter is about how to make your writing really stand out. It's about how you present your personality in writing—and how much of your personality you present. This in turn depends on your audience, and on the kind of letter or memo you're writing.

One thing is certain: You can't always use the same style and still write great letters and memos. So let's talk about how to be stylish.

What Is Style?

Style refers to the *way* in which something is done—as opposed to that something's content or substance. We all get dressed, but we dress in different styles. Many athletes who play the same sport, even the same position, have very different styles of play. All motion pictures are shot by exposing strips of film to light at 24 frames per second, but directors shoot movies in many different styles.

In writing, style centers on how much of your personality you show along with the material. Consider the following two memos, which both have very similar content.

To: Michael DeCamp

From: Jonas Erstadt

Re: Marketing Needs Task Force

You have been chosen as a member of the Marketing Needs Task Force. The task force will hold its first meeting on the first Thursday of next month and will meet on the first Thursday of each month thereafter until the end of the year. The goals of the task force are to assess the strengths and weaknesses of our current marketing operation in light of our customer base, the market place, and our product line.

You have been designated as the representative from the Technology Department in order to bring the perspective of that area to the marketing challenges we face as a company.

Please report to Room 714 at 9:00 a.m. on the first Thursday of the month for the initial meeting of the task force.

To: Michael DeCamp

From: Jonas Erstadt

Re: Marketing Needs Task Force

Congratulations. You've been chosen as a member of the Marketing Needs Task Force. We'll be meeting on the first Thursday of every month, from next month to the end of the year. Our goal is to assess the company's strengths and weaknesses in marketing, given our customers, markets, and products.

You'll be the task force's Technology Department representative. We need the perspective you can bring to the group.

Our first meeting will be in Room 714 at 9:00 a.m. on the first Thursday of next month. I look forward to working with you.

The style of the second memo is much more personal, isn't it? It's more personal because the writer is talking more directly to the reader. He is addressing the reader in a more personal way. He is talking to the reader as a person instead of presenting the information in a way that maintains distance. Style is about how much of your personality you present along with the material.

Shouldn't We Write Just the Way We Talk?

I did say that we should write the way we talk, and it's still great advice. Many business writers have trouble writing because they feel they should sound like professors from Oxford, resulting in an overly formal, stuffy way of writing. It's much better to sound like yourself on paper—but how *much* of yourself you should present along with the content is another story.

Here, as in other aspects of writing, it comes down to the subject and the reader. Going back to the two sample memos used earlier, you might adopt the more formal style of the first memo if you didn't know the reader, especially if you were in a senior position to him. However, if you know the reader and expect to work closely with him on the project, the style of the second memo would be better.

Your choice of style also depends on how formal the company is, which can vary even within an organization. As a loan officer trainee at a major New York commercial bank in the late 1970s, I was told to address the president of the bank by his first name, but to address the more elderly chairman as "Mister."

> **Trick of the Trade**
> Every organization has its own style. You can learn about a company's style by looking at its product literature and the letters and memos the employees write.

If you are a manager, you're going to run into many writing situations that call for a formal, impersonal approach. Delivering a written reprimand is a good example. You are focused only on the employee's behavior and how it must change. You're not trying to be personal; in fact, you want to maintain distance from the material you must deliver. There is a risk that the employee will fail to improve and will become an ex-employee. Under the circumstances, a personal approach would not be appropriate.

Choosing the Right Style

As with how you dress, it's useful to think of writing style according to how formal or informal you should be for the occasion.

A formal style is best when you are focused exclusively on the material. Manuals, textbooks, and academic journals are good examples of a formal style; so are police, medical, and insurance reports. All have in common the goal of presenting material as objectively as possible.

> **Watch Out!**
> You can get into trouble by choosing the wrong writing style. If you are overly formal, you may appear awkward or cold. If you are too informal, you might seem immature. The correct writing style will put you in the best light.

An informal style is best when you're relating to the reader as a person as well as relating the material to the reader. For instance, when you want to get attention, generate enthusiasm, or win cooperation you should use an informal style. Formal writing, no matter how eloquent, creates too much distance between writer and reader to forge much of a relationship—and in most letters and memos (but not all), you are trying to forge relationships. Business writing should be clear, direct, and interesting to the reader.

Here is a range of writing styles:

Stuffy ⟷ Formal ⟷ Personal ⟷ Informal ⟷ Casual

Business writing should never be stuffy or overly formal. On the other hand, it should never be too casual or chatty, either, except perhaps in e-mail messages to people you know and regularly communicate with by e-mail.

In most letters and memos, you should strive for a personal style. Just "talk on paper" in a matter-of-fact way about the material. Address the reader directly about common goals, what you're trying to accomplish, and what you need from him. A style in the personal-to-informal range is the one to use for most letters and memos to someone you know inside or outside the organization.

You can be informal and even casual in certain announcements; for example, one about the division's softball league or the company picnic. Other kinds of announcements, especially difficult ones like announcements of layoffs, require a more formal style to distance the writer from the unpleasant facts. Reprimands and letters of termination call for a formal style.

Sales letters should be in a personal style, but the style of a proposal should be more formal. That's because a proposal is more in the nature of a contract (a legally binding agreement) than a sales letter.

Business letters you write for personal reasons should take a personal tone. These include most thank-you letters and written apologies. Letters of rejection, however, should be in a fairly formal (but not totally impersonal) style, reflecting that you are not rejecting the reader—only his proposal or request.

Cover letters and other letters to potential employees or clients should have a personal but not casual style.

Let's Get Stylish

So how do you approach the issue of style? Whenever you sit down to write, three factors will shape what you create:

➤ Your approach to the material
➤ How you address the reader
➤ Word choice and sentence structure

Let's look at each of these separately.

Your Approach to the Material

Your approach to the material has to do with your mind set. The more objective your view of the material, the more formal your writing about it will be. By an "objective" view, I mean you're not personally involved. The more personally involved you are with the material, the more personal your writing about it will be.

A scientist writing up the results of an experiment must use an impersonal, formal style, even if he has devoted three years of his life to the experiment. He must at least appear to be personally uninvolved and to have an objective view of the material. Yet that same scientist writing a love letter had better be personally involved and put some emotion into it, or his ladylove might feel she's part of a failed experiment.

Compare these two paragraphs:

> *Regarding the prices of our products, respondents to our recent survey were negative: One-third of them stated that if they could buy from another supplier, they would.*

> *Clearly we are making enemies with our high prices. Many customers can't stand it. An astonishing one-third of the respondents to our recent survey would leave us if they could only find another supplier.*

Trick of the Trade
There will be times in business when you might not feel objective but have to adopt that posture—fake it, to use the technical term—in order to get your point across. There is nothing wrong with that.

Isn't the first paragraph more objective? It presents the material and lets it speak for itself. The writer's approach in the second paragraph is not objective. In fact, that writer goes well beyond the material to state that the company is making enemies, the customers can't stand the high prices, and that the one-third is "astonishing." She may be right, but she's not objective.

Either approach to the material can work, but which one you should use depends on the situation. If you were trying to simply report the survey results, you would use the approach in the first paragraph. If you were trying to persuade someone that the company's prices are too high, you might be better off with the second approach.

The key is to be conscious of your approach to the material, and to use the right one.

How You Address the Reader

As I wrote in Chapter 6, the more you use the words "we," "I," "me," "you," "us," and "ours," the more personal your writing will sound. Those pronouns are a big part of our daily conversations because they enable us to relate to others. To drop them from our writing when we are supposed to sound personal doesn't make sense.

By the same token, it stands to reason that if you want a more formal approach, you'll want to minimize your use of such words, especially the word "you." Instead of "we," use the term "the company" or "our organization" or the company name. If you're referring to your department, say "the department" or, if they report to you, "my people." Instead of "our goals" say "the company's goals" or "the department's goals."

Trick of the Trade
Whenever possible, it's a good idea to write and talk in terms of "we" and "us" and "our" when you're in an organization. It helps create team spirit and common goals.

Another issue is how directly you address the reader. Which sentence strikes you as more personal?

In the future, employees should park in the south section of the lot unless there is snow on the ground.

In the future, please park in the south section of the lot unless there is snow on the ground.

Most people would say that the second sentence is more personal. The writer is directing the comment to the reader and asking the reader to do something ("please park") rather than stating a more objective fact ("employees should park"). The second sentence has more impact, doesn't it?

Word Choice and Sentence Structure

Business letters and memos should be written in Standard English. However, Standard English allows for a wide range of styles.

What's That?
Polysyllabic words, or *polysyllables,* are words that have more than three syllables.

Within Standard English, watch out for those 25-cent words, the polysyllables. The more of them you use, the more formal your writing will sound. It can quickly make your work sound stuffy, as in the following example:

We need to facilitate the implementation of this plan immediately or maintenance of the company's revenue position will be impossible.

...which can be translated as:

We must act on this plan right now or we will lose sales.

It's best to minimize your use of certain formal-sounding phrases if you want your writing to sound personal. Otherwise there's the danger that your writing will take on an overly formal, even pompous style. Here's a list of some overly formal phrases along with some good substitutes:

Too Formal	Substitute
Enclosed please find	I've enclosed
In view of this	Given this
In the amount of	For
In connection with	Regarding, about
Due to the fact that	Because
At this point in time	Currently, now
I am prepared to	I can, I will
If you deem it acceptable	If you agree
Please don't hesitate to call	Please call

Use the phrases in the left column *only* when you're trying to sound very formal or even a bit stuffy (for example, if you're writing to someone who is stuffy, and you think it might help). Otherwise, stay with the phrases in the right column.

To make your writing even less formal, use more casual words. While some colloquial words will often work well in business writing, avoid slang, hip talk, street talk, and, of course, profanity.

Trick of the Trade

While it's good to sound like yourself on paper, it can be better at times to match your style to your reader. If you write informally to someone who is very formal or if you write formally to someone who is very informal, you may hurt your case. Most people like to deal with people who are like themselves. It helps to write in the way that's most comfortable for your reader.

Here's an example of a very casual note.

Dear Jim,

Thanks a million for helping out by staying late last night. I heard you were here until the wee hours. Sorry I had to leave for the airport. I owe you one.

Regards,

Bob

In most situations, something this casual would be more appropriate for a handwritten note or an e-mail than for a typed letter of thanks. Bob has also used clichés, which are best avoided. They lack originality, can sound flippant, and can bore the reader.

What's That?

A *cliché* is a phrase that has been used so often that it has become stale. Once a phrase becomes a cliché, it's almost useless to a writer who is looking for fresh ways to say things.

Here are just a few examples of clichés: *"dead in the water," "not one thin dime," "high as a kite," "he walks on water,"* and *"growing like a weed."* You can probably think of dozens of others.

Sentence structure is another way to adjust your style. I'm not talking about sentence length, a topic I covered in Chapter 6. This is about putting a sentence together.

Using Active Voice

Earlier in this chapter I pointed out the advantages of directness in business writing. One way of being direct is to use the active voice *("as Jim said at the staff meeting…")* rather than the passive voice *("as was said at the staff meeting…").* The passive voice creates an impersonal style of writing. It does help the writer and reader to stay objective about the material, but that too can be overdone.

What's That?
Voice refers to the relationship between the subject of the sentence (a noun) and the predicate (a verb). In active voice, the subject is doing the action described by the verb. In passive voice, the subject receives the action described by the verb. A noun is a person, place, or thing. A verb describes an action.

The subject of a sentence is the word that the sentence says something about. The subject usually appears at the beginning of the sentence. The predicate describes the action or state of being of the subject.

For example, in the sentence, "Jim sells cars," "Jim" is the subject and "sells" is the predicate (and, by the way, "cars" is the object). "Jim sells cars" is active voice. "Cars are sold by Jim" is passive voice.

Here are some example of sentences in passive voice:

Next year's goals will be announced on November 15th.

This plan should be changed as soon as possible.

Sales were made by everyone at the trade show except Mike.

Our old equipment is being auctioned by Louie the Liquidator.

Memos should be written clearly and concisely.

Compared with active voice, passive voice makes it more difficult to know who is doing what, which can make the writing unclear. Passive voice also requires some form of the verb "to be" ("should *be* put," "*were* made," "will *be* in place," "is *being* auctioned," and so on); thus it requires at least one more word than active voice. Finally, passive voice makes it harder to pin down responsibility.

The responsibility issue is one of the principal reasons people overuse passive voice in business writing. Many people don't like to identify who is doing what when they write. It makes them feel uncomfortable. As a consequence, however, they sacrifice clarity.

For example, suppose a boss writes a memo to her five employees saying, "The storage area should be cleaned up by Friday at 5:00 p.m." Each employee can think, "I'm glad she doesn't mean me!" It would be much better to say, "Steve and Mary should clean up the storage area by Friday at 5:00 p.m." That way, someone is clearly responsible for the task. Or she could write, "I would like all of you to clean up the storage area by Friday at 5:00 p.m." That at least holds them all responsible for the task.

Changing Passive Voice to Active Voice

Since sentence structure is a matter for step three in the writing process—the editing phase—there's nothing wrong with using passive voice, or even over-using it, in your draft. But when you edit your draft and want to improve your writing style and make it more personal, you'll want to change most passive-voice sentences to active voice.

Here's how to do that:

1. *Locate the passive voice.* Do this by asking yourself, "Is the subject of the sentence doing, or receiving, the action of the verb?"

   Next year's goals will be announced on November 15th.

   The subject is *goals* and the verb is *will be announced.* The subject is receiving the action of the verb (the goals are *being* announced).

2. *Find or supply the "actor"—the one who receives the action.* Sometimes the actor is part of the sentence, as in the earlier "Louie the Liquidator" example, but often you have to supply the actor, as in the "goals" example.

   Let's say the actor here, the person doing the action, is the president.

3. *Put the actor in front of the action and rearrange the sentence as needed.* Generally, once you put the actor in front of the action, the active voice sentence falls into place.

   The president will announce next year's goals on November 15th.

Here's how to change the other sample sentences above to active voice:

Passive voice: *This plan should be changed as soon as possible.*

Active voice: *We should change this plan as soon as possible.*

Passive voice: *Sales were made by everyone at the trade show except Mike.*

Active voice: *Everyone made sales at the trade show except Mike. Or, Everyone except Mike made sales at the trade show.*

Passive voice: *Our old equipment is being auctioned by Louie the Liquidator.*

Active voice: *Louie the Liquidator is auctioning our old equipment.*

Passive voice: *Memos should be written clearly and concisely.*

Active voice: *Write your memos clearly and concisely.*

Notice that there is no actor in the last sentence. Yet it is still active voice. How can that be? Because in this form the subject is referred to as "you, understood," which means that "you" is the subject without being mentioned. So that last sentence is understood to mean, "You (the reader of this memo), write your memos clearly and concisely."

Any direct order such as "Stop smoking," "Keep your hands off the subway doors," and "File your taxes early" has as its subject "you, understood."

When to Use Passive Voice

Most (about 65–80 percent) of the sentences in your business writing should be in active voice. However, you should use passive voice in the following instances:

➤ To occasionally vary your sentence structure and give the reader a change from active voice.

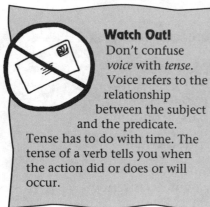

Watch Out!
Don't confuse *voice* with *tense*. Voice refers to the relationship between the subject and the predicate. Tense has to do with time. The tense of a verb tells you when the action did or does or will occur.

➤ When you can't (or don't want to) identify the actor who performs the action: *"Our chairman's car was broken into yesterday and his briefcase was stolen."*

➤ When you want to shift the emphasis a bit or because passive voice is the accepted way of making such statements. (But don't make this an excuse for overusing passive voice.) For example: *"This report was prepared by Larocca & Lambert Inc., an international consulting firm."*

Be sure you know the difference between active and passive voice and consciously choose which form to use. The more you use active voice, the clearer, livelier, and stronger your writing style will be.

Don't Be Tone-Deaf

Let's turn briefly to the issue of tone. Tone is related to, but separate from, style. While style has to do with the way the writer approaches and presents the content, tone has to do with the writer's *attitude* toward the subject and toward the reader.

Tone really refers more to an emotional state. A writer's tone can be serious or humorous, gentle or angry, open or sarcastic, friendly or hostile, enthusiastic or skeptical.

The best tone to take in most letters and memos is a positive, professional, supportive one. You may at times be tempted to take a negative, sarcastic, or even angry tone. Don't. It's a bad idea.

> ## Watch Out!
>
> Never allow a condescending or sarcastic tone into a final draft. It can creep in without your knowing it, so be watchful. Take a word like "obviously," which can sometimes sound like "as any bozo knows." Phrases like "total failure," "learned nothing," and "waste of time and money" belong on the cutting-room floor. Don't play judge, jury, and executioner in your letters and memos.

One great way to check that your tone is businesslike and positive is to have your spouse or a friend outside the business read the memo and tell you what they think. If they say something like, "It sounds strong to me," or "You aren't pulling any punches," you should probably tone it down (as the saying goes).

Say It with Style

The message of this chapter is: Say it with style. You can exert quite a bit of control over your writing style. Ultimately, however, your writing style, like your style of speaking or driving or dressing, emerges from your personality. Be aware that what readers will see is your personality, right there in print. Take time to develop yourself as a clear-thinking, direct, positive business person as well as a clear-thinking, direct, positive writer.

The Least You Need to Know

➤ Gear your writing style to the content, goals, and readers of the piece you're writing.

➤ Most business letters and memos should be written in a personal style, but some, such as reprimands, call for the distance of a more formal approach.

➤ You can adjust your writing style by adjusting your approach to the material, the way you address the reader, and your word choice and sentence structure.

➤ By using the active voice—having the subject of the sentence performing the action of the verb—your writing will be more personal, direct, and clear.

➤ Strive for a positive, supportive friendly tone in business letters; avoid negativity.

Nail Down the Basics

OK, this is it. Grammar. English usage. Rules! I'm afraid there's no alternative. We have to deal with it sooner or later. But I'll make this as painless as possible and keep the rules to a minimum.

In this chapter, you'll learn about the most common errors in grammar and usage, how to avoid them—and how to fix them if you can't avoid them.

Grammar Matters

Let's face it—there is no way that a letter or memo can be called great, or even good, if it's riddled with grammatical errors. And I do mean riddled. Such mistakes can make your writing seem like a riddle to the reader, even if it's clear to you.

Just because you have always said or written something a certain way doesn't mean it is correct. If your grammar is incorrect it reflects poorly on you, even if your readers can figure out what you mean. Incorrect grammar is the mark of an uneducated person, and most people in the business world value education. It's really that simple.

I'm not saying that lack of education makes you a bad person. It doesn't even mean you aren't intelligent. For various reasons, many intelligent people have not had much education. Meanwhile, many cheaters and liars have had wonderful educations and are able to cheat and lie in perfect English. Still, mastery of written and spoken English will help your career and enable you to express your ideas and feelings in any situation. There's no reason for you to go through life without that ability.

What's That?
Grammar is the set of rules that governs the way a language is used. It tells us how to arrange the words so that the language makes sense.

So if you slept through English class, or if you were awake but thinking of other things, here's a chance to get grip on the basics.

The Parts of Speech

To a professional writer, words are tools. A writer has to use the right tool for the job at hand, just like a carpenter or metalworker. Writers have to know their tools, just as carpenters and metalworkers have to know theirs.

The writer's tools, the words in the English language, are classified into the "parts of speech." Each part of speech has a different function. Table 12.1 gives you a quick rundown of the parts of speech in the English language, along with their functions and some examples of each.

Table 12.1   The Parts of Speech

Part of Speech	Function	Examples
Noun	Names a person, place, or thing	*man, city, building*
Pronoun	Substitutes for a noun	*he, that, which*
Verb	States an action or condition	*run, swim, is*
Adjective	Modifies nouns	*fast, good*
Adverb	Modifies verbs	*quickly, well*
Conjunction	Creates links	*and, but, or*
Preposition	Creates links with phrases	*by, for, at, in, with*
Interjection	Signifies exclamation	*Oh, Egad, Wow*
Article	Identifies a noun	*the, a, an*

A few more items:

Adjectives and adverbs are also called *modifiers*.

A *proper noun* is capitalized and names a particular person, place, or thing, such as John (person), Paris (city), or the Empire State Building (thing).

There are a variety of pronouns. These include *personal pronouns,* such as "he," "she," "you," "I," and "we," which substitute for nouns; *relative pronouns,* such as "who," "which," and "that," which substitute for nouns and create modifying phrases; and *reflexive pronouns,* such as "myself," "herself," and "themselves," which refer to the subject of a sentence.

A *phrase* is a group of words that (usually) acts as a modifier. For example, in the sentence "He was the best salesperson in the company," the phrase "in the company" is a phrase modifying "salesperson." Actually it is also a *prepositional phrase,* because it begins with the preposition "in."

Some examples of the uses of various parts of speech in sentences follow:

He and I got into the office early today.

Noun: office

Verb: got

Pronouns: he, I

Preposition: into

Conjunction: and

Adverbs: early, today

Article: the

Good managers demand and get the best work from every employee.

Nouns: managers, work, employee

Verbs: demand, get

Adjectives: good, best, every

Preposition: from

Conjunction: and

Article: the

You can be a good writer without knowing the parts of speech, but it does help to have that grounding. It's also helpful for me to be able to refer to the various kinds of words by their names when I'm focusing on grammatical errors, as I'll be doing for the next several sections.

Fixing the Most Common Errors

Here's a summary of the most common grammatical and usage errors business writers make:

➤ Dangling modifiers

➤ Lack of parallelism

➤ Faulty comparison

➤ Unclear pronoun reference

➤ Incorrect pronoun case

Dangling Modifiers

A dangling modifier is a modifying word or phrase that is misplaced in the sentence. The result is a lack of clarity, sometimes with humorous results. Here are some examples of dangling modifiers:

Scalded with coffee, the machine injured several employees. (The machine was not scalded; the employees were.)

Working all day long, John's project was completed on time. (John's project did not work all day long; John did.)

Happy at last, the plane finally got clearance to take off. (The plane can't be happy; who was?)

The Fixes

To fix dangling modifiers, rearrange the sentence and add or omit words as necessary to get the modifying phrase next to the word or words that it is modifying:

The machine injured several employees, who were scalded with coffee.

Working all day long, John completed the project on time.

We were happy at last when the plane finally got clearance to take off.

Lack of Parallelism

Parallelism refers to the practice of presenting a series of words or phrases in the same way. Lack of parallelism can make your writing harder to read and understand, as in the following sentences:

Mary has everything needed for success in market research, including asking good questions, the ability to listen, analytical skills, and handles herself with poise.

The key challenges facing Europe now are:

➤ *Unemployment*

➤ *Achieving competitiveness*

➤ *Greater unity*

➤ *A single currency*

The Fixes

The way to create parallelism is to decide what form of word you want to begin a list with and stick with it. The list can be either within a sentence or in a bulleted list. Don't switch around—if you want to use "-ing" endings, use "-ing" endings; if you want to use articles, use articles; if you want to use nouns, use nouns:

Mary has everything needed for success in market research, including the ability to ask good questions, listen to others, analyze results, and handle herself with poise.

The key challenges facing Europe now are:

➤ *Lowering unemployment*

➤ *Increasing competitiveness*

➤ *Achieving greater unity*

➤ *Establishing a single currency*

Faulty Comparison

Be sure that the words on the page compare exactly the things that you want to compare, which is not the case in these sentences:

The economy of California is bigger than Sweden.

Jim ate his dinner faster than the dog.

Harry's business acumen is better than most experienced entrepreneurs.

The Fixes

Add language and punctuation that clarifies the comparison:

The economy of California is bigger than Sweden's.

Jim ate his dinner faster than the dog ate its food.

Harry's business acumen is better than that of most experienced entrepreneurs.

Unclear Pronoun Reference

Pronoun reference is clear when the reader knows what a pronoun refers to. The references are not clear in these sentences:

International trade will greatly expand the size of the world economy. It is growing by more than 5 percent a year.

Kathy helped Louise with the analysis for this project, but she wrote most of it.

The Fixes

Add language and rearrange the sentences to make the reference clear, or use nouns instead of the unclear pronouns:

International trade, which is growing by more than 5 percent a year, will greatly expand the size of the world economy.

Kathy helped Louise with the analysis for this project, but Louise wrote most of it.

Incorrect Pronoun Case

The term *case* refers to the form of the pronoun you should use in the situation. You use *subjective case* (such as "I," "we," "he," "she," or "they") when the pronoun is the subject of the sentence. You use *possessive case* (such as "mine," "ours," "his," "hers," or "their") to indicate possession. And you use *objective case* when the pronoun is the object in a sentence or in a prepositional phrase.

The following sentences are all examples of incorrect case:

Between you and I, we can easily make our sales goals for next year.

Her and I are going to fly on Friday to the London conference.

Jim has a much better attendance record than me.

The Fixes

Use the correct case for the situation:

Between you and me, we can easily make our sales goals for next year. (<u>Hint:</u> "Between you and I" is a common mistake. The key here is the word "between." "Between" is a preposition and needs to be followed by an objective-case pronoun like "me," "him," "her," or "them.")

If this sounds too confusing, try taking away the "you and." Would you say "between I," as in "the man stepped between I and the TV screen"? No, you wouldn't, you'd say "between me." So "between you and me" is the correct choice.

She and I are going to fly on Friday to the London conference. (<u>Hint:</u> This one's even easier. Leave out "and I" and see how the sentence sounds without it. You wouldn't say "Her is going to fly on Friday," but rather "She is going to fly on Friday.")

Jim has a much better attendance record than I. (<u>Hint</u>: You're really saying, "Jim has a much better attendance record than I do." You would not say, "than me do," would you?)

Common Mistakes in Word Usage

Certain words in English are inherently confusing. They either sound the same but have different meanings (like "affect" and "effect") or the have similar, but nonetheless different, meanings (like "continual" and "continuous").

Here is a list of these easily confused words, along with their actual meanings and examples of their correct usage.

Affect and Effect

The verb *affect* means to influence or to change in some way. The verb *effect* means to cause or to bring about.

> *Economic conditions will not affect our business.*

> *This plan should effect an increase in sales.*

The noun *affect* (stress on the first syllable) is a technical term meaning behavior or demeanor. The noun *effect* means a change or result.

> *The employee's affect was inappropriate given the situation.*

> *Lower morale was the main effect of the cutback.*

All, Each

All is a collective noun that takes a plural verb. *Each* is singular.

> *All are invited to attend Jim's farewell party.*

> *Each is to donate five dollars for Jim's gift.*

As

Be careful when you use the word "as" because it can mean many different things, including "since," "while," "because," and "at that time" (for example, "as of last Friday...").

Change: *We made the sale as Peter talked about sports with the prospect.*

To: *We made the sale while Peter talked about sports with the prospect.*

Or: *We made the sale because Peter talked about sports with the prospect.*

As Such

The phrase "as such" often sounds awkward and is frequently overused. It's best to omit it or use other words.

Change: *We expect a bad winter. As such, we should arrange for snow removal.*

To: *Given that we expect a bad winter, we should arrange for snow removal.*

111

Assure, Ensure, Insure

Assure, ensure, and *insure* all mean "to make certain" or "to make secure." However, you *assure* another person of something. *Ensure* and *insure* can be used interchangeably, except when you mean to insure the financial value of something with an insurance policy.

> *He assured me that the check was in the mail.*

> *This new capacity will ensure (or insure) that we can meet increased demand.*

> *This policy will insure your building and equipment for $250,000.*

Bad, Badly

Bad is an adjective and should be used to define nouns (a bad cold, a bad job), and after verbs such as "feel" and "look." *Badly* is an adverb and therefore defines verbs.

> *It is natural to feel bad about being fired.*

> *You will look bad if you're not prepared for your meeting.*

> *A poorly maintained machine will perform badly.*

Can and May

The verb *can* means "to be able to." The verb *may* indicates probability.

> *Marty can sell anything.*

> *Marty may sell his beach house this autumn.*

Cannot

The word *cannot* is one word. It should never be spelled "can not."

Continual and Continuous

Continual refers to something that happens repeatedly or intermittently. *Continuous* means uninterrupted.

> *The watchdog barks continually, whether or not there are intruders.*

> *This machine produces a continuous sheet of steel.*

Center Around

The expression *center around* actually doesn't make sense, since the center of something cannot be around something else. Instead of "around," use the word "on" or "upon."

> *Our concerns center upon his competence.*

Compare with, Compare to

Use *compare with* when you are comparing things that are similar to one another, and *compare to* when comparing fundamentally different things.

> *Comparing the Porsche with the Miata will tell us a lot about sports cars.*

> *Compared to the horse and carriage, any car represents advanced technology.*

Complement, Compliment

A *complement* is something that makes something complete or the number it takes to make something complete. (<u>Hint</u>: think of the "e" in complete and the "e" in *complement*). A *compliment* is a favorable remark. Similarly, *complementary* means completing or filling a lack, while *complimentary* means favorable or free of charge.

> *With two more jurors, we will have the complement of 12.*

> *His boss gave him the sincerest compliment of all—a bonus.*

> *Irene will bring complementary skills to the department.*

> *Everyone likes to get a complimentary introduction.*

> *Call today for your complimentary set of steak knives.*

Data

Data is the plural of the Latin word *datum*, meaning a single unit of information. While formal usage would call for data to be treated as plural, it is acceptable in business writing for it to take either a singular or plural verb. If, however, the data is a single group of information, it's more correct to use a singular verb, as in the first example below.

> *The data is ready for you to pick up whenever you're ready.*

> *The economic data are contradictory at turning points in the business cycle. (but "data is" would also be acceptable)*

Decades

Decades should be written without apostrophes: *1860s* or *1980s.*

Discrete, Discreet

Discrete means separate and individual. *Discreet* means showing good judgment or being able to maintain secrecy.

> *The regulators look at each violation as a discrete event.*

> *He discreetly mentioned that her slip was showing.*

e.g and i.e.

The abbreviation *e.g.* stands for *exempli gratia*, which means "for example" in Latin. (Many people take it to mean "example given.") The abbreviation *i.e.* is from the Latin *id est*, meaning "that is." It's best to simply use the English words, since many people confuse these two abbreviations.

Change: *Government agencies, e.g., the DOD and CIA, often do business with companies.*

To: *Government agencies, for example, the DOD and CIA, often do business with companies.*

Or: *Government agencies, such as the DOD and CIA, often do business with companies.*

Change: *Our goal for next year, i.e., a doubling of sales, is simply impossible.*

To: *Our goal for next year, that is, a doubling of sales, is simply impossible.*

Or: *Our goal for next year, a doubling of sales, is simply impossible.*

Etc.

The abbreviation *etc.* means *et cetera*, which is Latin for "and others." *Etc.* is often overused in business writing and can at times create the impression that you're too lazy to mention the others or that there really aren't any others. It is often best to use the terms "such as" or "for example" and then mention several specifics. Also, it is incorrect to use *etc.* with "such as" or "for example" because it is redundant.

Change: *The person we seek needs sales skills, such as the ability to cold call, close, etc.*

To: *The person we seek needs sales skills, such as the ability to cold call and close.*

Fewer, Less

Use *fewer* for things that can be counted individually and use *less* for things that cannot.

This new line of snacks has less fat and fewer calories.

Former, Latter

Use the word *former* to refer to the first of two items mentioned and *latter* to refer to the last of two. When more than two items are mentioned, use words like "first" or "last of these" to be clear.

We have a chairman and a president. The former is responsible for overall strategy; the latter is in charge of day-to-day operations.

We need new products, new systems, and new ideas, the last of these being the most important.

Good, Well

Good is an adjective and *well* is an adverb.

> *She has good skills and she uses them well.*

> *He's got a good job and he's doing it very well.*

Imply, Infer

You *imply* something when you hint at it or indicate it. You *infer* something when you figure it out based on some evidence.

> *The boss was indirect, but he implied that a layoff could be coming.*

> *Since we have no plans to hire and we're losing money, I infer that a layoff is coming.*

Irregardless

"Irregardless" is not an English word. The correct word is *regardless*.

Change: *Irregardless of what he said, he's not going to fire anyone.*

To: *Regardless of what he said, he's not going to fire anyone.*

Its, It's

Be very careful of these two. They are often confused. *Its* is the possessive form of the pronoun "it." *It's* is the contraction for "it is."

> *It's going to be a bumpy ride in the next recession.*

> *The machine was pushed beyond its capacity.*

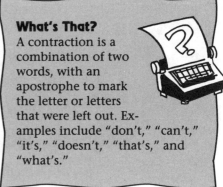

What's That?
A contraction is a combination of two words, with an apostrophe to mark the letter or letters that were left out. Examples include "don't," "can't," "it's," "doesn't," "that's," and "what's."

Lay, Lie

Lay means to put or place something somewhere. *Lie* means to recline.

> *If the stack of material is too heavy, lay it on the nearest desk.*

> *Any employee who feels dizzy should lie down.*

Numbers

The rule of thumb in business writing is to spell out the numbers one through ten and use numerals for those over ten. If a numeral over ten appears at the beginning of a sentence, either spell it out or reword the sentence so that it's not at the beginning. Page numbers should always be written as numerals.

> *As you'll see on page 5 of the report, we have approval to add four new employees, which will bring our total staff to 12.*

Principal, Principle

The noun *principal* means a person with position or authority, most specifically in an educational institution or a business. Principal also refers to a sum of money in a loan or fund.

> *We negotiate only with principals, not with agents or brokers.*

> *We calculate the interest on this loan on the original principal.*

The noun *principle* means a law or doctrine.

> *The principle of delegation is central to the art of management.*

The adjective *principal* means the most important.

> *Poor performance was the principal reason for his termination.*

The adjective *principled* (or *unprincipled*) means based on (or lacking) a principle or principles.

> *Principled behavior calls for fairness in all terminations.*

Reason Is Because

The expression *the reason is because* is redundant, which means uselessly repetitive. Either use the *reason is that* or the word *because*.

Change: *If costs are down, the reason is because inflation is low.*

To: *If costs are down, the reason is low inflation.*

Or: *If costs are down, it's because of low inflation.*

Regards, Regard

The word *regards* means "best wishes," while *regard* means "about" or "having to do with." People often use *regards* when they mean *regard*. However, *regard* can also mean "esteem."

> *Give my regards to everyone at the company.*

> *I'm writing in regard to your most recent delivery to us.*

> *I've always had high regard for Mike's management skills.*

Seasons

Don't capitalize the seasons of the year, unless they are at the beginning of the sentence or are part of a proper noun.

> *This summer we will see the usual increase in gasoline prices.*

Stationary, Stationery

Stationary means immovable. *Stationery* is paper and envelopes.

> *Place the unit in a stationary position before turning it on.*

> *Fine notepaper is available at any good stationery store.*

Time

The correct way to write *a.m.* and *p.m.* is with lowercase letters and periods.

> *Our office hours are from 9:00 a.m. to 5:30 p.m.*

Their, They're

Don't confuse *their* and *they're*. The former is the possessive of "they," while the latter is the contraction for "they are."

> *They're bound to forget their umbrellas once the rain stops.*

Very

Many people overuse the word *very* in their business writing. You're usually better off omitting it or finding a better adjective or adverb.

Change: *Sales rose very quickly last month.*

To: *Sales rose sharply last month.*

Or: *Sales skyrocketed last month.*

Your, You're

Your is the possessive form of "you." *You're* is the contraction for "you are."

> *You're sure to find your new Maximillion Copier to be a superior value.*

Warning: There are many spelling and usage errors that spell-checking programs in word processing software will not catch. Good examples include "from" and "form," "by" and "buy," "it's" and "its," "your" and "you're," and "their" and "they're." There's no substitute for careful proofreading.

Avoiding Jargon and Buzzwords

Try to stay away from jargon and buzzwords in your writing. Jargon can be hard to avoid, and used sparingly, it won't do much harm, provided your readers understand it. If you overuse it, however, your work will sound like technical writing instead of business writing.

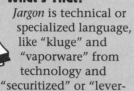

What's That?

Jargon is technical or specialized language, like "kluge" and "vaporware" from technology and "securitized" or "leverage" from finance.

Buzzwords are slang words that come into temporary favor, such as "paradigm" or "right-sizing" in business, or "lifestyle" in the vocabulary of the larger culture. "Lifestyle" is an example of a word that gained broad acceptance and entered the language.

Unless they have permanently entered the language, buzzwords tend to sound silly or overwrought on paper. Look for good Standard English words instead.

One form of jargon you must handle carefully is the *acronym*, which is an abbreviation formed by combining the first letters of several words. Unless the acronym is familiar to all readers, such as U.S.A., IRS, or IBM, when you first use one in a memo, write out the full name and then the acronym in parentheses. For example, write "return on investment (ROI)" and then just use "ROI" in the rest of the memo.

Remember, in most cases, there is really no substitute for good, solid Standard English in your business writing, and you certainly can never go wrong with it.

The Best Source for More Help

The single best tool for becoming a better writer, building your vocabulary, and avoiding usage errors is a good dictionary. If you have one, keep it near you when you write. If you don't have one, buy one and keep it handy. Some good dictionaries include *Webster's New Collegiate Dictionary*, *The American Heritage Dictionary of the English Language*, *The Random House College Dictionary,* and *Funk & Wagnalls Standard College Dictionary*.

There is hardly a professional writer of any kind who does not frequently consult his or her dictionary.

The Least You Need to Know

➤ Grammar is the set of rules that governs the way a language is used. These rules ensure that the language makes sense.

➤ Correct grammar is the mark of an educated person. Most of the people who will play a role in your success or failure in business will know whether or not you speak and write correct English, and they will judge you at least partially on that basis.

➤ Words are a writer's tools; the more you know about those tools and how to use them, the better a writer you will be.

➤ Keep a good dictionary handy when you write, and refer to it often.

Chapter 13

How It Looks Is How You Look

In This Chapter

➤ What it takes to create professional-looking documents

➤ What readers expect when it comes to appearance

➤ How to format letters and memos properly

This chapter is about cosmetics, not content. It's about how your letters and memos look, not how they read. In business there are professional ways of presenting words on paper, and then there are other ways.

Having worked so hard to make the content of your letter or memo as good as you can make it, you owe it to yourself (and to your readers) to make it look as good as you can. This chapter will show you how.

Neatness Counts

You probably remember teachers in elementary school saying as they announced a writing assignment, "Neatness will count." Those teachers were trying to save themselves the trouble of trying to read words obscured by messy erasures, smeared chocolate, and spilled cola. But they were also trying to help us establish a life-long habit of turning in professional-looking work.

First impressions are lasting impressions, and first impressions are usually visual. This applies to people, places, and things. How a person is dressed, how a yard is kept, and how food looks on the plate all have an effect on us before we talk with the person, enter the house, or taste the meal.

Similarly, how your memo looks when the reader first sets eyes on it will have an effect on him or her. If it's messy or improperly formatted, the reader may still read it (but maybe not). If the material is compelling enough, the reader may even overcome that first impression (but maybe not).

Don't take the chance that the appearance of your memo will work against you. Instead, turn out the most professional-looking documents that you can.

The Professional Look

Turning out professional-looking documents is an important part of a secretary's job—or should I say was? Unfortunately, there are just not as many secretaries in most organizations as there used to be. As recently as the mid-to-late 1980s, most managers and supervisors in large organizations, and many professionals, had access to the services of a secretary, if only on a shared basis.

The personal computer created both the means and the demand for us to all do our own "typing" (which is now called word processing). Like other changes wrought by technology, this is a good-news/bad-news situation. The good news is that now we all create professional-looking documents. The bad news is that now we all have to know how to do that.

There are four basic elements to a professional-looking document:

➤ Flawless error correction

➤ Proper format

➤ Customary layout of extra information

➤ Proper letterhead and stationery

Getting Rid of ~~Missteaks~~ Mistakes

Thanks to the personal computer, the standard in error correction today is "completely undetectable." In the age of the typewriter, readers would tolerate a slightly visible correction done with Wite Out®, Liquid Paper®, or correction tape. Now, however, it's actually becoming difficult (and impractical) to purchase a typewriter, because word processing is a far better technology and almost as inexpensive.

What's That?

Wite Out® and *Liquid Paper*® are brands of correction fluid. To correct a typewritten error, you brush a small amount of the fluid over the mistake, let it dry, and type the correction over it. However, if the correction takes up more space than the original, you usually have to retype the whole page.

Correction tape, which is built into many machines, serves a similar function. The tape covers the error with a sticky white powder, which you then type over. As with correction fluid, however, you often have to retype the page instead.

The advantage of the computer is that it stores the document on disk. This enables you to edit the document until you get it right, with a only fraction of the effort that retyping would require.

Given computer technology, readers' tolerance for errors has approached zero. They expect perfection. Many readers find spelling errors particularly irksome. Their first thought upon spying one is usually, "Couldn't they even run this through a spelling check? How lazy can you get?"

If you're not writing on a personal computer, you are placing yourself at a huge disadvantage when it comes to your personal productivity. This is true whether you're just starting your career or you're a seasoned senior executive who may be "keyboard shy." There is really no excuse for anyone in an organization—or working in a home-based business—to be writing on a typewriter.

Don't think that you have to spend big bucks on a computer. Because the technology changes so fast and companies are always upgrading to new machines, there's a healthy secondhand market for PCs.

If you buy from an individual, bring along someone who knows PCs and your needs. (You don't need the latest model if you're mainly doing word processing.) Many stores handle secondhand machines, and a good store will give you at least a 30-day warranty on one.

Whether you use a computer or not, your readers will have almost no tolerance for errors, typos, or misspellings. A computer will make your writing life much easier, but you will still have to proofread carefully, preferably more than once and after you have gotten some distance on the piece.

Watch Out!

Always, always, always use the spelling-check feature in your word processing software. If you used it on an earlier version of the document and have made any change at all, run it through again. It's so easy to make an error, yet so easy to correct it with a spelling checker.

Trick of the Trade

One of the best ways to ensure an error-free document is to have someone else read it. If you have co-workers, enlist one or two in a "buddy system" in which you proofread their work in return for their proofreading yours. There's nothing like a second set of eyes for catching errors.

Choosing the Right Format

The basic acceptable formats for business letters and memos haven't changed much in this century. This means that the human race pretty much figured out how these documents should look a while ago, and hasn't substantially improved on them lately.

In this section, I'll show you formats by indicating what goes where, rather than giving you actual sample letters and memos. The samples in the other chapters are all properly formatted. There are some variations, however, that you'll see in this chapter.

On the pages that follow are the basic formats for letters: The first two are for letterhead, and the second for situations when you need an inside address for your location. Remember, though, with many of today's word processing packages, it's easy to create your own letterhead—with a graphic, if you like.

Sample 1 on the following page shows the format for a letter on letterhead.

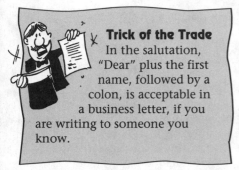

Trick of the Trade
In the salutation, "Dear" plus the first name, followed by a colon, is acceptable in a business letter, if you are writing to someone you know.

Given the informality of business in the United States (in contrast to Europe and Asia), it's often acceptable to use a first name simply on the basis of having spoken with the person on the phone. If you don't know the person, however, use "Mr." or "Mrs." or "Ms." plus the last name.

It's always best to write to a specific individual, but if you don't have a name of a person, use "Dear Sir:" or "Dear Sir or Madam:" rather than the somewhat old-fashioned "Gentlemen:" which may be considered gender-biased.

Note that non-indented paragraphs, rather than indented paragraphs, are considered standard today. That's one change from 30 or 40 years ago, when you would often see indented paragraphs.

Note also that these paragraphs have a "ragged" right margin as opposed to a justified right margin. Sample 2 shows the same letter with a justified right margin.

What's That?

The right margin of the text in a document can be either *justified*, that is, lined up so that each line of text ends in the same place on the page, or *ragged* so that the end points of the lines vary. The term *justified* or *right justified* refers to a justified right margin, while *ragged right* refers to a right margin that is not justified.

Documents are always *left justified*, of course, except for the first line of a paragraph, which may be indented.

Your Company Name

Company Street Address

City, State Zip

Telephone Number   Fax Number

Date

Mr./Ms. First Name, Middle Initial, Last Name

Title

Company Name

Street Address Floor or Suite (if applicable)

City, State Zip

Dear Mr./Ms./Mrs. Last Name:

First paragraph First paragraph First paragraph First paragraph First paragraph First paragraph First paragraph First paragraph First paragraph First paragraph First paragraph First paragraph First paragraph First paragraph First paragraph First paragraph First paragraph.

Second paragraph Second paragraph Second paragraph Second paragraph Second paragraph Second paragraph Second paragraph Second paragraph Second paragraph Second paragraph.

Third paragraph Third paragraph Third paragraph Third paragraph Third paragraph Third paragraph Third paragraph Third paragraph Third paragraph Third paragraph Third paragraph Third paragraph Third paragraph Third paragraph Third paragraph Third paragraph Third paragraph Third paragraph Third paragraph Third paragraph.

Fourth paragraph Fourth paragraph Fourth paragraph Fourth paragraph Fourth paragraph Fourth paragraph Fourth paragraph.

Sincerely,

Your First Name, Middle Initial, Last Name

Your Title

Sample 1: Format for a Letter on Letterhead.

> A ragged right margin is less dense and intimidating than a justified one.

Company Name

Company Street Address

City, State Zip

Telephone Number   Fax Number

Date

Mr./Ms./Mrs. First Name, Middle Initial, Last Name

Job Title

Company Name

Street Address Floor or Suite (if applicable)

City, State Zip

> A justified right margin creates a more formal block-of-text format.

Dear Mr./Ms. Last Name:

First paragraph First paragraph First paragraph First paragraph First paragraph First paragraph First paragraph First paragraph First paragraph First paragraph First paragraph First paragraph First paragraph First paragraph First paragraph.

Second paragraph Second paragraph Second paragraph Second paragraph Second paragraph Second paragraph Second paragraph Second paragraph Second paragraph Second paragraph.

Third paragraph Third paragraph Third paragraph Third paragraph Third paragraph Third paragraph Third paragraph Third paragraph Third paragraph Third paragraph Third paragraph Third paragraph Third paragraph Third paragraph Third paragraph Third paragraph Third paragraph Third paragraph Third paragraph Third paragraph.

Fourth paragraph Fourth paragraph Fourth paragraph Fourth paragraph Fourth paragraph Fourth paragraph Fourth paragraph.

Sincerely,

Your First Name, Middle Initial, Last Name

Your Title

Sample 2: Letter on Letterhead—Justified.

Whether you use ragged or justified right margins is largely a matter of personal taste, subject to the custom in your organization. I prefer ragged right and I believe most readers do. I also see it far more often. The ragged right margin creates more white space and a less "boxy" and more inviting look.

If you do use justified right margins, use a proportional font rather than a nonproportional font. A proportional font automatically adjusts the spacing between the letters in a word so that there are no gaping spaces between the words in a line. A nonproportional font can't make this adjustment, so you wind up with some large spaces between the words when you use a justified right margin.

The spacing between words is not an issue with a ragged right margin, which is another good reason to use ragged right margins in your letters and memos.

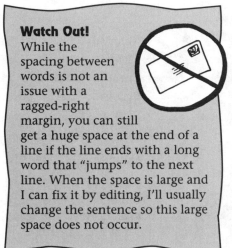

Watch Out!
While the spacing between words is not an issue with a ragged-right margin, you can still get a huge space at the end of a line if the line ends with a long word that "jumps" to the next line. When the space is large and I can fix it by editing, I'll usually change the sentence so this large space does not occur.

Accepted Closings

Besides "Sincerely," the accepted closings for a business letter include "Very truly yours," "Yours very truly," "Yours truly," and "Very truly" all of which are considered more formal than "Sincerely" (which I prefer and most often use). "Cordially" is still more informal. "Regards" and "Best wishes" can be used for a personal touch when you have a personal as well as business relationship with the reader and the subject matter is somewhat personal.

Sample 3 on the following page shows a letter formatted without letterhead. (This kind of letter is sometimes called a personal business letter to distinguish it from a business letter, which goes on letterhead.)

Your Street Address
City, State Zip
Date

Mr./Ms./Mrs. First Name, Middle Initial, Last Name
Title
Company Name
Street Address   Floor or Suite (if applicable)
City, State Zip

Dear Mr./Ms. Last Name:

First paragraph First paragraph First paragraph First paragraph First paragraph First paragraph First paragraph First paragraph First paragraph First paragraph First paragraph First paragraph First paragraph First paragraph First paragraph First paragraph First paragraph.

Second paragraph Second paragraph Second paragraph Second paragraph Second paragraph Second paragraph Second paragraph Second paragraph Second paragraph Second paragraph.

Third paragraph Third paragraph.

Fourth paragraph Fourth paragraph Fourth paragraph Fourth paragraph Fourth paragraph Fourth paragraph Fourth paragraph.

Sincerely,

Be sure to align the closing with your address at the top of the page.

Your First Name, Middle Initial, Last Name

Your Title

Sample 3: Personal Business Letter (No Letterhead).

This is the format you would use if you were writing to a company from your home. But even so, with a computer it would be easy to create personal letterhead, as in the following example:

John Smith
33 East 33rd Street
New York, New York 10022
(212) 999-9999

Personal Letterhead Created on a Computer.

Just as computers have created the standard of zero errors and no cover-ups or erasures, the reasonable standard has become some form of letterhead done on a computer. From the practical standpoint, this makes the inside address positioned to the right (as in Sample 3) obsolete. However, I include it here because it is acceptable, and—who knows?—someday you may find yourself without access to a computer and the need to write to a business from your home.

Sample 4 on the following page shows a format for a memo that has a justified right margin.

To:	First Name, Initial, Last Name, Title
From:	Your First Name, Initial, Last Name, Title
Date:	Month, Date, Year
Subject:	The Subject of the Memo
cc:	First Initial, Last Name (of each person who will get a copy)

First paragraph First paragraph First paragraph First paragraph First paragraph First paragraph First paragraph First paragraph First paragraph First paragraph First paragraph First paragraph First paragraph First paragraph First paragraph First paragraph First paragraph.

Second paragraph Second paragraph Second paragraph Second paragraph Second paragraph Second paragraph Second paragraph Second paragraph Second paragraph Second paragraph.

Third paragraph Third paragraph.

Fourth paragraph Fourth paragraph Fourth paragraph Fourth paragraph Fourth paragraph Fourth paragraph.

Sample 4: Format for a Memo.

Page Numbers for Letters and Memos

If your letter or memo is longer than one page, you should number each page at the top right corner, beginning on page 2, as shown in the following example:

First Initial and Last Name of Recipient   **Page 2**
Month, Date, Year

In practice, this would read:

J. Jones   **Page 2**
Nov. 12, 1998

and:

J. Jones   **Page 3**
Nov. 12, 1998

…and so on.

After this material at the top of each page, skip two lines before starting the text.

Page numbers are important because you *do not staple* the pages of a letter together. Page numbers also help the reader not only to keep the document in order, but also to discuss it on the phone more easily with you or with anyone else who gets a copy ("On page 3 it says that…").

On a memo, page numbers can be placed either at the top of the page as they would be for a letter or at the bottom of the page, either centered or in the lower right-hand corner.

Marginal Thinking

The standard size for paper in the United States is $8\frac{1}{2}$ by 11 inches. Do not use legal-size paper, which is $8\frac{1}{2}$ by 14 inches, for business correspondence.

Proper margins for a letter or a memo are from $1\frac{1}{4}$ to $1\frac{1}{2}$ inches on the right and left sides.

Letterhead can begin from one-half inch to $1\frac{1}{4}$ inches from the top of the page. This also applies to any other typing beginning at the top of a page, such as the page number lines, but not to the text itself, which should be $1\frac{1}{4}$ inches from the top or two lines below the page number lines.

The "To" and "From" lines for a memo should begin from 1 to $1\frac{1}{4}$ inches from the top.

The bottom margin should be from 1 to $1\frac{1}{2}$ inches.

> ## Watch Out!
>
> Never make a letter or memo appear crowded on the page in an effort to keep it to one page or any other length. It looks terrible. Either edit the text so that it fits comfortably on one page, or begin the text further down on the first page so that you push more onto the next.
>
> Never leave one line or less on a page all by itself. (Editors and printers call this a "widow.") Anything over one line is acceptable, but in practice any less than two lines plus a bit on the third line tends to look pretty lonely. For this purpose, do not count the closing, signature, name, or title lines of a letter as lines of text.

In practice, most of us who work with word processing software on a personal computer use the default settings for margins, which on most packages are $1^1/_4$ inches on all four sides. The *default setting* on a computer is the setting that the program automatically uses unless you manually override it.

Customary Layout of Extra Information

Often in a business letter, several lines below the closing, signature, name, and title of the sender, you'll see two sets of initials, separated by a slash, at the left-hand margin, for example:

Sincerely,

Thomas F. Gorman
President

TFG/mcm

This means that the document is from Thomas F. Gorman and that his secretary, Mary Celia McCaffrey, did the typing. This is formal practice for a secretary, and I include it for that reason.

If you are enclosing an attachment or additional information with a letter, it is customary to note that fact after the closing, signature, name, and title, as follows:

Sincerely,

Thomas F. Gorman
President

Attachment

TFG/mcm

or:

Sincerely,

Thomas F. Gorman
President

Enclosure

TFG/mcm

Finally, as noted in Chapter 3, you will often need to use a "cc" or distribution list to send out multiple copies of your document. Here's where the "cc" or distribution list would go in a business letter:

Sincerely,

Thomas F. Gorman
President

cc: J. Smith
     M. Doe

Attachment

TFG/mcm

or:

Sincerely,

Thomas F. Gorman
President

Distribution:

J. Smith
M. Doe
H. Hathaway
B. Rubin

Attachment

TFG/mcm

or:

Sincerely,

Thomas F. Gorman
President

Distribution: J. Smith
                 M. Doe
                 H. Hathaway
                 B. Rubin

Attachment

TFG/mcm

If the attachment or enclosure is integral to the letter, you would include it for those on the "cc" or distribution list as well. If it's not integral, it would be acceptable for those people to receive just the letter.

For memos, the information about the "cc" and distribution lists, the secretary, and the attachments and enclosures would be presented the same way, at the end of the memo after the text of the memo itself (since there are no signature, name, and title lines at the end of a memo), with one potential variation. As noted in Chapter 3, if they're not too long, you can put the "cc" or distribution list at the top of the memo; for example:

To:	First Name, Initial, Last Name, Title
From:	Your First Name, Initial, Last Name, Title
Date:	Month, Date, Year
Subject:	The Subject of the Memo
cc:	First Initial, Last Name (of each person who will get a copy)

or:

To:	First Name, Initial, Last Name, Title
From:	Your First Name, Initial, Last Name, Title
Date:	Month, Date, Year
Subject:	The Subject of the Memo
Distribution:	J. Smith
	M. Doe
	H. Hathaway
	B. Rubin

or:

To:	First Name, Initial, Last Name, Title
From:	Your First Name, Initial, Last Name, Title
Date:	Month, Date, Year
Subject:	The Subject of the Memo
Distribution:	J. Smith, M. Doe, H. Hathaway, B. Rubin

If a "cc" or distribution list is long, it should go at the end of the memo.

Letterhead and Stationery

The business world seems to be in a state of flux regarding standards for paper and stationery. Many people used to believe that paper and envelopes with a heavy feel, substantial rag content, and engraved letterhead were needed to create an impression of "class" and richness. Again, however, the personal computer is changing things.

The weight of paper refers to the number of pounds that a ream (500 sheets) weighs. In general, the heavier the weight of the paper, the heavier and "nicer" the feel in your hands—and the greater the cost. Standard paper for a laser printer is usually 20-pound paper, while higher-quality paper can go as high as 60 or 80 pounds.

> **What's That?**
> *Rag content* refers to the amount of rag (usually cotton) in paper. Good-quality paper usually has at least 25 percent rag or cotton. In general, the more rag or cotton in paper, the higher its quality and price.

Most businesses, even small home-based ones, are producing their letters and memos on computers hooked up to printers. The requirements of the technology have become more important than notions of what looks "classy." When you're doing mailings with computer-generated labels, the envelope that the label goes on becomes something of a side issue. After all, the label is going to look rather cheesy no matter how nice an envelope it's on, won't it?

On the other hand, really flimsy paper and envelopes will not look good. Since most paper is white and most print is black, the use of color and graphics on letterhead has become more of a mark of quality than the heavy, ivory-colored paper that banks and law firms used to favor.

If you are a freelancer or have your own business, you can prepare letterhead on your word processor. However, depending on your business, your budget, and the way you sell, it's often worth it to invest in professionally produced letterhead, envelopes, and business cards. Adding a color (beyond black) will cost you a bit more, but will make your material stand out, especially if you have a nice logo.

Your local copy shop can work within various price ranges. They can also usually refer you to a freelance designer. Ask the designer for samples of his or her

133

work and take the time to develop a common understanding of your goals and price range. Although you can get by without a designer, a good one can help your letters get noticed. Just don't go overboard.

Remember, when you write letters longer than one page, your subsequent pages must match your letterhead. I have received letters in which the letterhead is gray, tan, or off-white and pages 2 and 3 pure white. This looks bad and is not acceptable.

When you have letterhead prepared by a print shop, you have two choices. Either have your letterhead done on standard white paper of the same weight that you will use in your printer, or buy a large enough supply of the nonstandard paper (whatever the color and weight) so that you won't run out before you run out of letterhead.

Practically speaking, you're probably better off putting your letterhead on standard white paper that matches what you use in your printer. First, it is always available; second, if you try to buy paper through printers, they'll often tell you they're not in the paper business and to order direct from the supplier, which can take time and be a hassle; and third, white paper produces the highest contrast against black ink and makes for easier reading than colored paper.

Print Quality

In the days of the typewriter, print quality was not a major issue. If you needed a fresh ribbon in the typewriter, you replaced it. If you had a broken "k" and the letter didn't come out clearly, you had a repairman replace it. But if the typewriter was working properly, you got clear, readable text.

Printers hooked to computers can be another story. Before ink-jet printers and laser printers became affordable, dot matrix printers were widely used. However, dot matrix printers deliver poor print quality. Today, good ink-jet printers and laser printers are the standard for business letters and memos. Laser represents the true state of the art, but a good ink-jet delivers almost equally good results.

Of course, if you still type your letters, make sure your ribbon is in good shape.

What's That?

Ink-jet printers create letters by shooting ink onto the page. *Laser printers* burn the letter onto the page. *Dot matrix printers* apply the ink with tiny pins grouped in the shape of the letter.

Ink-jet and laser printers both produce acceptable print quality. Dot matrix printers generally do not, because the pins do not produce clean lines at the edges of the letter.

Looking Good

Professional-looking documents do not just happen, any more than clear, readable text just happens. You have to choose the right format, have proper margins and spacing, and make sure that the type is readable.

This is common sense. No matter how good something is, people base their first judgment on how it looks.

The Least You Need to Know

➤ It's worth the extra effort to make sure that your documents look professionally prepared.

➤ Proper format is key to the appearance of a letter or memo. Put things where they belong or readers will think about your weird format, instead of about your message.

➤ Always use proper margins and never crowd words onto the page to save space. If your text doesn't fit on one page, either edit it to fit or add another page.

➤ The standards for the appearance of business documents today are driven by, and have been incorporated into, personal computer technology. If you have any significant amount of business writing to do, you should probably be doing it on a computer.

Part 4
What Should I Write and When Should I Write It?

Do you get the feeling that there's an unlimited number of business situations calling for a letter or memo? Well, as a matter of fact, it's true. But things are simpler than they look. To prove it, I've grouped these situations and the kinds of writing that they demand into some basic categories. The specific letters and memos you will learn about in this section will cover over 90 percent of the writing situations that you'll come across in business.

Each of these situations has its own demands, depending on your role in the organization and your relationship to the reader. These demands also have to do with the situation itself. For example, is this the first letter you're writing on the subject, or is it the third? Are there legal implications in what you are writing? We will cover these aspects in this section.

You will also find many outlines and samples that you can use as models. You will be able to use phrases, sentences, and even paragraphs from some of these samples almost word for word. But often you'll have to adapt them a bit to your particular situation and style of writing.

That's the way it should be. You should take these samples as starting points and then take them as far as you can. Improve them. Make them your own. Strive always to develop your own style and to sound like yourself. After all, that's where the fun comes in.

Chapter 14

GET IN THERE AND WIN, WIN, WIN!!

Asking for Action So People Will Act

In This Chapter

➤ How to take the right tone in making requests

➤ Making the case for your request

➤ Ways to make sure readers do what you request

Most business letters and memos, except for notes of thanks and apology, are requests for action in some form. When you write a cover letter for your resume, a sales letter, or a proposal, you are requesting action. But to narrow things down a bit, this chapter covers memos in which you ask someone to do something that he more or less has to do.

Usually, the person has to do what you're asking because of his role in the organization. He may work for you. If not, the requested action may simply be part of his job. Of course, that does not guarantee that he will do what you ask and do it when and in the way you want it done. So this chapter shows how to write memos that get cooperation.

What Do You Want Done?

The first issue is to establish what you want done. In the planning stages of your memo, you must be very specific about this in your mind and in your outline. Readers will interpret your request according to their own frame of reference, which could very well be different from yours.

Exactly how specific you need to be with the reader depends mostly on the reader. With some readers, including those who lack experience or expertise, you must be very specific. For example, if you ask an experienced painter to paint an office, he knows that he must first prepare the surface. An amateur may have to be told this.

How specific you need to be also depends on the complexity of the action requested and how fussy you are. If you're requesting that the cafeteria bring a cold lunch tray to a conference room, that may be all you have to say. If you expected shrimp salad and cold poached salmon, and instead got ham and cheese on rye, you should have been more specific.

The more specifics you include, the better. In most organizations, too little communication, not too much, is the problem.

Simple Requests

By a simple request I mean one that your reader should be fairly receptive to. In these cases, doing the requested action is generally part of the reader's job and complying with the request, should not present many difficulties. Here's a simple formula for a simple request:

1. Lead with the general request.

2. Present the details of your request.

3. Thank the reader for his or her help.

You can also add a follow-up step if you feel it would be useful, as shown in Sample 1 on the following page.

Sample 2 is a request for information.

Notice how both samples use format to highlight the action requested. Headlines are used to good advantage in the first memo, while the second uses bullets. Notice that these bullets are actually small boxes that the reader can use to check the items off as he gathers them. Many word processing packages will allow you to customize bullets in this way. (But don't get too fancy or cute.)

Any time there is a date, time, and place where the reader must be physically, highlight that information. Ways of doing this are shown in Samples 1 and 3.

To: Louis Brillate, Manager of Food & Beverage Services

From: Alice Gerald, Director of Operations

Re: Request for Luncheon on February 12th

I'm writing to request lunch for eight to be delivered to an upcoming all-day meeting. Here are the details:

> Day and Date: Thursday, February 12th
>
> Time: 12:30 p.m.
>
> Place: Second Floor Conference Room
> (Room 217)

Alice uses a format that helps readers find the most important information quickly.

Desired Menu:

Since this will be a working lunch, I believe cold sandwiches would be best. A buffet-style layout would allow each person to make their own sandwich. Please furnish silverware rather than plastic disposables since the attendees are senior people.

Given the time of year, we would also like a hot soup (your choice). We can serve the soup ourselves from a heated tureen.

Soft drinks, tea, and regular and decaf coffee, plus your choice of dessert, will round out the meal.

Cost Center:

You should charge this luncheon to cost center #313.

I'll give you a call on the 11th to confirm these arrangements. Thanks in advance for helping to make this meeting a success.

Sample 1: Request for a Luncheon.

To: Jim Millerchip, Director—Sales

From: Paul Kasade, Vice President—Marketing

Re: Request for Detailed Sales Figures

> Underscoring, bullets, and white space make Paul's memo more readable.

I would appreciate your giving me the following sales data for this year <u>through the month of June</u>, by Friday, July 24th, for my upcoming management meeting in Aspen:

- ❑ Monthly total sales figures
- ❑ Monthly sales figures by product
- ❑ Monthly sales figures by sales district
- ❑ Quarterly total sales figures
- ❑ Quarterly sales figures by product
- ❑ Quarterly sales figures by sales district

Please include your comments on specific sales figures that are plus or minus 10% off the original projections prepared last November. These comments should explain each 10% variance.

<u>Note</u>: Please send the figures to me both in hard copy and on a disk in a Lotus 1-2-3 spreadsheet.

Thanks for your assistance. These numbers plus your comments will help me prepare for this important meeting.

Sample 2: Request for Information.

To: All Employees

From: Kristen Katz, Manager of Employee Benefits

Re: Mandatory Attendance at Health Benefits Meeting

Effective January 1st, the company will change some provisions of the employee health plan. We will be holding meetings to inform employees of these changes and of choices you will have to make by December 1st. Attendance is <u>mandatory</u>.

Meeting Schedule

The schedule of these meetings is as follows:

For employees whose last names begin with the letters A–M:

      Day and Date: <u>Tuesday,</u> October 12th

      Time: 9:30–10:30 a.m.

      Place: Tenth Floor Auditorium

> Kristen uses formatting tools to present potentially confusing information clearly.

For employees whose last names begin with the letters N–Z:

      Day and Date: <u>Thursday</u>, October 14th

      Time: 9:30–10:30 a.m.

      Place: Tenth Floor Auditorium

Thank you in advance for you attendance.

Sample 3: Announcing a Mandatory Meeting.

Too often writers bury the information about the time and place of a meeting somewhere in their third paragraph. The format of Sample 3 ensures that the reader can't miss that important information.

Sample 3 was written by someone in authority addressing many people whom she does not know personally. As a result, the tone is less personal. The authoritative tone suggests that the writer has probably seen poor attendance at these meetings, or that the company is legally required to hold them. This explains the commanding style of this simple request.

Complex Requests

More complex requests may involve more complex tasks. Perhaps you need to request something that the reader does not necessarily have to do, or you're following up on earlier requests. Such situations demand that you exercise persuasiveness and establish follow-up strategies.

How to Be Persuasive

Being persuasive does not mean pleading. It means making a case for your request. What does your case rest on? Unless you are the reader's boss, if your only rationale is that you really, really, really want the person to comply with your request, you need to support your case.

Good communicators try to identify mutual goals. Even if your request will benefit only you or your department, you can play upon the fact that people like to appear helpful. By making a request, you give your reader—let's call him Joe—an opportunity to be helpful—and perhaps run up a "credit balance" with you. If you've helped Joe in the past or can help him in the future, he'll have a reason to help you now.

Another tactic is to appeal to Joe's higher instincts by pointing out how his help will benefit the entire organization. Most people want to be "team players," and helping others is part of playing on a team.

Sample 4, a memo from the head of the mailroom to the company's managers, shows persuasive writing.

To: All Managers and Administrative Personnel

From: Henry Clavin, Manager, Mailing & Shipping Services

Re: The Need for Cost-Center Codes on Outgoing Mail

By summarizing the memo's message, this subject line saves the busy reader time.

Please be sure that your <u>cost-center code</u> is written in the upper right-hand corner on all outgoing mail. We have recently received many pieces of mail without cost centers on them.

While I understand that everyone is busy, we in Mailing & Shipping Services are also busy. The volume we handle does not allow us to put cost-center codes on outgoing mail. When we do have to put cost-center codes on outgoing mail, it slows up both that mail and delivery of everyone else's incoming mail.

If you do not know your cost-center code, you can get it by calling me at ext. 653 or Mary Beth Morris in Accounting.

Thank you in advance for your cooperation.

cc: M.B. Morris

Sample 4: Using Persuasion.

Watch Out!
When making requests, don't offer to do the work yourself. You will gain nothing and risk losing good will if your offer is taken up by some readers and not others.

Note how the writer acknowledges that everyone is pressed for time. That helps create common ground. The point that everyone's mail is delayed when the mailroom has to look up cost centers will not be lost on those who do put cost centers on their outgoing mail, only to have their mail slowed up by those who don't. That puts peer pressure on those who don't use cost-center codes.

Finally, notice that Henry offers help in case some readers do not know their cost-center codes.

Using Threats

Depending on the situation, it can be useful to include a threat or consequence in the memo. This should be a strategy reserved for the second request, if the first one does not get results. Sample 5 shows the second request on the cost-center issue.

Read Sample 5 carefully. It demonstrates how to use a threat properly, as well as how to use format—in this case, underscoring and italics—to highlight key information. Note the use of "Second Request" in the subject line.

Note also that Harry has obtained a vice president's approval before making this threat. If you are ever in doubt about your authority or the practicality of a consequence, be sure to check it out with someone above you.

Watch Out!

Be very careful with threats. Never use them in first requests unless you have a very good reason. Try to make them sound like consequences, not threats. Be sure you can follow through on the threat, that it is practical, and that you have the authority to make it.

Finally, if you must make a threat, link it to what you're trying to accomplish. Don't threaten an unrelated action or something out of proportion to what you're requesting.

To: All Managers and Administrative Personnel

From: Henry Clavin, Manager, Mailing & Shipping Services

Re: <u>Second Request</u>: Please Use Cost-Center Codes on Outgoing Mail

As a follow-up to my earlier memo, I repeat: *Please be sure that your <u>cost-center code</u> is on all outgoing mail.* While almost all outgoing mail now comes to us with cost centers, there are still exceptions.

> Format reinforces the stronger tone of this second request.

<u>Please note</u>: As of the first of next month, any outgoing mail that comes to the mailroom without a cost center <u>will be returned to senders</u> so they can put the cost center on it. I have spoken with Mike McFadden, Vice President, Operations, and he has approved this course of action.

Again, if you do not know your cost-center code, you can get it by calling me or Mary Beth Morris in Accounting.

Thank you for your cooperation in this small but important cost-control measure.

cc: M. McFadden
     M.B. Morris

Sample 5: Second Request, Including Threat.

Follow-Up Strategies for Requests

The best way to follow up a written request, especially if a second request doesn't get results, is by phone. No matter how personal you are on paper, writing is less personal and easier to ignore than a phone call or a face-to-face meeting. For example, instead of a third request, Henry Clavin should call the managers of areas that still don't put cost-center codes on their mail. As a fourth step, he could visit them personally to discuss it.

When two written requests don't get the desired result, call and ask (nicely) what the problem is. People don't usually ignore requests just to annoy you. Something is keeping them from complying. Try to find out what that is and work with them to overcome it, or if necessary, adjust your time frame while they get things sorted out.

An Outline for Requests

Try using the following general outline for memos in which you make requests:

To:

From:

Date:

Subject:

Opening, Paragraph 1: Mention the overall request and the time frame.

Body, Paragraph 2: Give details of the request.

Paragraph 3: Give the rationale for the request (or consequences of not complying, or both).

Add other paragraphs as needed.

Closing: Thank the reader and add follow-up if necessary.

The Least You Need to Know

➤ Be very specific about what you are requesting, in planning and in the memo itself.

➤ Use format to highlight important information, particularly the time and place of meetings.

➤ Remember to gain cooperation: Identify mutual goals, sound authoritative, include threats on second requests, and follow up on your requests.

➤ Limit written requests to two memos, follow up by phone, and then, if practical, follow up in person for the fourth request.

➤ Be sure you have the authority or the back-up you need when you make a request, particularly if you make what could be interpreted as a threat.

Announcements That Get the Word Out

Memos that make announcements are one of the chief ways managers at all levels communicate with employees. Announcements are not particularly difficult, but like any form of business writing, they have their own requirements. This chapter will show you these requirements and how to meet them.

What's New?

Essentially, announcements tell employees of changes in the organization. Management often uses announcements to make employees aware of:

➤ Personnel changes

➤ Policy changes

➤ Special events

Because they go to groups of people, memos that make announcements tend to have an official tone. But they can take a personal or even lighthearted tone in certain instances, such as an announcement for the annual Christmas party.

Announcement memos are also a key tool for recognizing people and welcoming new employees. When someone joins the staff, it is not simply "nice" to announce that fact. Your announcement recognizes her existence, welcomes her to the team, and paves the way for people who'll be meeting her on the job.

Similarly, people who work on a particularly successful project or a special event should be recognized. People enjoy being recognized on paper. (That's why most of us like seeing our name in the newspaper, provided we haven't been arrested.)

The announcements that don't get issued are often the ones that cause the most trouble—when someone joins or leaves an organization, or when there's a major change in organizational structure and it goes unannounced or is announced too late.

Good Timing

The timing of announcements is important. An announcement issued too late can be an embarrassment. It can make management look uncaring or out of touch, as if the last thing on their minds is keeping employees informed. On the other hand, an announcement issued too early can turn into an embarrassment if the news being announced doesn't happen or if details turn out to be wrong. Pay attention to timing.

For example, if someone new is joining the organization, his first day on the job is a good time to issue a memo announcing he's come on board. If you send it before then and he winds up not joining, it could be embarrassing. On the other hand, I've seen such announcements go out weeks after the fact, as if it took forever to get around to it.

> **Trick of the Trade**
> If you have to make an announcement that readers will see as late, acknowledge that fact early in the memo. For example, you can use a first line such as "With apologies to Steve Murphy for the lateness of this memo, we welcome him to Campbell Associates." or "While most of you have read about our recent merger in the newspapers, we'd like to cover several items related to this important event."

Similarly, if the organization is merging with another one, you shouldn't announce it too early: The major stockholders need to know first, and, again, it will be embarrassing if the deal falls through. However, a merger is often announced weeks after everyone has been gossiping about it and reading about it in the newspapers, which makes management appear out of touch.

Pick the right time: not so early that it's not an actual fact, and not so late that it seems like an afterthought.

If, on the other hand, you are announcing an upcoming annual event such as the company picnic or the blood donor drive, give people six to eight weeks' notice on the first announcement. Do a follow-up two to three weeks before the event, then issue a reminder the week before.

People Come, People Go, People Get Promoted

Announcing personnel changes is usually straightforward. The most important element, as important as timing, is having your facts straight. If you announce incorrect information, you defeat the purpose of the memo and may insult the person you're writing about.

When Someone Joins the Organization

It's fun to announce good news. Sample 1 announces that someone is joining the organization. The sample follows basic custom for this kind of announcement. The traditional opening line is "Please join me in welcoming…" This is hard to improve on. It's also customary to include some background information: former employer, skills the person will contribute, and some personal information, with education the most often included.

Use good judgment in deciding how much personal information to include. Some people will not want their hobbies or musical tastes disclosed. Very few would want a divorce mentioned. The best way to ensure that this kind of memo will not offend its subject is to show it to the person, but that really shouldn't be necessary if you think carefully about what's appropriate. Take a warm and personal (but not gushing) tone. Don't brag about the employee's accomplishments or go into great depth about the company's expectations of the person.

The audience for such announcements will range from those who will report to the person on up to everyone in the company, depending on how senior the new employee is. As a basic guideline, anyone who will be reporting to or regularly dealing with a new person should receive an announcement when that person comes on board.

When Someone Leaves

Trying to avoid an unpleasant topic, many organizations do not issue announcements when people leave. Meanwhile, the rumor mill spins fast and furious. When anyone in senior or middle management leaves, in my view there should be an announcement.

This is one of the few kinds of memos in which it's OK to be vague. The reasons for someone's leaving tend to reflect poorly either on the person leaving (if he was fired) or on the organization (if he found a better position elsewhere). It's best to be obscure about the person's reasons for leaving and future plans, unless of course he is simply retiring.

The memo in Sample 2 announces a termination.

> **What's That?**
> *Middle management* is the layer of management between senior managers and supervisors. Middle managers usually have managers or supervisors reporting to them.

To: All Marketing Employees

From: Louise Quant, Vice President of Sales & Marketing

Subject: Ron Geiger, Our New Director of Marketing

> Louise gives just the right amount of information.

Please join me in welcoming Ron Geiger to the position of Director of Marketing. Before joining Reliable Manufacturing, Ron was Manager of Marketing at a midwest building supplies distributor. Ron's experience with distribution systems and point-of-purchase display brings us the skills we need to further penetrate the retail market.

Ron holds an MBA from Northwestern's Kellogg School of Management and a BA from George Washington University. He has just moved to Middleville with his wife and two daughters and enjoys movies, family outings, and playing blues guitar.

Over the next several days, Ron will be learning more about our company and meeting with each of you personally.

Sample 1: Announcing a New Employee.

To: All Employees

From: Hedrick Jones, President

Subject: Personnel Change

> A short memo is enough to acknowledge someone who was fired or suddenly quit.

This is to announce that effective tomorrow, Larry Lane will be leaving Amalgamated Ltd. to pursue other interests. For now, the duties associated with Larry's position of Vice President, Corporate Strategy, will be divided among senior management.

Please join me in wishing Larry all the best in his future endeavors.

Sample 2: Announcing a Termination.

Most people, reading between the lines of Sample 2, will realize that Larry was terminated. The clues are that the change is effective the next day ("effective immediately" would be even more obvious), that Larry's plans are vague, and that he was not thanked for his contribution.

You may be wondering, if everyone knows that Larry was terminated, why not mention it and the reason? The answer is that people's privacy must be protected. Besides, there could be potential legal issues in making such an announcement.

But if the memo is going to say so little, why write it at all? The answer is, to acknowledge Larry's moving on officially and to announce the disposition of his duties.

The memo shown in Sample 3 announces a more pleasant event.

> **Watch Out!**
> When someone leaves for any reason, it creates emotional and operational dislocations. An announcement, even a bland one, at least partly addresses this. Not issuing a memo makes the sense of dislocation seem even worse, especially to those who reported to the person.

As a basic rule of thumb, the degree of warmth and personal detail to include in a memo about personnel changes depends upon the person leaving the organization, her length of service, and her reason for leaving.

When Someone Is Promoted

Announcements are particularly important when someone is promoted, because in many companies the promotion doesn't seem "real" to the person being promoted or to his or her co-workers unless it is announced. Sample 4 includes the basics of this type of announcement.

The goal in this letter is to announce the promotion, but also to indicate—subtly and briefly—that it is deserved and that others who are qualified and work hard will also be promoted.

> **Trick of the Trade**
> In general, keep memos announcing personnel changes short. Their purpose is to announce changes, not explain them in depth.

To: All Employees

From: Peggy Gilbert, Vice President, Human Resources

Subject: Thank You, Sheila O'Shay

This subject line captures the spirit of the memo nicely.

Please join me in wishing the very best to Sheila O'Shay, who will be retiring from the bank at the end of this month after 37 years of service.

Sheila joined the bank as a loan documentation clerk when we were still First Farmers' Trust and had only two offices. She rose steadily through positions of increasing responsibility in the credit function and became a loan officer in 1982. Sheila's superb business development skills led to her promotion to Vice President of Lending for the eastern district in 1990.

During her career, Sheila also raised four children with her husband Charles, an electrical engineer.

Sheila has certainly earned her retirement, which she and Charles will spend here in Meadowville and at their winter home in Scottsdale, Arizona. We will all miss her.

Those who worked with Sheila are invited to join us for a cake-and-coffee toast for her on Friday the 24th in the Third Floor Conference Room at 4:00 p.m.

Sample 3: Announcing a Retirement.

To: All Employees

From: Peggy Gilbert, Vice President, Human Resources

Subject: Promotion of James Neville

Specific details about the person being promoted brings Peggy's announcement to life.

Please join me in congratulating James Neville, who will be promoted to Director of Technical Services effective June 14th.

Jimmy joined us in 1994 as a programmer and quickly rose to Senior Programmer, then Systems Analyst, and, most recently, Manager of Technical Support. Jimmy's hands-on knowledge of our systems coupled with his managerial skill and his MBA, which he recently completed in his off-hours, well qualify him for this position.

Sample 4: Announcing a Promotion.

Announcing Organizational Changes

The most common organizational changes that need announcing are policy and structural changes. Although the major goal here is to announce rather than explain, policy and structural changes usually call for more explanation than personnel changes.

The memo shown in Sample 5 announces a change that's sure to be unpopular (at least with the managers).

People usually temper bad news with vague language and elaborate buzzwords. This fools no one. In fact, many people lose respect for people who deliver mealy-mouthed messages. Most adults can deal with the truth if it's delivered fairly and personally, as in the following memo.

In Sample 5, the threefold message is clear without being harsh: Management can't be rewarded when the company is not profitable; we're not going to take it out on the employees (not yet anyway); and we have work ahead of us. That's it. It's all there.

Sample 6 shows an example of a straightforward policy announcement.

To: All Managers and Supervisors

From: Mike Cummings, Chief Executive Officer

Subject: Salary and Promotion Freeze

> Mike's tone is appropriate: seriousness and regret, coupled with fairness and authority.

I am sorry to announce that effective immediately and for the rest of this year, there will be a salary and promotion freeze in effect for all management personnel. This freeze does <u>not</u> affect clerical, professional, and technical staff.

The base salaries, job grades, and titles of all managers and supervisors will remain at current levels during the freeze. No new requests for increases or promotions will be considered during this time. Any increases or promotions now in process will be frozen regardless of where they are in the process.

This freeze is necessary because we have not been profitable for the past two quarters and are projecting a loss for this quarter. Although we are taking steps to restore profitability, we cannot in good conscience give raises and promotions to management under the circumstances. I and all of senior management are also subject to the freeze.

Management must accept responsibility for the state of the company and lead the return to profitability. Thank you in advance for joining me in this effort.

Sample 5: Announcing a Freeze on Salaries and Promotions.

To: All Sales Personnel

From: Bruce Threadgill, Vice President, Marketing

Subject: Price Increase for Next Year

> Bruce anticipates objections and addresses them directly.

Effective with contracts written on or after January 1st, prices of all our products will increase by 3.5%. Each of you will receive the new price list within the next week.

Management recognizes that this aggressive pricing may hurt the sales of some products in our line. However, we are willing to take that hit in order to earn higher profits on the products that will continue to sell well.

We will hold a series of meetings during the first two weeks of December to discuss strategies for presenting this increase to our customers. The times and places of these meetings will be announced on the Monday before Thanksgiving Day.

Sample 6: Announcing a Policy Change.

Announcements for Special Events

Special events include anything from the annual holiday party and blood donor drive to legal matters, mergers and acquisitions, financial performance, or general news reports about the company.

Recurrent Scheduled Events

Announcements of regular annual events are straightforward, as Sample 7 shows.

The idea in this memo is to convey the twin messages of good times and safety. Notice that, although I didn't use them on previous samples in this chapter, you can use tools such as indentation, boldface, and headlines in announcements.

Announcing Structural Changes

Employees must be promptly advised of any changes in the organizational structure that can affect them. An example of a memo that does this effectively is shown in Sample 8.

To: All Employees at Corporate Headquarters

From: Jamie Fortunado, Vice President, Human Resources

Subject: Holiday Party

It's that time of year again! Happy holidays from all of us in Human Resources.

Here are the details on this year's annual holiday party:

Day and Date:	Thursday, December 17th
Time:	7:00 p.m. to midnight
Place:	The Boom Boom Room 444 East 57th Street

Jamie uses format and tone effectively to get her message across.

A hot and cold buffet will be served from 7:00 to 9:00 p.m. There will be an open bar for the entire evening and dancing to the sounds of dee-jay Cool Klee on the second floor from 9:00 p.m. to midnight.

Special Note on Transportation

All employees are urged to take the transportation provided by the company from The Boom Boom Room to their homes. Vans will leave for Long Island, New Jersey, and Connecticut at 12:15 a.m. Employees within the five boroughs of New York can take taxis (shared, when possible) and submit their receipts for full reimbursement.

Let's make this the greatest (and safest) holiday party ever! See you there.

Sample 7: Announcement of a Regular Event.

To: All Sales Personnel

From: Neil Lemmon, Senior Vice President, Sales

Subject: Reorganization of the Sales Function

Neil states his main message in the first sentence.

This is to announce a reorganization of the sales function effective next Monday, April 3.

Essentially we will be reorganizing Sales along product lines. This will provide greater product specialization than our present regional organization. This is in response to our customers, who have repeatedly said that we need to improve our product knowledge.

The details will be presented this coming Friday. Basically, we will collapse our 14 districts and five regions into five sales departments organized by product line, as follows:

➤ Copiers

➤ Commercial photography products

➤ X-ray and other health care systems

➤ Military optics

➤ Industrial devices

We expect this to be a far more efficient structure resulting in better product knowledge and higher sales.

Sample 8: Announcing a Change in Organizational Structure.

Announcements Regarding News Events

Public relations professionals repeatedly advise companies to be as open as possible during times of crises. Although the legal staff must often play a role in responding to negative publicity, Sample 9 offers one basic approach for communicating about it internally.

When addressing news stories, stick with the main point of the story. Be sure you understand how true or false it is and confirm the degree of truth or falsity for the company's employees—to the extent that legal counsel allows. It's not advisable, from the standpoint of communications and morale, to keep employees in the dark. But neither is it advisable to discuss details in an internal memo about a legal matter in process.

To: All Employees

From: Lisa Marino, Director, Corporate Communications

Subject: Recent News Stories About the Company

As most of you are aware, the company has recently been the subject of negative stories in several newspapers and magazines and on radio and television. This memo will clear the air.

The substance of the stories is that our lawnmowers are unsafe and have caused severe injury.

> Lisa earns her readers' respect by stating the need to keep details confidential, without appearing evasive.

For legal reasons I cannot go into the situation in great detail. However, I can tell you that in all but two of the 12 cases, the charges appear to be completely groundless. In two cases it does appear that there may be some liability of some kind on the part of our company.

All of us at Blade Industries remain committed to making the best and safest products that we can. Our products are consistently rated among the highest in safety by independent institutes and in injury statistics. We have every intention of maintaining that record of safety.

Sample 9: Announcement About Negative Publicity.

An Outline for Announcements

Here is a basic outline for announcements:

To:

From:

Date:

Subject:

Opening, Paragraph 1: Mention what you are announcing and the effective date (if there is one).

Body, Paragraph 2: Give some details about the person, event, or change.

Paragraph 3: Give additional details if necessary.

Add other paragraphs as needed.

Closing: Add a closing if necessary (but often it is not).

The Least You Need to Know

➤ Announcements, by definition, go to groups of people within the company, so a somewhat impersonal tone can be acceptable on some of them.

➤ Announcements must be timed properly. It's best to send out the announcement just as the news is happening or soon after it has happened.

➤ The purpose of an announcement is to announce a change or an event, not to explain it.

➤ Keep announcements short, usually to one page.

➤ It's acceptable to use the same language repeatedly in similar kinds of announcements. For example, open with "Please join me in welcoming…" when announcing a new staff member, or "Please join me in congratulating…" for a promotion.

Chapter 16

Writing Up Poor Performance

In This Chapter

➤ When to issue a written reprimand

➤ Your role and the role of Human Resources

➤ How to get the result you want

As far as I'm concerned, there is no form of business writing more difficult than the reprimand. A lot of people must agree, because in almost every company I've ever worked, I've seen cases of poor performance tolerated. They were tolerated because the manager either didn't know what to do, or more often, could not get up the strength to do it.

It takes strength to write a reprimand. It's hard to tell people, in a calm, specific way, that they're not doing their job well. Nobody likes getting a reprimand, and some people don't know how to respond constructively to one. But although giving reprimands is difficult, it is necessary at times, and you need to know how to write one.

What's That?
A *reprimand* is an order from a manager or supervisor to a subordinate to change his or her behavior. This can mean the subordinate must stop doing something, start doing something, or do something differently.

When Should You Write a Reprimand?

You need to write a reprimand when you've asked a subordinate to change his behavior and he has not done so. Suppose someone keeps arriving late for work. You might ignore it the first time, ask about it the second time, and the third time, tell him that he must start arriving to work on time every day. You will probably mention that you and other people depend on him to be there on time, and that good business practice demands it.

After one more verbal warning, it would certainly be appropriate to "write him up," as the saying goes. During that final verbal warning, you should warn him of the written reprimand. ("If you're late again within the next 30 days, I'm going to have to write a formal reprimand.")

The subject of improving employee performance is beyond the scope of this book. Large companies have guidelines and policies for these situations. In a small company, such guidance may come from the head of Human Resources, your boss, or perhaps even the president.

Remember, you owe someone a verbal warning before moving on to a written reprimand, and if necessary, to termination.

The Role of the Human Resources Department

If your organization is large enough to have one, the Human Resources (or Personnel) department can be very helpful when you deal with problem employees:

➤ They can be a sounding board and help you get a perspective on a difficult employee; they see these situations all the time.

➤ They can tell you about the process the company has in place to address such situations.

➤ They can review what you write to ensure that it's reasonable, legal, and in line with company policy.

➤ They can back you up in meetings with the underperforming employee.

Generally, however, Human Resources won't write your letters of reprimand for you. It's your responsibility as a manager to deal with employee performance issues.

Focus on the Problem

The goal in writing a reprimand is to focus on the problem, not the person. At times, it's easy to become angry at someone who seems uncooperative or uncaring about his job. You may feel that the person is trying to annoy you or wants to be fired. While you may come across such people, most performance problems are caused by deeper issues, such as trouble at home, past failures, being in the wrong job, substance abuse, or a poor work ethic.

None of these issues should be the subject of your memo. Don't get into mind reading or trying to be the person's therapist or social worker. You are her boss, her manager on the job. Your role is to signal that she needs to change her behavior, not her personality. So you must focus on behavior. That means you must focus on facts.

Begin Planning Early

You cannot write an effective reprimand without solid planning. Planning here goes beyond writing an outline: You must gather and record facts very early in the process. Use a memo to the file, as discussed in Chapter 3, to record your facts as you go along (see Sample 1 on the following page).

Memos to the file like this one, or other informal *written* records of what the employee did, when he did it, and what each of you said, are key steps in the process. Don't rely on your memory. Having these facts helps you to write the reprimand by keeping you focused on behavior, and it helps protect you from charges of unfairness.

Regular performance appraisals are another key way of recording lapses in employee performance. Most large companies have formal appraisal systems, and every company needs one. Be sure to refer to the employee's personnel file and recent appraisals before writing a reprimand.

This kind of fact-finding takes the place of brainstorming when you write a reprimand.

> **What's That?**
> A *performance appraisal* (or review) is a formal, written review of an employee's performance, strengths, and areas for improvement. Managers give these reviews to subordinates regularly, usually once a year, but in many companies as often as quarterly, which is preferable.

Memo to the file from Timothy Sappington

Re: Dennis Wallace

Date: September 9, 1997

> Specific details create an effective record in case problems with this employee continue.

This memo is to note two conversations I had with Dennis Wallace. One happened today at about 10:15 a.m. The other occurred last Friday.

Dennis has been spending excessive amounts of time on personal telephone calls. I spoke with him about this last Friday, and he first told me "I'm not on the phone that much at all," and then, "I've got problems at home." I told him to please sharply reduce the amount of time he spends on personal calls.

Yesterday afternoon, I received the phone bill detail for last month and analyzed the usage for the five people in my department. Dennis's usage is more than triple that of the next most frequent user. (In fact, the duties of this department, including Dennis's, require few calls outside the building.) Also, he appears to be on the phone as much as ever since I spoke with him about it a week ago.

This morning, I told Dennis that he cannot continue to use the telephone at this rate. I reminded him of our policy of keeping personal calls to a total of ten minutes a day, and told him that I was concerned about both the expense and, even more, the time taken from his work.

Dennis told me again that he has problems at home. (He and his wife are considering adopting a child and are finding the decision very difficult.)

I told him that I realize that his and his wife's decision is a hard one, but that this is a place of business. I told him that if his phone usage does not return to normal levels within the next week—and remain there—I will have to issue a written warning to him.

Sample 1: Memo to the File Regarding Poor Performance.

An Outline for a Reprimand

Once you have your facts together and you've decided that the written warning is necessary, you need an outline. The following shows a basic working outline for a reprimand.

To:

From:

Date:

Subject:

Statement of the problem: Specifically state what the overall performance problem is.

Evidence of the problem: Give specific instances of the problem. This may take a few paragraphs, or you can use bullets. Mention deviations from company or department guidelines, policy, and expectations.

Steps taken so far: Mention conversations you have had, prior written warnings, and anything you've done to help the employee improve.

Your expectations: Clearly state what you expect from the employee in the future; mention any assistance that you will provide.

Conclusion and next steps: Note that, if the employee's performance does not improve immediately and remain at the improved level, further steps—up to and including termination—will be taken.

This outline includes all the major points you must cover, and in the correct order. You are simply giving the employee written notice that if her performance does not improve right away and remain at the improved level, she will be fired. The entire memo should not run more than two pages.

Trick of the Trade

It's important to note in the letter of reprimand that the employee's performance must improve and *remain* at the improved level. Too often, an employee will improve temporarily and backslide after the pressure is off.

The Letter Itself: Loud and Clear

By the time you get to the point when you actually need to write a letter of reprimand, you clearly have a performance problem on your hands: The employee has not responded to your requests to improve. Therefore, the letter must be a loud, clear wake-up call for the employee.

The language of such a letter should not be personal. You're not trying to establish rapport. You're not even trying to be persuasive. Rather, you are officially documenting the fact that the employee is not performing up to standards and that this is unacceptable. You are supporting that charge with facts. You are allowing for the possibility that the employee's performance may still improve, but you're also allowing for the possibility that it may not.

Using the Outline

Sample 2 shows a sample letter of reprimand based on the outline and using facts drawn from Sample 1.

Trick of the Trade
Be sure to have your boss and someone in Human Resources examine the memo and approve your course of action.

This kind of memo places the responsibility for improvement directly on the employee, where it belongs. The memo is impersonal and displays no emotion. Finally, it puts the employee on notice that he may face termination if he continues his current behavior. In most companies, this kind of written warning is necessary before suspending or terminating an employee for performance problems, except in cases of proven or admitted theft, drug abuse, sexual harassment, and similar issues.

To: Dennis Wallace

From: Timothy Sappington

Date: September 23, 1997

Re: Excessive personal telephone calls

> Timothy states the possible consequence of the employee's poor performance in a way that cannot be misconstrued.

This memo documents the fact that your usage of the company telephone for personal calls is excessive and unacceptable.

I have spoken with you on three occasions regarding this problem, on September 2, 9, and 16, and you have made only marginal improvement. After noting your personal calls during the month of August, I began getting weekly usage reports from our Telecommunications Data Center. Since I first spoke with you about this issue, your personal calls to your home number exceeded a total of 90 minutes on 12 different days and 60 minutes on another eight days. Company guidelines limit personal calls to a total of ten minutes a day.

Although I understand that you are dealing with a personal situation, you must understand that our company is a place of business. You are incurring excessive costs and taking time and attention away from your work. You must immediately reduce the amount of time you spend on the phone on personal calls to ten minutes a day or less.

Our conversations on this matter have been largely unproductive. If you need to use vacation time or unpaid leave in order to deal with your personal problem, then you should do so. If you need an adjustment to your working hours, we can consider that as well (although I cannot guarantee it). I have suggested these steps in our talks, but you have been unresponsive.

You must improve your job performance in this area immediately or further remedial steps, including suspension without pay or termination, may be taken.

Sample 2: Letter of Reprimand.

What's Next?

Even if you would rather have him out of the company, after he receives this memo the employee has the right to try to improve his performance. If he does and if he maintains his performance at the improved level, he is in the clear, unless he substitutes another unacceptable behavior. If he substitutes another kind of poor performance, you should move quickly (after one verbal warning, at most) to another written reprimand and toward termination.

Watch Out! When an employee who has received a written reprimand remains defensive and fails to improve, things rarely work out well. The best course of action is swift termination.

If an employee improves, it's customary in most companies to note that fact at the next regular performance appraisal. A savvy employee might ask you to document his improvement some time after the letter of reprimand. If this happens, ask for guidance from Human Resources or your boss.

In many cases, unfortunately, you'll find that you have to go to the next step toward termination.

The Final Warning

The next step can be suspension or termination, as stated in the letter of reprimand, or another warning. Suspension is rarely used. If the employee isn't improving, suspending him is not about to help matters. The next step is usually termination. However, in order to be as fair as possible and to avoid charges of wrongful termination, many large companies require a final written warning.

Sample 3 shows an example of such a warning.

Note that the tone of Sample 3 is impersonal, unemotional, and factual, yet clear and strong. Don't say you're sorry or disappointed. Use the approach of good old Joe Friday on *Dragnet:* just the facts.

Termination Letters

Sadly, some people fail to improve their performance and must be terminated. In a large company, the termination letter is usually written by Human Resources. In a small company, however, the task may fall to you.

Keep it short and factual, as shown in Sample 4.

To: Dennis Wallace

From: Timothy Sappington

Date: September 30, 1997

Re: Final Warning: Excessive personal telephone calls

As a follow-up to my memo of September 23rd, this memo documents the fact that your usage of the company telephone for personal calls remains at excessive and unacceptable levels.

> By quantifying the employee's poor performance, Timothy builds a solid case for the next step: termination.

During this past week, since receiving written warning, your personal calls have totaled five hours and 42 minutes. This is an average of more than 60 minutes per day. My memo of September 23rd mentions the acceptable limit of ten minutes, and that was your target.

This memo represents a final warning. If you do not immediately bring your level of personal calls to within acceptable limits, further remedial steps, including suspension without pay or termination, will be taken.

Sample 3: Final Warning.

To: Dennis Wallace

From: Timothy Sappington

Date: October 7, 1997

Re: Termination of Employment

> Because the run-up to termination was handled well, the notice of termination can be short and to the point.

Effective immediately, your employment at this company is terminated. Please remove any personal belongings from your desk and office and vacate the premises as soon as possible.

The reasons for this step have been well documented in memos dated September 23 and 30 and center upon your excessive use of the company telephone for personal calls.

We wish you the best in your future endeavors.

Sample 4: Letter of Termination.

Document, Document, Document

Proper termination comes down to a number of things, including good judgment, clear expectations, solid interpersonal skills, and sound company policy. All of these should be reflected in proper documentation. As shown in this chapter, you must document the remediation and termination process correctly or you can cause major headaches for yourself and your company.

The Least You Need to Know

➤ Verbal warnings, which you should document in memos to the file, are the first step in working with an employee who needs to improve his performance.

➤ If the employee does not improve his performance in response to verbal warnings, move quickly to a written reprimand.

➤ All of your writing regarding an employee who needs to improve his performance should be impersonal, factual, clear, and strong.

➤ Be sure to get guidance from Human Resources and your boss as you go through the process; have them read over your letters of reprimand.

Chapter 17

Sales Letters: Your License to Print Money

In This Chapter

➤ A proven approach to writing sales letters

➤ How to talk to the reader about features and benefits

➤ How to increase the chances of getting a response

You see them all the time in your mailbox and in-box. You probably read some of them. Call them sales letters, direct mail pieces—anything but junk mail. There's too much money at stake in this multibillion-dollar-a-year industry for them to be junk.

Although you're probably not a direct-mail pro, there's a good chance you'll have to write a sales letter or something very like one in the course of your career. If you work for someone else, it's a great skill to have in your portfolio. If you're self-employed, you might find prospecting and selling by mail to be a great source of business. That's what I've found as a consultant and business writer.

The topic of direct mail, which includes mailing lists, reply mechanisms, collateral material, and much more, has filled many books. This chapter will show you something basic: how to write a sales letter that opens doors—and wallets and purses and checkbooks.

> ### What's That?
>
> A *mailing list* is a list of the names and addresses of people who will be the target of a direct mail campaign.
>
> *Reply mechanisms* are ways for the reader to get in touch with you, such as postage-paid return envelopes and postcards, and toll-free telephone numbers.
>
> *Collateral material* means brochures and other kinds of product literature that accompany the sales letter.

The Challenge: Getting Attention

If you think there's too much direct mail out there, you're in good company: People in the industry agree. It's a problem for them, and they call it "clutter." Their solution, of course, is not to stop sending out their letters, but rather to get theirs to break through the clutter and grab readers' attention.

At the least, a sales letter has to be well written. If you can make it sparkle or sizzle or skyrocket (what is it about "s" words, anyway?), so much the better. These letters also have to speak to the reader in a personal way.

Most of all, you must have something to offer that addresses a need the reader sees as important. This means that whatever you're offering has to solve a problem, fill a need, save money, or make money for the reader.

The battle for reader attention has led the industry to develop various bells and whistles to engage the reader. These include so-called involvement pieces that give the reader something to do, such as moving a sticker from the collateral material to the reply card. Although these often work, the most fundamental things you need for success in selling by mail is a good offer, a good letter, and a great mailing list.

A Word About Mailing Lists

As we all know, the reader is king. The people on the mailing list are the readers. Depending on your business, this list can number from ten people up into the tens of thousands. In building your mailing list, you get to choose your audience, so this step is extremely important. No matter how great your letter is, if it's going to the wrong people, you'll get nowhere.

As a small-business person, I've found that the best way to compile a mailing list is by myself, by hand, over time. I go to the library and search professional and industry directories. I collect names from newspapers and magazines. I keep the lists of attendees from every event I go to. Then I enter all of these names into my database of prospects. (Often I have to get on the phone to get addresses and titles and so on.) Key point: I don't do large-scale mailings, so this is practical for me.

If you need to do large mailings, say over 500 or 1,000 pieces, you'll probably need to rent a list from a mailing list broker. There are several very large ones in the U.S., as well as many smaller outfits. They can be found in the Yellow Pages in major cities. Call and they'll gladly send you a catalog.

You can also rent the lists of organizations or publications whose members or readers you want to approach by mail. But the direct-mail business is a subject unto itself, and beyond the scope of this book.

> **Trick of the Trade**
> If you are a consult-ant or small-business person, you should defi-nitely consider compiling a computer-accessible list of names and addresses and regularly doing some prospecting by mail. All it takes is a good word-processing package that will enable you to create a table of this information and then merge that list with a sales letter. This is also a great way to test an idea that you might have, to see if it will really work with real prospects.

Two Ways to Write a Letter

You can write either a long sales letter or a short one. By "long" I mean more than two pages. A typical format is four to six pages on oversized paper, done so that the letter folds out. By "short" I mean a page or two. One page can be very effective, and stands the best chance of actually getting read. In this book we deal only with short sales letters.

Short and Sweet Sales Letters

My formula for short, three-paragraph sales letters has been the same for more than ten years, because it works:

Dear _____:

First paragraph: Dramatize a problem that the reader can relate to.

Second paragraph: Tell the reader that you can solve this problem (and how you can).

Third paragraph: Ask for action or tell the reader either how to get in touch or that you'll be in touch.

There's nothing magical about it. It's just the old hard-sell, gussied up:

> "Tired of sleeping on that tired old bed? Tired of waking up tired?" (The Problem)

> "Then try the new SuperMat Sleep-Easy. Your back will know the differ-ence." (The Solution)

> "Visit your local SuperMat today. Check the phone book for one near you." (The Way to Get the Solution)

It works. It's as reliable as ready, aim, fire. (Yes, unfortunately, sometimes you miss.)

Sample 1 demonstrates this formula in action.

April 12, 1998

Ms. Wendy Quinn
President
Quinn Distribution
945 Washington Street
Knoxville, TN 99999

Dear Ms. Quinn:

Are you disappointed or angry that so much of your money goes to taxes each year? Do you feel that your taxes are as low as they possibly could be? Would you like to cut your annual tax bill by next April 15th?

I am a certified public accountant specializing in tax and estate planning for business owners. A number of my clients in the distribution business have found that their taxes dropped dramatically—by up to 25% in some cases—with my tax planning strategies. These strategies are, of course, entirely legal. Some of these strategies could keep more of your money in your pocket.

Next week, I'll be calling you to arrange a meeting at your convenience. If you give me 30 minutes, I'll give you a new way of thinking about your taxes.

I look forward to speaking with you soon.

Sincerely,

Jack Murray

President

Sample 1: A Short, Sweet Sales Letter.

> Opening with one or more questions immediately involves the reader.

What's at Work in This Letter?

Aside from the formula I mentioned in the previous section, there are several other things at work in Sample 1. Let's analyze them paragraph by paragraph.

In the first paragraph, the copy strategy is to use questions to dramatize the problem. (The date of the letter—right around the annual federal tax deadline—means that these are timely questions.) As I pointed out in Chapter 8, questions tend to engage the reader. If you use questions, don't use more than three in a row, four at the most if they're short, because you might overwhelm the reader. You can use bullets to list the questions and increase white space. Questions are a common copy strategy, so come up with ones that the reader will find really interesting.

In the second paragraph, the writer positions himself as the solution to tax problems. In doing this, he must establish credibility, which he does by mentioning that he's a certified public accountant who has helped clients in the reader's industry. He also quotes a dramatic number—quoting numbers in your copy adds credibility. Most people, and especially business people, are impressed by numbers. He also tries to ease any fears that the reader may have about the legality of these strategies.

The third paragraph tells the reader that Jack will be in touch to make an appointment. The (unstated) action requested is, "Please take my call and give me an appointment." In one sentence he also mentions the amount of time requested and reinforces the core message of the letter by mentioning the benefits again.

The fourth, one-line paragraph in the letter is a cordial closing that rounds things off nicely.

This letter stands a good chance of being read, since it's short and fairly engaging. Unless the reader is paying practically nothing in taxes, she will probably at least take Jack's phone call and listen to his pitch.

What's That?
Direct-mail professionals use the term *copy strategy* to refer to the approach that the letter will take toward the reader and the subject. The term *copy* refers to text of any kind.

Features and Benefits: The Difference and Why It Matters

The major problem in most sales letters written by amateurs is that the copy stresses features rather than benefits.

Here's the difference: *Features* are about the product and service; *benefits* are about the reader. When you talk about features, you're talking about what you are selling. When you talk about benefits, you're talking about how what you are selling can help the reader.

For example, if you say that something you're selling is durable, that's a feature. The benefit is that it won't break down and cost the customer time and money. If you say that the software you sell has drop-down menus and a great "Help" facility, those are features. The benefit is that it's easy for the customer to learn and use.

In service businesses like consulting, sellers tend to tout features without tying them to benefits. Here are some examples of what I mean:

> "Acme Consulting Services was established in 1984 to serve the financial services industry."

> "Our client base includes some of the largest banks and securities firms in the nation, while our staff of over 40 market researchers, strategic planners, and product development specialists holds more than 25 graduate degrees."

> "All of the methods we use on client engagements have stood the test of time, yet we keep abreast of new approaches."

And so on. This is typical of the kind of writing that is all about the seller rather than about the prospects and their needs. The way to avoid writing like this is to focus on how the characteristics of the company can help the reader. Here's how you might rewrite these three points to do just that:

> "Because Acme has specialized in financial services since 1984, we understand the problems you face. You don't have to spend weeks and months—and money—on the consulting assignment teaching us your business."

> "Our staff of over 40 includes market researchers, strategic planners, and product development specialists. This versatile group can work with your people to help you reach your business goals."

> "Our methods have stood the test of time, which means, frankly, that we do not use our clients as guinea pigs. However, we also keep abreast of new approaches in order to bring you the best of them—the ones that will work in your business."

You see? Prospects tend to see comments about how great you are or how great your client list is as self-serving. And they *are* self-serving, unless they are linked to a benefit for the client. Readers care about things like saving time and money and reaching their business goals. Those are benefits.

So the way to write about benefits is to take a feature of your product or service and translate it into a benefit, as in the following examples:

Feature	Benefit
The color is red	You'll stand out in a crowd
The motor is strong	You'll enjoy the power at your fingertips
We work quickly	You can give us the project on short notice and still make your deadlines
We're inexpensive	You save money
We deliver high quality	You get it done right the first time
This glass is bulletproof	You'll be safe from terrorist attacks

Whatever it is, if it's a feature worth mentioning, it's worth tying to a benefit.

More Examples of Good Sales Letters

Sample 2 shows an example of a sales letter for a business product.

As Sample 2 shows, you are certainly not limited to three paragraphs. This letter employs several tactics worth pointing out:

➤ It starts by quoting an independent study. Whenever you can quote a source other than yourself to dramatize a problem, it adds credibility.

➤ The writer explains how his company is able to deliver these savings. This helps overcome the reader's natural skepticism.

➤ The guarantee also helps overcome skepticism and sales resistance, and it dovetails nicely with the request for the reader's current prices: Standard Products can't beat a price without documentation, can it?

➤ The letter uses an eye-catching P.S. to flag a deadline. Any time you add a deadline, whether driven by a special sale, free premium, or extra savings, it tends to increase your response rate—the percentage of the pieces of mail you send that generate a response.

By the way, on most mass mailings, a response rate of 1–2 percent is considered good. That may strike you as low, but on some mailings, one-half percent is considered a good return. Direct mail is "a numbers game."

Sample 3 shows a sales letter for a consumer product.

Trick of the Trade
Generic salutations like "Dear Client" and "Dear Jazz Fan" are obviously far less personal than those using the reader's name. Whenever it is cost-effective (sometimes it just isn't), have an internal address and a personal salutation inserted by computer. It's not necessary to insert the reader's name into the body of the text.

Trick of the Trade
A P.S. on a sales letter can be very effective. Often it is the first (and sometimes the only) part people read, so make it compelling. If possible, mention making or saving money.

179

Standard Products Incorporated
900 Lowell Bank Station
Millstone, CT 04587

Mr. Mark Peters
Vice President
Peterson Brokerage Services
245 Lincoln Blvd.
Los Angeles, CA 09008

> Effective formatting can save a sales letter from going straight into the recycling bin.

Dear Mr. Peters:

A recent study by the American Photocopying Institute showed that <u>photocopying costs have risen 7%</u> in each of the past two years. The study showed that the increase is not due to the cost of copiers. Rather it is the skyrocketing cost of supplies, particularly paper and toner.

I'm writing to you because I can help you cut these costs sharply. In fact, if you own your own copiers or lease at favorable terms, Standard Products Inc. can <u>guarantee</u> that your cost per copy will actually <u>decrease</u> over the next year.

Standard Products can give you this guarantee because we buy in huge volume from various manufacturers and thus win deep discounts. Also our state-of-the-art distribution network <u>minimizes warehousing and shipping costs</u>. We pass these savings on to you by beating whatever price you're now paying.

Of course, low prices mean nothing without high quality, so we also guarantee the quality of our paper, toner, and other supplies. The copies you get with our supplies will be as good—or better—than your current copies.

To get these savings, you only have to do one thing: Pick up the phone and call us at 1-800-555-0300. Tell us your current volume of usage and what you're now paying for paper and toner, and we'll fax you a proposal the next business day. (To give our guarantee of lower prices, we do require documentation of your current prices, so be ready to mail or fax us a recent invoice.)

Don't let another year of cost increases rob your profits. **Call us at 1-800-555-0300 today.**

Yours truly,

Leon Davies
President

P.S. If you place an order with us by the 15th of this month, we will take an <u>additional</u> 10% off the price of that first order. Call now and start saving!

Sample 2: A Sales Letter for a Business Product.

Victory Security Systems
45 Dakota Street
Miami, Florida 00440
1-800-555-6600

> This disclaimer simultaneously raises the issue and disarms objections.

Dear Homeowner:

Unfortunately, crime is on the rise in our city and shows no sign of decreasing. I am not, however, writing to frighten you, but to make you feel more secure.

Your Best Protection

Law enforcement officials everywhere agree that a top-quality home security system is your best protection against forcible home entry. Top-quality systems are the only kind we sell at Victory, which means that you get:

➤ Total protection against forcible entry, whether you are at home or away

➤ An easy-to-use system that you can set or disarm in the dark with just one finger

➤ Protection against false or accidental alarms

➤ Guaranteed three-hour installation and easy 24-month payment terms

We offer a 35-year record of protecting customers in Greater Miami. Our service personnel are bonded, and we can provide numerous local references for your review. Our commitment is to provide only the level of security that you need. However, you must ask yourself: Should I continue without the home security I need?

Act Now to Protect Your Home and Family

Call us at 1-800-555-6600 today for a complimentary analysis of your home security needs. If you call for this free analysis within the next five business days and show your Victory Security Analyst this letter, he will give you a **free Victory Pad Lock** on the spot. This is the lock that stands up to the .357 Magnum at close range, as seen on TV.

Don't you owe this call to yourself and your family? Don't you deserve the protection recommended by law-enforcement officials against forcible home entry? Of course you do. Call today and learn how to protect yourself.

Sincerely,

Andrew Victor
President

P.S. Remember: You get a free Victory Pad Lock just for letting us analyze your security needs.

Sample 3: A Sales Letter for a Consumer Product.

The best writing of any kind appeals to both the head and the heart; that is, to the thinking and the feeling sides of the reader. The subject matter in Sample 3 lends itself to an emotional appeal, which the writer exploits. Whenever possible, try to appeal to basic needs like money, security, and status.

Increasing Your Response Rate

Again, direct mail is a numbers game. Whether you send six pieces, 60, 600, or 60,000, the better your response rate, and the more business you can do. To ensure that you have the highest possible response rate, be sure you:

➤ Start with an up-to-date mailing list of properly targeted prospects.

➤ Translate each important feature of your product or service into a benefit for the reader.

➤ Make an offer that has some time limit or time factor associated with it.

➤ If possible and appropriate, include a compelling P.S., because people generally read them.

➤ Unless you think the list is a complete dud, try a follow-up mailing or even follow-up phone calls to selected prospects.

Provided you can afford the expense, don't give up too fast on direct mail if you believe it can work for your business. Repeated exposure lets people know that you intend to be around for a while and gets them used to seeing your name and your offer. That familiarity ultimately leads to more business.

The Least You Need to Know

➤ The easiest formula for writing a sales letter is to dramatize a problem, present your product or service as the solution, and ask for action or tell the reader how you will follow up.

➤ Much of your success depends on selecting or building the right mailing list.

➤ A sales letter must speak directly to readers about how they'll benefit from dealing with you; don't just tout features.

➤ Enhance your credibility by quoting independent sources whenever possible.

➤ To create a sense of urgency, include the element of time ("If you act now…"), offer a special discount, or offer something for free to prompt the reader to act.

Chapter 18

Writing to Get Media Attention

In This Chapter

➤ How to approach newspapers, magazines, and other media

➤ What makes an idea newsworthy

➤ Do's and don'ts when approaching the media

A *query letter* is the term professional writers and editors use for letters that pitch story ideas to newspapers and magazines and to radio and television shows. A *press release* is not really a letter or memo, but rather a special form of writing to the media. However, you should know about press releases, particularly if you are in sales or marketing or in business for yourself, so I include them in this chapter.

Getting publicity has become an extremely valuable skill in our media-oriented society. This chapter will show you how to go about it.

Why Try to Get Publicity?

Publicity is media coverage of your business or product or of people in your business. You can get publicity if you have something to say that editors or producers see as newsworthy or as interesting to their readers or viewers. You cannot pay an editor or producer to "run your story." You can, however, pay a public relations firm to help you get your story into the media. You can also pay the media to run advertising, but that is not publicity.

What's That?

Editors are the people who decide what stories go into a publication. They also oversee the entire publishing process, from developing and assigning story ideas to writing and photography to layout, design, and production.

Producers decide what stories and guests get covered on a radio or television program. They also oversee all the work necessary to get the show on the air.

A *public relations* (or PR) firm works with clients to design and execute a media campaign. This includes targeting publications, editors, shows, and producers; developing story ideas; writing query letters and articles; and coaching clients on how to deal with the press.

The right public relations firm or freelance PR professional can be a big help in getting a story out to the media. But they can be expensive, and you have to work closely with them to get the best results. This chapter will show you how to get media coverage on your own.

However you get it, media coverage can be well worth the effort, for several reasons:

➤ Media coverage can give your company, product, or service a level of credibility that you just can't buy with advertising; people know that advertising is paid for, but an article or news story is taken as objective information.

➤ You can clip stories and articles from print media and send copies to prospects and customers with a nice note that starts off, "In case you missed it in *The Gazette*, I thought you'd be interested in a recent article they did on a new product of ours."

➤ Over time, if you are covered often enough in the media, you acquire the status of "expert" and then you keep getting coverage with relatively little extra effort.

Query Letters That Get Attention

Editors receive query letters every day. Since editors are busy and their volume of reading is extremely high, they have to decide quickly what they're going to spend time on and what goes right into the "circular file."

Sound familiar? Everyone decides what to read or toss in seconds, so you've got to get attention fast.

How?

You already know the general rules, so I'll just quickly remind you of them:

➤ Your letter has to be well written.

➤ It has to be properly formatted.

➤ It has to address the needs of the reader.

What Editors Need

That last point is crucial. The most common complaint that editors have about query letters is that "the writer obviously never read my publication." Too often, people pitch editors ideas that won't interest their readers, that would offend their advertisers, or that were already covered recently in their publication. Editors toss these letters immediately.

Editors need ideas for articles that will interest their readers, be acceptable to the advertisers, and will not have been done to death, or that at least offer a new spin on an old topic. This means that you must target publications properly and develop fascinating ideas.

How to Target Publications

The publications you want to target are the ones read by the people you want to reach. If you sell high fashion, you want coverage in *Vogue* and *W;* if you sell rock-and-roll CDs, you want your company's artists written up in *Rolling Stone* and *Spin;* if you sell business equipment, you want the *Wall Street Journal* and *Business Week*, and so on.

If you target a publication properly, you'll automatically be on the road to connecting with the editor. That's because you'll be trying to reach the same readers that she's trying to reach.

Now it's obvious that you don't pitch an idea for a piece on the Canadian floor covering market to *Seventeen* magazine and that you don't target *Linoleum World* with an article on how to get rid of zits. However, at a more subtle level, each publication has its own point of view, style, and "voice." Some are serious, some irreverent; some cover personalities, some don't. The only way to get a fix on these issues is to read a few issues.

Many libraries stock any of several good directories of magazines and newspapers, including *Ulrich's International Periodicals Directory* or *Standard Periodical Directory* for magazines, and *Editor and Publisher International Yearbook* for newspapers. Writer's Digest Books publishes an annual directory, available in bookstores, called *Writer's Market,* which lists hundreds of magazines and newspapers (as well as book publishers). Another source, although it's less readily available (and quite expensive), is *Bacon's Publicity Checker*, also available in a CD-ROM version. A good business library will often have a copy of *Bacon's*.

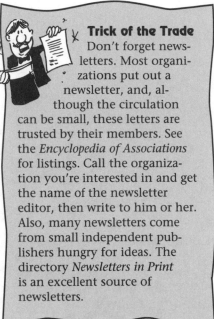

Trick of the Trade
Don't forget news-letters. Most organizations put out a newsletter, and, although the circulation can be small, these letters are trusted by their members. See the *Encyclopedia of Associations* for listings. Call the organization you're interested in and get the name of the newsletter editor, then write to him or her. Also, many newsletters come from small independent publishers hungry for ideas. The directory *Newsletters in Print* is an excellent source of newsletters.

What's That?
A *by-line* tells you who wrote the article in a newspaper or magazine. Sometimes a bio note or author's bio will give a bit of information beyond the name: "So-and-so is president of Speedpar Industries, a manufacturer of automotive products."

When you target publications it's natural to get excited about the big, household names, but it can be a mistake. *Time*, *Newsweek*, *The New York Times*, *The Wall Street Journal*, and other national publications get hundreds of query letters and press releases a week. They also have large staffs that develop article ideas. And they tend to be general in their coverage, interested only in topics with very broad appeal. Given all this, you can often do better targeting local or regional publications that are more tightly focused on the readers you most want to reach.

Your target publications and radio and TV shows, with the names, titles, addresses, telephone and fax numbers, and even e-mail addresses of the editor or producer, make up your press list (or media list). Keep this list updated in a computerized database so you can efficiently do mass mailings (which I'll cover in Chapter 27).

Targeting the right editor or producer is essential. Don't assume that they will pass your material along to the right person in their outfit, and don't suggest that they should or you'll appear unprofessional. When you build your press list, get on the phone and ask who the best person would be to send ideas or news items to. Many general-interest publications have special editors for investing, small business, new products, technology, education, retail, lifestyle, food, home improvement, and so on.

If you're interested in getting your idea or item into a specific column, write to the editor or author of that column. Sometimes, if the author doesn't have a by-line, you'll have to call and ask who writes the column. This is especially true for columns called things like "People on the Move" or "Company News" that consist of many short entries.

How to Develop Story and Article Ideas

To develop ideas, get into brainstorming mode (see Chapter 5) and think along typical story lines. These include:

➤ Event-driven stories, which focus on a recent news item or major event (for example, a visit by a dignitary, a sharp rise or drop in the stock market, or a recession)

➤ Issue-driven stories, which focus on trends (for example, a wave of layoffs or the aging of the workforce), lifestyle (for example, time-pressed, two-paycheck households), and other issues

➤ Personality-driven stories, which focus on people in your organization or those you sell to (for example, your CEO is a skydiver or your largest customer is a French billionaire)

➤ Internally driven stories, which focus on events within your company (for example, a new product or a reorganization)

If your idea is event- or issue-driven, make sure you find an "angle" for your company or products or services. Remember, you're writing to get publicity, not for the joy of giving editors great ideas.

If the idea is personality- or internally driven, you need to relate that to an event or a topic. Editors are not in the business of promoting your company. If you tie something about your company into an event or trend, you justify mention of your company by linking it to something newsworthy.

Developing story ideas takes work. Professional PR people often find it difficult, and they never stop thinking about it. It comes down to brainstorming and deep thinking, reading widely, listening to others, and always seeking connections between your company and the "outside world."

Watch Out!
Editors notoriously avoid "puff pieces," which are articles that simply tout your company or its people or products. If you pitch one, you're wasting your time and undermining your credibility with that editor.

Outline for a Great Query Letter

Here's an outline for an effective query letter. The basic elements are:

Dear _____:

The lead: Compose an attention-grabbing opening for your first paragraph.

Pitch and rationale: In one or two paragraphs, explain the article idea and why readers will be interested.

Why you're qualified: Explain why you're qualified to write the article, or, if you're just pitching yourself as a source, to talk about the subject.

Delivery details: If you are writing the article, mention when you would deliver it, in what form, and any other details.

Close: Add a cordial closing.

This general outline will work for articles that you would write, or for ideas that you pitch for the editor to have done by her staff or to assign to a freelancer, with you or someone else in your company acting as a source.

Sample 1 shows a letter for an article to be written by the person doing the pitch. Notice how it follows the outline.

If you have any kind of published writing, even from the school paper, that shows that you can write, include a copy as a "clip" if you are positioning yourself to write the article.

Sample 2 pitches an idea for a column rather than proposing to write an article.

Jim Rivers Executive Recruiting
400 Water Street
Hannibal, MO 05661
1-800-959-8000

February 12, 1998

Ms. Ellen d'Amico
Managing Editor
Careers After College
201 Broadway
Cambridge, MA 02139

Dear Ms. d'Amico:

> An editor will take a specific proposal for an article more seriously than a vague one.

This June, tens of thousands of graduating students will start their careers in business. Yet how many of them are really prepared for the challenges of today's uncertain workplace?

To help them in career planning and interviewing, I propose a 2,000-word feature article with the working title, "Creating the Chameleon Career." The chameleon career helps people deal with the constant change of today's workplace. It means developing portable skills, constantly gauging the market, and being ready to move quickly from employment to self-employment—and back again.

In my 15 years as an executive recruiter, I've seen what it takes to survive downsizing and recession and to prosper during expansion and growth. I have published several articles in newsletters (see the enclosed clips) and would do a professional job on this piece.

I could have the completed article on your desk within four weeks of your giving me the go-ahead. Please give me your reaction to this article idea at your earliest convenience.

Thank you for your consideration.

Sincerely,

Jim Rivers
Managing Director

Sample 1: Request to Submit an Article, Addressed to an Editor.

Mr. Mark Darymple
Editor—New Product News
The Gazette
888 Main Street
Deerville, MN 99999

> This letter is targeted to exactly the right person.

Dear Mr. Darymple:

Our newest product—a high-tech import from Japan—will hit the streets on May 25th. It's The WristPhone: a telephone that's a bit bigger than a digital sports watch and is worn the same way. Because people already wear watches, the product includes a digital watch, but The WristPhone is far more than a timepiece.

Our Japanese partner, CyberPhone Industries, has miniaturized cell-phone technology so that the clarity of communications on this tiny phone equals or exceeds that of most portable phones. A miniature speakerphone serves as both the microphone for talking and the speaker for listening. While small, the touch-tone pad resembles the one on an ordinary cellular phone and is easily accessible.

The WristPhone will initially be available in one size for men and women and only in black, with a choice of 12 fashionable straps. The retail price of $395 includes a one-year warranty on parts and labor. Billing for calls is through normal cellular-phone service providers at normal cell-phone rates.

If you would like to see a demonstration of this exciting new product, we can arrange one in your office. If you have a cellular phone service, we could let you use The WristPhone for a day so you can review the product. I'm also available for an interview at 1-800-555-9999 ext. 243.

I appreciate your consideration.

Very truly,

Jerry Spengler
Vice President, Marketing

Sample 2: Pitch for an Idea for a Column, Addressed to an Editor.

Whenever you write to the press, aim for an enthusiastic but businesslike tone. Editors resent any hint of a condescending tone or an approach that says, "Here's an idea that's going to blow your readers out of their chairs." Even worse is saying, "If you don't like this idea, we're ready to go elsewhere."

Trick of the Trade
Be aware that most magazines work with lead times that can be much longer than you might think. For a monthly or quarterly publication, submit article ideas at least three to four months in advance.

A simultaneous submission is one going to more than one editor at a time. Most editors don't like simultaneous submissions of article ideas if you intend to write the article. If you're just submitting an idea, that's different. If you do make a simultaneous submission of an article that you propose to write (I don't suggest this), mention it.

The query letter represents the most personal approach to an editor or producer, most of whom prefer to get mail rather than calls from people they don't know. The press release, although less personal, is an even more essential publicity tool.

Press Releases

The press release, also known as the news release or media release, has its own rules and quirks, but essentially it's a recognized means for an organization to release a news item (or what it hopes is a news item) to the media. A press release can go out to several publications and shows or to thousands at a time.

Anyone and any organization can send a press release to a newspaper, magazine, or radio or TV show. As with any written communication, having a specific person to send it to is important. However, a press release is not a one-to-one means of communication. It's designed to broadcast a message through the media. Editors and producers therefore understand that this item is going to many of them simultaneously.

Press releases used to go out by mail, and often still do. However, the fax machine is becoming the delivery mechanism of choice for press releases. If your media list is in a computerized database and you have a telephone line and the right communications software, you can send a press release by fax to hundreds, even thousands, of editors right from your personal computer.

In fact, the computer and fax machine have made it so easy to send press releases that they now come flying out of the machines at editors all day long. The staggering volume at many publications again raises the question, How do you ensure that your material gets read?

Press Releases That Get Attention

Your press release must be well written, of course, and it must be in the proper format, or it will immediately appear to be the work of an amateur.

The matter of getting attention comes down to content. An editor at a nationally distributed newspaper recently told me, "Frankly, most press releases aren't really about anything newsworthy. They're about things the company would like to get into the news, but they're not often about anything that our readers would find interesting."

Press releases, by their nature, have something to do with your organization. It makes no sense for an organization to release a news item about something not connected with its business. The challenge, then, is to first decide what is and isn't newsworthy, and second, when possible, to develop an angle connected to the outside world. I say "when possible" because it's acceptable to send out a press release that is just company news—if it is significant. If it's not very significant, either don't send it out, or first work up an angle connected to the outside world.

Outline for a Press Release

The basic form and outline for a press release looks like this:

For: Company Name

Company Address

Contact: The name and phone number of person to contact for more information

FOR IMMEDIATE RELEASE (or the release date)

Headline

Lead paragraph: Get as many exciting facts as you can into this paragraph, including what your organization does if it's not well known.

Second paragraph: Add more detail and expand on a fact or two from the first paragraph.

Third paragraph: Add more detail and expand on another fact or two from the first paragraph.

Fourth paragraph: Add more detail and expand on another fact or two.

Double-space the text and leave a ragged (not justified) right margin. Try to keep the press release to one page. If you go to a second page, type MORE at the bottom of the first page, and at the top of the second page, type the name of your business and the word "Continued." Don't go beyond two pages. At the end of the text, type END.

Sample 3 shows an example of a good press release, using The WristPhone as the subject again. Note the differences between a query letter and a press release.

For: Monarch Mobile Communications
     557 Alexandria Blvd., McLean, Virginia 99999

Contact: Jerry Spengler, Vice President, Marketing, 1-800-555-9999 ext. 243

FOR IMMEDIATE RELEASE

> Quotations in press releases help reporters write their stories.

Cellular WristPhone Now In from Japan

McLean, Va.—Dick Tracy won't need his wrist radio anymore and the cellular phone category could see a shake-up in the months ahead. The $395 WristPhone, which will hit retail stores this weekend, fits on your wrist and includes a digital watch. New miniaturization technology from Tokyo-based Monarch partner CyberPhone Industries makes the tiny telephone possible.

According to Monarch President Terry Maltby, "Without a doubt, this technology delivers clarity of sound equal to or better than current cellular phones. This should change the game in cellular phones." Monarch, which makes a line of six different cellular phones, plus several wireless home phones, is the first U.S. company to offer a wristwatch-size phone.

Recognizing that consumers are already wearing watches, the company included a digital watch in The WristPhone. Maltby states, "The phone weighs almost as little as a digital watch. It's nicely styled with a black casing and a choice of 12 different wristbands." The keypad on The WristPhone looks like that of a regular touch-tone phone, only smaller.

Over 300,000 WristPhones have been sold in Japan. Monarch, the exclusive North American distributor, expects to sell that many in the U.S. and Canada over the next 12–18 months.

END

Sample 3: Press Release.

The best approach is to try to give the editor everything he or she will need to write a short article on the topic. In practice, if a press release gets "picked up" (used in some way by the newspaper, magazine, or show), it is as the basis of a short article or as a source of information or a quote in a larger piece. For this reason, it's good to include a quote or two in a press release. Journalists like quotes.

Making Your Own News

If you have the time, resources, and ambition, you can create your own news. I'm not talking about committing a spectacular crime or running for office, but doing a survey or a study. Many companies do a study annually or every two years so they have a reason to get into the news periodically. The survey should, of course, be tightly connected to your business.

Sample 4 is a press release based on a survey by the fictitious Jim Rivers Executive Recruiters.

Some surveys get picked up by major media every year and become mini news events in their own right.

Regardless of the news or item, a well-crafted query letter or press release is your best tool for getting media attention.

For: Jim Rivers Executive Recruiters
       400 Water Street, Hannibal, MO 99999

Contact: Jim Rivers, President, 1-800-555-3333

FOR IMMEDIATE RELEASE

> Two paragraphs can be enough if you really have something to say.

New Grads Face Tough Job Outlook

Hannibal, MO—An annual survey shows that this year's graduating college seniors face the toughest job outlook of the 1990s. The survey of 350 employers, done every year since 1987 by Jim Rivers Executive Recruiters, reveals that most companies are still digesting recent hires from the past several years and have not seen the growth that would warrant strong hiring this year.

This is not to say that there are no jobs for grads this year. "It's just going to be more competitive this year. The past several years have been a seller's market. New grads could pick and choose. This year the advantage has swung back to the employers," said Jim Rivers, president of the company that sponsors the study. Rivers added that job-search skills, such as targeting prospective employers and interviewing well, typically enable qualified grads to land jobs within four months of graduation.

END

Sample 4: Press Release Based on a Company Study.

Do's and Don'ts When Writing to the Media

Do:

➤ Present an item that can be judged newsworthy.

➤ Try to write in an interesting but objective manner.

➤ Give facts, instead of opinion, to the degree possible.

➤ Use proper form in your press releases.

➤ Include a quote or two in press releases.

Don't:

➤ Pitch self-serving "puff pieces."

➤ Take a condescending or bombastic tone.

➤ Promise an article (or anything) that you can't deliver.

➤ Let any typos or factual errors slip through.

➤ Give up after one or two attempts.

The Least You Need to Know

➤ If you want attention from the press, build and maintain a well-targeted, computerized media list.

➤ Use a query letter to pitch article ideas to editors and producers, but send only one article idea to an editor at a time if you intend to write it.

➤ Use a press release to get word out to numerous people in the media at the same time.

➤ In all of your writing to the media, understand that their concern is not your needs, but their readers' interests.

➤ If you target the right publications and present good ideas to them often enough, you will eventually get through, but it takes time to learn the right approach.

Chapter 19

OH MY!

Decent Proposals (and Letters of Agreement)

In This Chapter

➤ How proposals lead to agreements

➤ The elements of good proposals and agreements

➤ Protecting yourself in business deals

Most business deals require "something in writing." That something in writing can be anything from a long, formal contract to a short, informal letter of agreement. Deals have to start somewhere, and they often start with a written proposal. In fact, as you'll see in this chapter, the written proposal can become the basis of the final agreement.

The purpose of writing up a business deal, whether for the sale of equipment or for a consulting engagement, is to clarify the responsibilities of everyone in the transaction. Who must do what? When and where? What is the price? What are the terms and time of payment? What is to be delivered? By whom?

This chapter is not actually about contracts. To deal with contracts you need an attorney, and I'm not an attorney. What it is about is writing clear, businesslike proposals and letters of agreement—what are, in effect, simple contracts.

Is It Worth the Paper It's Printed On?

A *contract* is a legally enforceable agreement between two or more people or organizations. Many people don't realize that verbal contracts are just as legal as written contracts. They are, but without something in writing it's harder to enforce a contract because it becomes "your word against mine." That's why if someone is not willing to put something in writing, it's wise to wonder if they will follow through.

It takes three things to make a legal agreement: an offer, consideration, and acceptance.

Let's say that you are the one making the proposal, the one selling something, or offering to do a piece of work. Your *offer* might be to sell your car to someone or to shoot a video for a company.

What's That?
A *counteroffer* is usually the result of bargaining. If you offer to sell your car for $5,000 and the other person says, "How about $4,000?" that person has made a counteroffer.

Consideration is what you will get in return. Usually this is money, but it could be something that you take in a trade. For example, you could trade your car for a motorcycle of similar value or you could shoot the video in return for free advertising.

Finally, you don't have an enforceable agreement without *acceptance*. This means that the other party has to accept your offer or you both agree to a counteroffer. It's usually a good idea to have the acceptance in writing.

Keep these basics in mind when you're writing proposals and agreements: offer, consideration, and acceptance.

How to Write an Attractive Proposal

As in most writing, the first step in writing a proposal is to understand your purpose and your reader. The purpose of most proposals is to get a piece of business: You want to sell something, usually to someone at a company (or you probably wouldn't need a written proposal).

Trick of the Trade
You may have several readers for your proposal. In most companies, it takes more than one person to OK a deal. Learn as much as you can beforehand about each person who must "sign off" on your proposal.

That someone is your reader. In the discussions before your proposal, be sure to learn as much as you can about the needs of the people to whom you're selling. That way you can address these needs in your proposal.

The more of the readers' needs that you address in the proposal, the better your chances of making the sale, but watch out. You also have to address *your* needs. It's all well and good to try to meet the customer's need for a low price, but can you make a profit at that price? The customer may need delivery by a certain date. Can you meet that deadline while maintaining your quality standards and not getting burned out?

It's easy to overpromise when writing a proposal. Agreeing to meet an unrealistic deadline is a common mistake. So is throwing in "extras" that the client wants but doesn't want to pay for. When writing a proposal, think realistically about what you can deliver, about how long things take, and about how much profit you'll make if you do what you propose.

The secret of writing an attractive proposal is to do all that you can to meet the client's needs *and* your needs. This means doing some fact finding before writing the proposal. You must learn what the client's needs are and how your product or service can meet those needs. You must learn about the prospect's expectations, how urgent her need is, and about her deadlines. You must also learn your client's views on pricing and quality. Everyone wants high quality at a low price, but that's usually not realistic. Be honest and try to learn whether she prefers low price over high quality or is willing to pay for high quality.

Ask Questions

Your best tools at this point are questions. Before you write your proposal, ask the prospect:

➤ What problem do you want to solve with this purchase? What's the ideal solution?

➤ What's the most important aspect of this deal: price, quality, timing? If you had to pick one as most important, which would it be?

➤ Who will be involved in the decision to make this deal?

➤ Who will be affected by this purchase? What stake do they have in the deal?

➤ How long has this need existed? Is it now urgent? Why?

➤ When would you like to see this completed? What is your deadline?

Ask your prospect for his "wish list," the list of things that he would want you to deliver in an ideal world. Tell him that you probably can't deliver everything on his wish list, but you want to come as close as you can. Then ask him to prioritize the items on the wish list from most to least important. The resulting list will allow you to see what he'd like to get out of the deal, what he sees as most important.

You'll have other questions, of course, depending on your product or service. But these are the basic ones. They are part of any sales process, but they're especially important when you sell by proposal. The more you know about the reader's needs, the better the proposal.

Outline for a Proposal

Here is an outline for a proposal. A proposal can run anywhere from one or two pages for a simple deal up to dozens of pages for a complex one.

Introduction	Summarize your understanding of the prospect's needs and mention what you're offering to meet those needs.
Deliverables	The equipment you will sell, or, if you are proposing a consulting assignment, the tasks you will perform; mention any guarantees in this section.
Time frame	The delivery date or deadline for completing the tasks.
Responsibilities	The things that you and the client are responsible for, including items such as whether you will deliver the equipment or the client will pick it up.
Compensation	The amount you will be paid and the terms and schedule of payment.
Conclusion	Mention that you are sure the client will be satisfied and you appreciate the opportunity to bid on this business.

A *bid* is an offer by a party to sell goods or services for a certain price. Often a company will request bids from several outfits. This frequently occurs in advertising, construction, and major equipment purchases. Many companies have a policy of getting three bids on any deal over a certain dollar amount, for example, $5,000 or $10,000.

An *RFP* or "request for proposals" is a document put out by an organization to solicit competitive proposals and bids. Often, especially if issued by a government agency, an RFP will ask for great detail in the proposal. If you respond to an RFP, your proposal must address every point in it.

The section heads used in the outline, Introduction, Deliverables, and so on, can be the actual section heads in your proposal, or you can change them to better suit your needs.

Sample Letter Proposals

Sample 1 shows an example of a simple letter proposal for a product. A good-faith payment, as mentioned in the sample under "compensation," is a percentage of the total amount of the sale (usually not more than 10 percent), paid before work begins to demonstrate the buyer's commitment.

Synergy Systems Inc.
444 Alameda Drive
Palo Alto, California 99999
1-800-555-9999

Ms. Orla McKeon
President
Zip Consulting Inc.
888 Montgomery Street
San Francisco, CA 99999

Dear Ms. McKeon:

Thank you for meeting with us over the past several weeks to give us an understanding of your business and your computing needs. Please convey our thanks to Jim, Marion, and Steve as well.

This letter proposes a solution that we believe will meet your needs for a user-friendly networked personal computing environment that can grow with you as your business grows. The parts of this proposal are:

➤ Introduction

➤ Deliverables

➤ Time frame   *These bullets tell the reader how the proposal is organized.*

➤ Compensation

➤ Conclusion

Introduction

Over the past several weeks, Synergy Systems has met with various members of Zip Consulting to learn about your needs for a personal computer network. This network should enable people in the company to work as a team, have access to one another's files (except those marked "private"), and be linked to a time-tracking system for billing. The system must also allow you to send files to clients for review and approval. This letter proposes such a network.

Deliverables: The System, Training, Support, and Warranty

The System:

The system will be configured as follows: *These bullets clarify what will be delivered.*

➤ One Acme model 5000 client server

➤ Eighteen Acme A500 personal computers with keyboards, mice, and monitors

➤ Six Acme model 465 laser printers and three Acme C400 color printers

➤ Synergy Systems series 999 network with all software and support

➤ Synergy Systems Sweet Suite (including five multimedia packs), plus the TimeTrack system to be linked to your accounting system

The system includes all wiring and full installation and documentation.

Training, Support, and Warranty:

Our price includes five days of training by our instructor for all personnel who will be using the system and all personnel that Zip wishes to attend. This means that you are purchasing five 7-hour days of our instructor's time, on-site at Zip.

Sample 1: A Proposal for the Sale of a Product.

Synergy Systems will provide support by telephone from 8:00 a.m. to 6:00 p.m. for one year. We will also provide a one-year parts-and-labor warranty on all components of the system. This means that if any part of the system malfunctions because of a failure in quality or workmanship, we will repair it (or, at our option, replace it) free of charge for one year from the installation date. We cannot, however, reimburse Zip Consulting for any other loss resulting from the failure of this system.

As we discussed, your technical staff is responsible for removal and disposal of your current system.

Time Frame

Our proposed installation date would be 10-12 calendar days from the date that Zip accepts this proposal. We will require three days to install and test the system. These dates can be moved forward or backward as you require.

Compensation

The cost of the new system, including installation, training, and support as mentioned earlier, will be $85,000. You will find the cost of the individual components and the applicable discounts broken out on Attachment "A."

Continued support for the second year will be priced at $9,000, which includes all upgrades to the system.

Should you wish to purchase any training and consulting time beyond the five days included in this proposal, you will be billed at $1,200 per day or $200 per hour.

Our terms of payment are 10% of the total as a good-faith payment upon signing this agreement, 40% upon completion of the installation, and 50% within 30 days of completion of installation.

Conclusion

We believe that our proposed network solution represents the best way for Zip Consulting to achieve its goal of creating an interactive work environment with a built-in time-tracking system that feeds the billing system.

Thank you for giving us the opportunity to submit this proposal. We at Synergy Systems look forward to helping Zip Consulting toward its goals with the best in networked systems and support.

To accept this offer, please sign in the space provided below, or if you prefer, in a return letter of your own, and mail it to my attention with a check in the amount of $8,500 for the good-faith payment.

If you have any questions or there are points that you would like to discuss, please call me.

Sincerely,

> Close with an invitation to the reader to call with questions or to talk over the proposal.

Gar Gartland
President

Accepted by:

_____ Date: _____

Orla McKeon
President

Sample 1, Continued: A Proposal for the Sale of a Product.

How a Proposal Works

When you make a proposal, you formally present your offer and request a decision. Many firms find it a good practice (and a source of cash) to request a good-faith payment, although this is not strictly necessary. What is necessary is to get written approval of a written proposal. It would be nice if we could do business "on a handshake," but I don't recommend it. Settling for verbal approval of a written contract is asking for trouble.

Your prospect may simply sign your proposal and return it, or she may negotiate to modify the proposal. Keep in mind that a proposal is just that, a proposal. Proposals are by definition subject to counteroffers, negotiation, and modification. Some people don't even start seriously considering a deal until they see something in writing, then they begin negotiating. When there's something to be signed, most companies give it serious consideration.

This means that you can expect a bumpy ride on the road to many deals. A proposal will often sit on someone's desk for a while. Sometimes it's because your deal is relatively low priority; sometimes it's because the person's not comfortable with the proposal and doesn't know how to follow up.

To give him an opening, you can telephone and ask about the proposal. For example, say, "Hello, Jim. I sent you my proposal last Thursday, and I'm wondering if you folks have had a chance to look it over." If he hasn't, at least you may get things moving.

If things seem to have stalled, try saying, "If you're not comfortable with some aspect of the proposal, I'd like us to talk it over. We'd like to do business with you and if there's anything you feel needs to be addressed, we can certainly discuss it."

If he has a problem with your proposal, he may open up at that point. Once it's on the table, you can then perhaps get negotiations moving forward.

Sample 2 and Sample 3 show a cover letter and a proposal for a service rather than a product.

Presenting your proposal in modular form, with various tasks and bullets, enables the prospect to clearly see what you offer. It also enables her to negotiate, for example, by saying, "What if we forget about this task, or what if we go with a smaller quantity? How does that affect the price and delivery?" Again, such negotiation is often part of the process.

As you'll see if you contrast Samples 1 and 3 with the sample sales letters in Chapter 17, a proposal is not a sales letter. A sales letter opens the door so that you can learn about the prospect's needs and then craft a proposal that meets those needs.

> **Watch Out!**
> Sometimes a company will get two or three proposals and then play one supplier off the other. This is just one more aspect of business deals. If a prospect tells you he's got a lower price and asks you to match it, first ask him in detail what he's getting for that price. Be sure he's comparing "apples and apples." If he's not, point it out.

> **Trick of the Trade**
> Including an expiration date on your proposal can help you move the sale forward. It can also help you avoid rush jobs. If you don't have a deal by the expiration date, you can then push back the completion date.

Precision Market Research Associates
111 Sam Houston Drive
Dallas, Texas 99999
1-800-555-2333

Mr. Philip Verakus
Vice President, Marketing
All Brand Motors Leasing Corp.
490 Turtle Creek Road
Dallas, TX 99999

Dear Phil:

Thanks for having Steve and me in on the 12th to learn about your market research needs. I think we have a good understanding of your goals in Dallas/Fort Worth and of the information you'll need in order to create a marketing plan to meet those goals.

As promised, I've attached a proposal for a survey designed to get the information you need. When you've had a chance to review this proposal, please give me a call if you have any questions, comments, or modifications.

Steve and I look forward to working with you on this important project.

Sincerely,

A positive close creates the right tone.

Jeff Chu
Managing Director

Sample 2: Cover Letter for a Proposal.

Market Research Proposal

<u>Prepared by</u>:

Precision Marketing Associates
Dallas, TX

<u>Prepared for</u>:

All Brand Motors Leasing Corp.
Dallas, TX

February 1998

Introduction

This document proposes that Precision Marketing Associates (PMA) survey the luxury auto leasing market in Dallas/Fort Worth for All Brand Motors Leasing Corp. (All Brand) in the spring of 1998.

The goal of the survey is to gather information on the following aspects of the luxury car leasing market in Dallas/Fort Worth:

➤ Market share in Dallas/Fort Worth for the major luxury car manufacturers

➤ Market potential for luxury car sales and leasing

➤ Consumer and business attitudes toward leasing

➤ Key factors in the lease versus buy decision

➤ Consumer and business purchase and leasing plans over the next three years

Tasks and Deliverables

PMA will be responsible for the following tasks and deliverables:

> Dividing research and consulting projects into phases helps readers clearly understand the process.

➤ *Task 1:* Development of a 30-minute questionnaire designed to get the above-mentioned information

➤ *Task 2:* Development of a randomly selected list of 3,000 consumers and 1,000 businesses in Dallas/Ft. Worth

➤ *Task 3:* Completion of 200 telephone interviews (that is, completed questionnaires) with consumers and 100 interviews with business owners or "the person responsible for company cars"

➤ *Task 4:* Analysis of the results in a two-hour presentation at All Brand's offices

➤ *Task 5:* Detailed written analysis of the results of the survey to be delivered in two parts: one for the consumer market, and one for the business market

Steve Misel and Joan Krupt at All Brand will have input during Tasks 1 and 2 (including approval of the questionnaire developed in Task 1) and will be able to observe interviews in progress during Task 3.

As we agreed, All Brand will not be identified in any way by our interviewers. All aspects of this survey, including All Brand's sponsorship, will be kept strictly confidential by PMA and its employees.

Sample 3: A Proposal for the Sale of a Service.

Time Frame

As we agreed, the telephone interviews will be conducted in May 1998. We will hold the on-site meeting (Task 4) by the end of June and deliver our final written analysis by July 15, 1998. This means that we will have Tasks 1 and 2 completed by April 30, at the latest.

Compensation

Our complete price for this survey of the luxury car leasing market in Dallas/Ft. Worth, based upon the five tasks outlined earlier, is $24,000.

Expiration Date

> An expiration date creates a sense of urgency, or at least closure.

We have prepared this proposal in light of our current knowledge of our commitments in the weeks and months ahead. Thus this proposal, including the definition of the tasks and the price quotes, will remain in effect through March 7, 1998.

Conclusion

Given our experience in market research and understanding of your information needs, we at Precision Marketing assure you that we will deliver research that meets your highest expectations.

We look forward to working with you on this important project.

_____ Date: _____

Jeffrey Chu
Managing Director
Precision Marketing Associates

_____ Date: _____

Stephen Misel
President
All Brand Motors Leasing Corp.

Sample 3, Continued: A Proposal for the Sale of a Service.

A Letter of Agreement

In many cases, the proposal becomes the agreement when it's signed by the person authorized to make the deal for the client company. Sometimes, however, you need an actual letter of agreement in order to document a verbal agreement.

Sample 4 on the following page shows a short letter of agreement

Party Down Company
999 Wilshire Blvd.
Beverly Hills, CA 02910
1-800-555-9999

Mr. Robbie Manning
888 Beverly Glen
Beverly Hills, CA 02910
Subject: Agreement for Services for October 19th

> *Attachments (not shown) contain material that is too long and complicated for a letter.*

Dear Robbie:

This letter will confirm our conversation this morning regarding arrangements for your birthday party to be held at 888 Beverly Glen from 10 p.m. to 4 a.m. on Friday, October 19th.

We will provide food and drink as listed on Attachments "A" and "B," as well as live music from the six-piece dance band, The Grifters, who will play 45-minute sets on the hour from 10:00 p.m. to 3:00 a.m. We will also provide the services of The Magic Marker, the Santa Monica-based caricature artist, from 1:00 a.m. to 2:30 a.m.

You will send us the guest list so that we receive it by September 1st. We will mail invitations with RSVPs, as we agreed. See Attachment "C" for a sample invitation and return card.

We will also provide a 200-person tent, and arrange for set-up on the morning of the 19th and break-down on the 20th. We will supply all decorations (balloons, streamers, favors, noise-makers, and three life-size ice sculptures of you).

Our staff of chefs, kitchen assistants, food servers, waiters and waitresses, bartenders, and buspersons will total 60 people and will begin arriving at your home at about 4:00 p.m. on the day of the party.

Our all-inclusive price for this event will be $45,000 (as detailed on Attachment "D") and payments are due as follows:

➤ $15,000 nonrefundable deposit with the return of this signed letter

➤ $15,000 on October 1st

➤ $15,000 on the morning of October 19th

We appreciate having the opportunity to make your birthday this year a truly memorable event.

Sincerely,

> *It's essential to be clear about what payment is due when, and what portion is nonrefundable.*

Devan Blaine
President

Accepted by: _____   Date: _____
　　　　　　Robert Manning

Sample 4: A Letter of Agreement.

What Do You Propose?

There are situations in which you can get a sale right from a sales letter. As you know, sometimes the documentation of a deal can be as simple as a receipt.

However, if you're selling relatively big-ticket equipment or services for an employer or if you're in business for yourself, it pays to know how to present a proposal on paper. It also pays to know a good proposal from a poor one, another lesson of this chapter.

The Least You Need to Know

➤ The basic elements of a contract are an offer, consideration, and acceptance.

➤ Verbal contracts are just as legal as written contracts but harder to enforce, which is why most business deals require something in writing.

➤ A proposal should clearly state what you will do, what you will deliver, what you will be paid, and the time frames for these items.

➤ Proposals are subject to negotiation, which is a normal part of doing business.

➤ Proposals often become written agreements when they are countersigned by the person authorized to make the deal for the prospect company.

➤ Use a simple letter agreement to document a straightforward verbal deal. In business, it always pays to have something in writing.

Dear Deadbeat, ...

Shine, Don't Whine: Complaints and Collection Letters

In This Chapter

➤ When you should write to complain

➤ Complaining to get results

➤ How to write a series of collection letters

If something can go wrong, it will: That's Murphy's Law. Mess-ups are a natural part of life. When you're the one paying, however, chances are you need the person or business responsible to fix the problem fast. Often that means complaining in writing.

When Things Go Wrong

When you pay for a product, you expect to get what you pay for. You expect on-time delivery of the correct item, and you expect the item to perform the way you were told it would. Likewise, when you buy a service, you expect professional conduct and results. That's not always what you get.

In such cases you have two choices: You can ignore the problem or you can complain. If you complain, you can either do it effectively or ineffectively.

Effective complaining gets results. Complaining to your boss, your co-workers, your spouse, or your neighbor doesn't—unless, of course, they created the problem. Complaining to yourself won't help either. Crying, cursing, and swearing may give you a sense of release or righteousness, but it won't fix the situation.

None of this will fix the situation because it disregards a basic rule of effective complaining: Complain to the right person. There are other rules. Let's look at them all.

Rules for Effective Complaining

It's natural to get angry when you've been wronged by a supplier, professional, or landlord. That's why it's so easy to become embroiled in costly, time-consuming losing battles. We need rules to guide our interactions with the people causing the frustration. Here are some useful ones:

➤ Propose a specific solution.

➤ Keep the moral high ground.

➤ Complain to the right person.

➤ Keep good records of all contacts.

➤ Be persistent.

Let's see how each of these translates into an effective letter of complaint. The rules that follow also apply to complaining in person or by telephone. (I'll cover when to use which medium later in the chapter.)

Propose a Specific Solution

Suppose a new piece of equipment you ordered was delivered this morning. A clerk in the mailroom signed for it without opening the box. When the box was delivered to your office, you opened it to find that the piece of equipment was badly damaged. You called the supplier, who said that you would have to bring it to the nearest authorized service center to have it repaired, but that they will pay for the repairs, which shouldn't take more than a week.

If you're happy with this solution, great, but not many of us would be. After all, the supplier's "solution" creates work and delay for you. In this case, you need to state what an acceptable solution would be and to insist (nicely) that the supplier implement it. Having your own solution in mind before you call gives you a benchmark by which to judge the supplier's solution and keeps you focused on getting things fixed.

Keep the Moral High Ground

Anger and useless (rather than useful) threats will cause you to forfeit the moral high ground. That's what you have when the other person knows you're in the right. Even when someone has not delivered as promised, you'll hurt your position if you take your anger out on others.

Complain to the Right Person

Sometimes we find ourselves amazed at the poor service we receive. It's astonishing to call a company that has messed up your order only to find someone with no sense of sympathy or urgency, let alone sorrow. When you run into a bad attitude, move on to that person's supervisor, quickly. Complaints in writing to the executive levels, including the chairman or president, can be very effective. The executive will pass the problem on, but his name on it ensures fast action.

The right person to complain to is one who is willing *and* able to help you. Occasionally, someone just can't help you. He may be in the wrong department or lack the needed authority. The first step, then, is to identify someone with authority and a willing attitude. Notice I said "person" and not "people." One person willing to champion your cause is better than five people who are mildly interested.

Keep Good Records of All Contacts

An important reason to complain in writing is to create a "paper trail" documenting your problem. Keep records of all phone conversations about a problem, and include:

> **Trick of the Trade**
> Early memos to the file documenting phone conversations will help you do a better, faster job on any letters of complaint you need to write later.

➤ Name, title, and phone number of the person you're speaking with

➤ Day, date, and time of the call

➤ Key points of the conversation

➤ Exact quotes for promised follow-up steps (or any offensive statements)

➤ Date and time by which you should have the solution

It's essential to keep pushing for a solution, and that can require persistence.

Be Persistent

When you have a problem, you need fast action. By "be persistent," I don't mean that you should be willing to fight a ten-year war. I mean that you should contact the company involved often over a short period of time. This ensures that solving your problem becomes a high priority for them.

> **Trick of the Trade**
> If you're getting nowhere with the head of the company, state your intention to complain to a licensing or regulatory agency, the state attorney general's office, or through the courts. And be willing to do so.

When to Write

The telephone is more personal and faster than writing, so use it first when you need a situation fixed. Complain in writing when you get no satisfaction by talking on the phone or when you'll need documentation.

Writing is also necessary to reach someone at a high level in a large organization. Unless you're a major customer, the secretary usually won't connect you to the chairman or president, but a letter will reach that executive or someone else who can help you.

Another reason to write is to "cc" another party on the document. For example, if you've tried and failed to get a situation resolved, you can "cc" your state attorney general, which might increase the pressure.

Analyzing the Reader

Nobody likes receiving complaints, so before you even send your letter you know that your reader is not going to be happy to receive it. The best approach, at least in the first letter, is a strong but reasonable one, with overtones of friendliness, if possible. I say "if possible" because if you're writing because you didn't get results on the phone, your mood is not likely to be friendly.

The goal is to persuade the reader to take responsibility for fixing your problem fast.

Outline for a Letter of Complaint

Here is a basic outline with the main elements of a good letter of complaint:

Dear _____:

Opening: Cite your relationship with the company and why you do business with them, and introduce your problem.

Second paragraph: Explain the problem and what steps, if any, have been taken to resolve it; document instances of the problem and of failure to solve it.

Third paragraph: Tell the company your solution and when you want it implemented; if it will help your case, mention any acceptable alternatives.

Fourth paragraph: Close as pleasantly and positively as you can and mention a specific follow-up step and date.

Yours very truly,

Watch Out!

Keep letters of complaint short—no more than two pages, and preferably one. You may think that the more you write, the better results you will get, but it's not so. Focus on the result you want rather than on a person's or company's incompetence.

A Sample Letter of Complaint

Sample 1 on the following page shows a first letter following several unsuccessful attempts on the telephone.

The letter in Sample 1 addresses an all-too-common issue in business: the recurring problem. Recurring problems are the kind you often end up writing about, because they don't get solved with phone calls.

When you write about these problems, propose your solution and leave the time frame regarding recurrence open. For example, it may not be reasonable for Orla to propose that Synergy Systems replace the network if it *ever* crashes again, but she certainly is right to insist on a new system if there's a crash in the next several weeks, given that repeated repairs have not worked. For the same reason, Orla is smart to be a bit vague about the time frame, although Peter at Synergy Systems may insist on more precise language. In fact, he may reject Orla's solution, but at least she has it on the table.

Another Letter of Complaint

Sample 2 addresses a different kind of problem.

Notice that the letter shows a personal touch and even some humor. Light humor can lessen the unpleasantness of complaining and win cooperation. Some people will simply avoid angry or irritated people. That's not to say you should never display anger, but rather that you should use whatever tone—light or angry—you believe will get results.

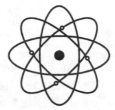

Zip Consulting Inc.
888 Montgomery Street
San Francisco, CA 99999
1-800-555-9999

Mr. Peter Jordan
Director—Customer Services
Synergy Systems Inc.
444 Alameda Drive
Palo Alto, California 99999

Dear Peter:

As we at Zip Consulting have discussed with you in phone conversations over the past several weeks, we continue to have problems with our Synergy Systems network. We chose Synergy Systems because of your quality and service claims, and we have been pleased with the network—when it works.

Unfortunately, the system still crashes regularly, creating downtime and loss of work in progress. We can no longer continue in this fashion.

As I write this, your repair people are here again to resolve "the crashing problem." This is their fifth visit in the past two weeks (on the 3rd, 5th, 9th, and 11th). This is in addition to some nine hours of phone consultation between your technical people and ours. Each time we have been assured, and twice you have personally assured me, that the problem would not recur. Yet our network has been down since 10:00 a.m. today.

<u>At this point I insist that, if the network crashes again, Synergy Systems replace the network with a new one at no cost to Zip Consulting.</u> While I realize that Synergy Systems is making good-faith assurances that the crashing problem will not recur, I am not optimistic. Our entire former computer system was replaced by Synergy six weeks ago. Therefore there can be no doubt that the problem resides in the software or hardware or in the installation provided by Synergy Systems.

Please understand that today's downtime, repairs, and assurances regarding this network are the last that we will accept. Under the circumstances, I see replacement of the system if it fails again within the next several weeks as the only fair solution.

Very truly,

Orla makes sure her message gets through to the reader.

Orla McKeon
President

cc: Jeff Chu, President, Synergy Systems

Sample 1: Complaint Following Several Ineffective Phone Calls.

**Correct Copy Center
771 Washington Ave.
St. Louis, MO 99999
1-800-555-9999**

Ms. Mary Russo
Credit Manager
Acme Paper Products, Inc.
8080 Main Street
St. Louis, MO 99999

Dear Ms. Russo:

Using humor can make a complaint letter less unpleasant for the reader.

I am writing to resolve, once and for all, a misunderstanding between our companies that began last January. We have been customers of Acme for more than five years, buying $2,000–$3,000 worth of paper from you every month. We want to continue to do business with you, but your collection department is making it tough. A merchandise dispute and billing error (on Acme's part) is threatening to become World War III.

Four months ago, on June 14th, your driver left a shipment of paper on a platform behind our building <u>after hours</u>. We had not requested or agreed to an after-hours delivery. Severe thundershowers that night ruined the entire shipment, valued at $1,688.50.

The next day we called your shipping department to tell you that we refused to accept delivery and to resend the order. Someone, presumably from Acme, picked up the damaged paper later that day (June 15th) and on the 16th we received the new order, which we paid for with the next monthly invoice.

Since then, we have received numerous collection calls and letters aimed at getting payment from us for the first $1,688.50 delivery, which we refused. We never accepted the delivery and were never invoiced for it. Acme has not produced signed delivery papers and never will, because we did not accept delivery of the damaged paper.

Yesterday, a David Jameson threatened to stop selling to us if this bill was not paid within five business days. When I explained the situation to him, he said, "All I know is that you owe us $1,688.50. When will I see it?"

Please direct your collection department to stop calling us and sending us letters demanding payment for this shipment. Attached are the original invoices for the past four months, together with copies of our checks in payment of these invoices.

You folks have an accounting error that you must correct as soon as possible. Thank you for your prompt attention to this matter.

Sincerely,

Steven Barber
Comptroller

Sample 2: Letter to a Collection Department.

An Opener and a Follow-Up

Samples 3 and 4 represent two stages in a complaint process.

Note the use of the fax machine on the letters about the heat. Writing provides documentation, but the only way to get same-day delivery is by fax or messenger. Overnight service and Express Mail provide next-day delivery in the U.S., but in urgent situations that may not be fast enough.

Watch Out!
Before you make threats, have your facts straight. Try to find out why your problem hasn't been addressed. Allow for the possibility that there's a legitimate reason for a failure.

As is the case with written reprimands, when you have to complain in writing, you already have a bad situation on your hands, because talking has not worked. Often, therefore, you have to move quickly to strong measures. That is particularly true when safety, productivity, or large sums of money are at stake.

January 18, 1998   <u>**By Fax**</u>

Mr. Henry Cheetham
Cheetham Property Management
888 Norway Street
Middletown, CT 99999

Re: Severe Lack of Heat and Communication

Dear Mr. Cheetham:

> Short sentences create a sense of urgency.

I am writing regarding the continual lack of sufficient heat in our offices over the past three business days. I have called your office at least twice a day on each of these days. Mrs. Stacey has told me that you "are aware of the situation" and "that you are trying to get it fixed." She also told me that she has given you my messages to call me. However, you have not returned my calls.

Both the heat and the communication situations are unacceptable. We must have heat and have it regularly. We are using space heaters, which raise our electricity bill and create a fire hazard. As a landlord, you surely realize this cannot continue. As a businessman, you know that not returning my phone calls isn't helping. Whatever the explanation of this situation, I want to hear it. More importantly, I want the situation fixed.

Given the severity of the cold, the interference with our productivity, the increase in our electric bill, and your lack of communication, I am notifying you that <u>we will reduce our next rent payment</u> by an amount that I view as fair unless this situation is fixed immediately.

I await your reply.

Very truly,

Michael Klepper
President

P.S. If you are unable to communicate with me for some legitimate reason, please let me know through Mrs. Stacey and advise me what to do.

Sample 3: First Stage in a Complaint Process.

January 20, 1998   <u>**By Fax**</u>

Mr. Henry Cheetham
Cheetham Property Management
888 Norway Street
Hartford, CT 99999

Re: Severe Lack of Heat and Communication (Second Letter)

Dear Mr. Cheetham:

This is a follow-up to my letter of the 18th. Given that we still have barely any heat and I have not heard from you, I am taking the following steps to remedy the situation unless I hear from you by 5:00 p.m. today.

First, I will call a heating repair service to restore adequate heat in this office. If the service demands payment on the spot as a condition of doing the work, I will pay them but will expect Cheetham Property Management, as owner and landlord, to be responsible for the bill. If they do not demand on-the-spot payment, I will have them bill Cheetham Property Management.

Second, I will deduct at least one-half of next month's rent in compensation for the time, trouble, electricity, and productivity the lack of heat has cost us.

Third, I will lodge a formal complaint against Cheetham Property Management with the Commercial Building Authority. The complaint will focus on the unsafe, uncomfortable conditions in this office over the past week and on your failure to communicate with us.

I await your reply.

Very truly,

> Using "First," "Second," and "Third" helps the reader focus and remember.

Michael Klepper
President

P.S. Again, if you are unable to communicate with me for some legitimate reason, please let me know through Mrs. Stacey and advise me what to do.

Sample 4: Second Stage in a Complaint Process.

Collection Letters

Collection letters are similar to complaint letters in that both attempt to get someone to do something they should already be doing, in this case, paying their bills.

Credit 101

Most goods and services that move from business to business in the U.S. are sold on credit. It's a good system, speeding up transactions by making sales and shipments move faster and enabling the buyer to see the goods before payment.

Different businesses extend credit on different terms. *Terms* refer to the length of time the buyer has in which to pay and to any special discounts that the seller may offer. While the most common terms are "payable within 30 days," another common arrangement is "2/10 net 30," which means that the buyer can take a 2 percent discount if he pays within ten days of receiving the invoice. Otherwise, he must pay the full amount of the invoice within 30 days.

In practice, two things happen. First, many buyers pay a bit more slowly than the terms allow. They do this because they don't have the money, or they have it but want to earn interest on it longer. Second, some buyers pay very slowly or not at all.

Once a company is 30 days past-due, meaning that they haven't paid the invoice within 30 days of the due date, it usually becomes a collection account.

> **What's That?**
> A company receives goods on *credit* when they get the goods first and pay later, usually within 30 days. The most common alternatives are to pay when the order is placed or to pay on delivery of the goods. The latter is known as *COD*, meaning "cash on delivery."

The Collection Process

Small companies have a person and large companies have a department that collects past-due accounts. This is usually done by first sending letters and then making phone calls to someone (usually in the Accounting department) at the company that is past due.

> **Trick of the Trade**
> A slow-paying company may be in serious financial trouble and able to pay only a few creditors. They will generally pay the most essential suppliers first and then the others. If you have reason to suspect that you are in the latter group, use strong collection tactics early or you may not get paid.

Virtually all companies that sell on credit have a series of letters that begin gently and become more aggressive—and, ultimately, threatening—with each letter.

Sample Collection Letters

Most companies have a set of collection letters that go out more or less automatically at the right times. Samples 5–10 are of increasingly strong collection letters.

Watch Out!

If you are an independent operator, a freelancer, or a small business owner, be careful whom you sell to and be aggressive about collections. By "aggressive," I mean get on them as soon as they are past due. Let them know (in a nice way) that you simply can't afford to "carry them."

Dear Valued Customer:

Are you aware that your account is past due?

According to our records, your account is past due in the amount of $1,494.91. Please pay this amount when you receive this letter, if you have not already done so. If you have, I thank you for your payment and ask that you kindly disregard this notice.

Ted Armstrong
Credit Manager

> An early-stage collection letter should allow for the possibility that the reader has already sent payment.

Sample 5: For an Account That Is 30 Days Past Due.

Dear Customer:

Protect your credit rating! Your account is past due in the amount of $1,494.91. To protect your credit rating and to avoid delays in having your orders processed, please pay this amount immediately.

Thank you for your prompt attention to this matter.

> Always mention the amount you are owed.

Very truly yours,

Ted Armstrong
Credit Manager

Sample 6: For an Account That Is 60 Days Past Due.

Dear Customer:

Your account is seriously delinquent! Please remit $1,494.91 to the address above immediately.

Your credit rating is a valuable business asset, which you are putting at risk.

Given that our previous requests have not resulted in your paying this bill, we will have to take other measures if we do not promptly receive payment.

Very truly yours,

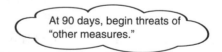

> At 90 days, begin threats of "other measures."

Ted Armstrong
Credit Manager

Sample 7: For an Account That Is 90 Days Past Due.

Dear Customer:

Your account is seriously delinquent and in danger of being referred to our legal department or a collection agency. To avoid these unpleasant consequences, please remit $1,494.91 to the address above immediately.

Very truly yours,

At this stage, the collection letter should be short and strong.

Ted Armstrong
Credit Manager

Sample 8: For an Account That Is 120 Days Past Due.

Dear Customer:

Unfortunately, your account is almost six months past due. If we do not receive payment of $1,494.91, we will begin legal action to recover this amount plus expenses or, at our option, we will refer your account to a collection agency.

To avoid one of these unpleasant consequences, please send $1,494.91 to the address above.

To avoid legal action or referral to a collection agency, you must pay your account in full within 10 days.

Very truly,

Ted keeps his options open.

Ted Armstrong
Credit Manager

Sample 9: For an Account That Is 150 Days Past Due.

Final Notice

Dear Customer:

Your account is six months past due in the amount of $1,494.91. At this point, we have no choice but to begin legal action to recover this amount plus expenses or to refer your account to a collection agency.

The only way to avoid one of these unpleasant consequences is to pay $1,494.91 at this office within 72 hours of receiving this notice.

This is the final notice you will receive from us. If your account is not paid in full within 72 hours, you will soon receive notification of legal action or action by a collection agency.

Very truly,

Giving the reader limited time to pay may get quick action.

Ted Armstrong
Credit Manager

Sample 10: For an Account That Is 180 Days Past Due.

What's That?

A *charge-off* (or *write-off*) is an uncollectible account. Uncollectible accounts are usually referred to a collection agency, a business that collects past-due debts. The company charging off the account subtracts it from sales as a business expense. If any written-off money is recovered, it is counted as revenue.

Collection Do's and Don'ts

Collecting past-due accounts is no one's idea of fun. Here are some guidelines to make it as effective as possible:

Do:

➤ Keep letters short and impersonal.

➤ Have a systematic schedule for sending collection letters.

➤ Mention the amount every time.

➤ Use words such as "unpleasant" and "unfortunate."

➤ Use phone calls along with collection letters.

Don't:

➤ Imply moral judgment in your letter.

➤ Use language such as "deadbeat" or "fraud."

➤ Make threats that you cannot or will not act upon.

➤ Spend more money on collection efforts than the account is worth.

➤ Harass the debtor.

A freelance or a small business cannot afford non-payment. To collect a past-due account, call the debtor and build a relationship with someone who can authorize payment.

The Least You Need to Know

➤ Before complaining by letter, complain by telephone.

➤ Be sure to complain to someone who is willing and able to solve your problem.

➤ Have a solution in mind and use it as a benchmark to judge any proposed solution; if the solution is not acceptable, say so and go higher.

➤ Have a set of collection letters that you send on a schedule; use the telephone too.

➤ If you own a small business, be careful whom you sell to, and be very aggressive and more personal in your collection efforts.

Chapter 21

So Sorry: Rejections, Apologies, and Answers to Complaints

In This Chapter

➤ Acknowledging receipt in a neutral way

➤ Rejecting the proposal, not the person

➤ Dealing delicately with written apologies

➤ Handling customer complaints in writing

Rejection letters are a required courtesy when you must refuse a written request, invitation, or proposal. It may be a request for a donation, an invitation to speak at an event, or a proposal for a new line of products. Whatever it is, your task is to reject it.

Letters of apology are necessary when your organization has offended someone in some way and must express regret. One special form of apology is answering customer complaints. These letters can be tricky.

This chapter will show you how to deal sensitively with each of these writing situations. But first let's look at a common response letter in business, the letter of acknowledgment.

Acknowledgment Letters

An acknowledgment letter is a good initial response to a request, invitation, or proposal. It lets the sender know that you've received the document and that you'll be evaluating it.

Letters acknowledging receipt of resumes often state, via a form letter, that there will be no further communication unless the organization is interested. Other acknowledgment letters should be individually tailored.

Acknowledging a Resume

Sample 1 acknowledges receipt of a resume.

The letter is short and courteous and places no obligation on the company to communicate further unless they want to interview the applicant.

Unless the company specifically solicited that applicant's resume, there is no need to say that the company will be in touch after reviewing the resume. Such a promise accomplishes nothing and only creates more work for the company.

Acknowledging an Individual Request

Sample 2 is a more individually tailored letter acknowledging receipt of an invitation.

This letter does two helpful things: It mentions the criteria on which the invitation will be judged (an area of great mystery for many people making requests), and it mentions the time frame for a decision—useful information for those lining up sponsors for the race.

Dear Applicant:

> The second sentence of the second paragraph makes writing a rejection letter unnecessary.

Thank you for submitting your resume to Amalgamated Industries.

I have directed it to the proper people in our organization, who, in the weeks ahead, will be evaluating your experience and qualifications in light of our needs. If you do not hear from us shortly thereafter, then we do not currently have an appropriate position. In that case, we will keep your resume on file for future reference.

Again, thank you for your interest in Amalgamated.

Very truly,

Hanna Gabler
Director of Recruiting Services

Sample 1: A Form Letter Acknowledging Receipt of a Resume.

Dear Ms. Baker:

> A specific comment about the event adds a personal touch.

Thank you for inviting National Auto Parts Inc. to sponsor a car in next year's Rough Rider 1,000. The race certainly sounds exciting.

In the course of its business, National Auto receives many sponsorship requests and proposals. We evaluate each one individually in light of our budgets, business goals, and, of course, the nature and timing of the event. This generally takes about six weeks.

When we have evaluated the sponsorship opportunity you have presented, I will contact you with our decision. Meanwhile, thank you for thinking of National Auto Parts.

Sincerely,

Jackson Campbell
Director, Special Events

Sample 2: Acknowledgment of an Invitation.

Acknowledging a Proposal Conditionally

On rare occasions, proposals can lead to legal trouble, especially in fields where ideas and creativity are a professional's bread and butter. Take the movies. Trouble can arise when a studio does a film that resembles one someone proposed (or thinks he proposed).

This has led people in certain businesses to be wary of unsolicited proposals. In idea-driven businesses, prudence may require protecting yourself regardless of which side of the desk you're on.

Sample 3 acknowledges receipt of a business proposal but sets a condition before agreeing to review the proposal.

A *waiver* is a statement in which you give up (or "waive") a right in exchange for something. For example, a record company may waive its right to keep an unhappy artist under contract in exchange for ownership of his previous songs. Or a wrongfully fired employee may waive her right to sue in return for a cash settlement.

Watch Out!

If you submit a proposal and there is a condition for having it reviewed, you will need to weigh the potential cost of the condition against the potential gain of having it reviewed and getting a deal. Most companies are not out to steal ideas, but legitimate disagreements do occur, pointing up the need for caution and legal advice.

Dear Mr. Harrison:

Thank you for your proposal regarding an opportunity for the Consolidated Toy Company to invest in your proposed line of motorized insects for children.

As a leader in the toy industry, Consolidated receives many new product proposals. At times these proposals resemble product ideas or actual products that we have in development in-house or with an outside organization or individual. Occasionally, that resemblance can lead to disputes over the ownership of the idea.

"We have a policy" is a useful phrase when you have to enforce a policy.

Therefore, to protect our interests, we have a policy of not evaluating any business or product proposal unless we have a signed waiver protecting Consolidated from any form of legal action relating to the proposal. Please understand that this waiver completely protects Consolidated should your proposal resemble an idea or product that we are considering or developing.

If you are willing to sign this waiver, please let me know and we will send it to you. (You may wish to consult your own legal advisor in this matter.) When we receive the signed waiver, we will review your proposal and notify you of our decision. If you do not wish to sign this waiver or if I do not hear from you within two weeks of the date of this letter, we will return your proposal without reviewing it.

Thank you in advance for your understanding regarding our policy, and thank you for your interest in Consolidated Toy Company.

Yours very truly,

Richard Worth
Corporate Counsel

Sample 3: Conditional Acknowledgment of a Proposal.

Rejection Letters: A Matter of Timing

Ideally, rejection letters should be sent as soon as you have made a decision—but not so quickly as to give the impression that the request or proposal was so laughably absurd that it took you all of five seconds to make up your mind. On the other hand, if you send a rejection weeks later, it may look as if responding was a low priority.

Worse, if the request is time-sensitive, you may have delayed the other person, particularly if you're hard to reach by phone. For example, invitations to an event—to speak on a panel or to sponsor a table at a luncheon—should be answered well before the event. You should answer within a week or two after receiving the request, assuming you received it at least eight to ten weeks before the event, as is customary.

It's OK to take longer in situations where the sender knows you face high volume. A college applicant, job applicant, or author knows that the admissions committee, company, or publishing house has hundreds, often thousands, of requests to deal with, so they can be tolerant. Nonetheless, six to eight weeks is reasonable in most cases. (College applicants realize that they're all notified at the same time, so this rule doesn't apply to them.)

For business proposals, four to six weeks is considered normal, unless the sender requests a speedier decision. Keep in mind that this chapter is about rejection, not acceptance, letters. If you wait five weeks to tell someone you accept their proposal, you may find they've gotten a deal elsewhere.

If the proposal mentions a deadline for responding, take it seriously—that is, if you're interested in the deal. Although some people use a deadline just to try and generate action, often the deadline is legitimate.

Watch Out!
People with good proposals often submit them to more than one outfit at a time. They are "supposed to" tell you if that's what they're doing, but sometimes they don't. If you're interested in a proposal, respond quickly or you may lose the deal.

High-Volume Rejection Letters

Since anyone with ink, paper, and a stamp can send you a written request, it's possible to spend most of your day writing rejection letters.

This happens, in fact. That's why so many high-volume rejection letters are form letters. Rejection letters from universities to applicants, from personnel departments to job seekers, and (I'm sorry to say) from publishers to authors are impersonal form letters because they cannot devote the resources to writing individual letters.

What's That?

A *form letter* is a letter prepared with standard wording that can be sent to many people. It can be as impersonal as "Dear Applicant," or it can be used as the basis of a more individually tailored letter in which some paragraphs are standard and others are customized to the reader.

Rules for Rejection

When you write a rejection letter, keep the following rules in mind:

➤ Reject the request, invitation, or proposal, not the person who made it.

➤ Be as specific as you can, but don't go into detail about your reasons for rejecting something.

➤ Give some encouragement or "leave the door open" if appropriate.

Letters of rejection should be somewhat impersonal. In theory, at least, your rejection of the proposal is not a judgment on the person or organization that submitted it. In practice it might be; but it's unprofessional to let that show. Stay focused on the request. It will help you to stay objective and keep you from moving from an impersonal style to a cold one. Of course, this advice assumes that you are not personally acquainted with whomever submitted the request, invitation, or proposal. If you know the person, your style can be more personal.

Be specific about the reasons for the rejection, so that the person knows that you actually considered the request, but not so specific that she can "pick apart" your position and come at you again.

If possible, give some kind of encouragement that leaves the door open. This softens the blow and preserves good will between the parties. Remember, you may someday work with that person—or have to submit a proposal to her! Your rejection will be more easily forgiven and forgotten if you're courteous.

Samples 4–8 show these rules in action.

Letters of Rejection

Sample 4 is a form letter for rejecting resumes.

This letter could be made even more personal. For example, it could cite a specific interest, experience, or skill of the applicant's that was impressive ("Your advertising background was particularly interesting."). Or it could give more specific reasons for the rejection ("We are seeking someone interested in remaining in sales rather in moving to marketing.").

A more individual letter for rejecting a job applicant after an interview can be found in Sample 5.

How personal or impersonal your style should be depends on your relationship with the applicant. For instance, rejecting a relative of a senior officer of the organization will require a more personal letter than rejecting a stranger.

Sample 6 rejects a request for a donation.

Notice how the writer of this letter manages to convey warmth without departing from the formal style of the rejection. Sample 7, a rejection of an invitation to speak at a conference, uses a similar strategy. In both cases, causes external to the applicant are cited as reasons for not participating.

Sample 8, a rejection of a business proposal, is more matter-of-fact.

Dear Applicant:

We regret that the volume of resumes that we receive does not allow us to respond individually to each one.

We do, however, review each one individually. This means that your resume was reviewed here in Human Resources and then sent to managers in the areas of our organization where there could be a match between your background and our needs.

At this time, unfortunately, there does not appear to be such a match. We will, however, keep your resume on file and contact you should a potential need for your services arise.

Thank you for your interest in Amalgamated Industries.

Sincerely,

The use of a form letter is acknowledged, but the reader is assured of individual attention.

Paul Markham
Director, Human Resources

Sample 4: Rejection of a Resume.

Dear Mr. Malmson:

Thank you for meeting with Mr. Johnson, Ms. Reynolds, and me this past Thursday to explore career opportunities at Amalgamated Industries. Each of us enjoyed meeting you.

Currently, however, we do not see a fit between your interests and experience and our needs. As you know, we have far fewer positions than qualified applicants.

We wish you all the best in your career. Thank you again for your interest in Amalgamated Industries.

Sincerely,

Mentioning that some qualified applicants must be rejected softens the blow.

Paul Markham
Director, Human Resources

Sample 5: Rejection of a Job Applicant Following an Interview.

Dear Mr. Bennett:

We have reviewed your request for Amalgamated Industries to sponsor a table at this year's Eagle Scout Annual Awards Dinner. We regret that we cannot play a role in this event at this time.

Please know that our decision was not an easy one and was based upon internal budget issues rather than on the worthiness of the request or our desire to assist the Boy Scouts of America.

Please accept my best wishes for the success of this event.

When declining to make a contribution, blame your budget.

Sincerely,

William Greene
Director, Corporate Affairs

Sample 6: Rejection of a Request for a Donation.

Dear Ms. Avery:

Thank you for asking me to be the keynote speaker at the Autumn Gala Conference of the Venture Capital Association of America.

I would truly enjoy having the opportunity to address the participants at this important event, but unfortunately, I cannot, given prior commitments for that week.

Thank you for the invitation, which I was honored to receive.

Sincerely,

Lawrence is intentionally vague about his reasons for turning down the invitation.

Lawrence Jacoby
President

Sample 7: Rejection of an Invitation to Speak at a Conference.

Dear Mr. Dannon:

Thank you for your proposal regarding the opportunity to invest in your contemplated line of automated corkscrews.

We have reviewed the proposal carefully and have decided that, given our current business goals and commitments, we will not invest in this project. I have enclosed the copy of the proposal you sent us.

Thank you for thinking of Amalgamated Industries and please accept my best wishes for the success of your project.

Lisa wisely returns the rejected proposal—and documents returning it in her letter.

Lisa Coady
Vice President, Finance

Sample 8: Rejection of a Business Proposal.

When rejecting proposals, it's good business practice as well as a matter of courtesy to return the proposal to the sender, as the writer in Sample 8 does. The sender should have included a self-addressed stamped envelope with the proposal, but even if he did not, it should be returned.

Keep Rejection Short and Sweet

As you see, these letters are all short, straightforward, and courteous, but light on explanation. You may have heard the saying, "Least said, soonest mended." Although rejection in a business situation isn't meant to give offense, there is the possibility that the person at the other end will be offended. At the least, he will be disappointed.

Rejection is rejection, after all, and nobody likes it. The less you say, the easier the rejection will be to accept. Going on about the reasons will sound hollow. Being complimentary will sound patronizing. Being too apologetic will sound insincere.

When it comes to rejection, keep it short and sweet.

The Sorrow and the Pity

You may need to write a letter of apology when you or your organization offends someone by saying or doing something, or by not saying or doing something. For example, your organization might forget to invite a board member to a function or could deliver the wrong item to a customer, triggering a complaint. Answers to customer complaints are the most common form of written apology in business.

Apologies for a personal offense are best done in the most personal way, meaning in person or on the phone. No matter how personal your style of writing, speaking with someone directly is always more personal.

Letters of Apology

Let's say it falls to you to write a letter of apology after your organization has offended someone. Samples 9 and 10 give two examples of how to do this.

The first one, Sample 9, should be sent by messenger along with a nice, expensive flower arrangement. When you've made a mistake, there is little to do but admit it and hope that you haven't made an enemy. In fact, a follow-up phone call after this letter would be a good idea in a case like this one. At the least, you'll find out whether your apology has been accepted.

Sample 10 is an apology for a different kind of mistake.

Again, a simple apology is often all that is required. Very little, if any, explanation is called for. Explanations quickly start to sound like excuses, and excuses have no place in a true apology.

Dear Mrs. Chatsworth:

I just learned from Mr. Hillary that you are, understandably, upset that you were not invited to our Annual Toast and Roast, which was held last night.

I apologize for this oversight and take full responsibility for it. My only defense, admittedly a poor one, is that I am new to the job of coordinating this event. I was working from last year's invitation list and did not realize that you had joined our board of directors since then.

Your presence was missed, and when I realized that I had neglected to invite you to this event I was, as you may imagine, horrified.

Please accept my apology and forgive my dunderheadedness. I assure you that it will never happen again.

Sincerely,

> Every apology letter should contain one sentence of "pure apology"— here, it's the first sentence in the second paragraph.

Terry Daniels
Coordinator, Special Events

Sample 9: A Letter of Apology for an Oversight.

Dear Mr. Redmond:

Please understand that we did not intend to offend anyone—least of all veterans of the U.S. military—by referring to our Memorial Day Sale as our "D-Day Invasion." It was an unfortunate choice of words for which I take full responsibility.

I am sorry for this irreverent reference to one of the most tragic and heroic events in military history. Please accept this apology from all of us at Main Street Auto Sales, where we will be sure to think our advertising themes through more carefully and considerately in the future.

Sincerely,

> Without evading responsibility, Scotty makes it clear that no offense was meant.

Scotty Steward
President

Sample 10: Apology for an Offensive Choice of Words.

Do's and Don'ts of Apologizing

Here are some dos and don'ts for apologizing on paper (or verbally for that matter):

Do:

➤ Admit your mistake and take responsibility for it.

➤ Point out that you meant no offense.

➤ Mention that it will not happen again.

➤ Send or offer some kind of tangible peace offering, if appropriate.

Don't:

➤ Try to weasel out of it or offer long explanations.

➤ Blame someone else (I know, it's tempting).

➤ Get cute, apologize too profusely, or patronize the reader.

➤ Blame the person to whom you're apologizing (for example, by implying he is too sensitive).

Answering Customer Complaints

When you receive a customer complaint in writing, you should answer it in writing unless the situation is so urgent that a telephone call is indicated.

One very real issue in addressing some customer complaints is how much responsibility to assume. We live in a society in which agreeing that your product was responsible for even a slight injury can land you in court.

Sample 11 is a letter that offers sympathy (and a free premium) without assuming responsibility.

The letter acknowledges that the little girl got a rash after using the product, but it does not in any way admit or agree that the product caused the rash.

Of course, there will be times when your organization is clearly at fault. Sample 12 attempts to soothe an angry customer who was treated badly.

> **Watch Out!**
> They way you handle certain written complaints may have legal implications. If you're at all in doubt, get legal advice on wording when answering complaints.

Dear Ms. Mulvaney:

I was sorry to learn that your daughter Kimberly apparently developed a reaction to Just Ducky Bubble Bath.

All of our products are hypoallergenic and thoroughly tested for safety before going to market. It is very rare that one of our products, used according to directions, will injure a user. Thank you for alerting us to this situation.

We regret that Kimberly developed a rash on her back after using Just Ducky, and we wish her a speedy recovery. As a token of our good will, please accept the enclosed complimentary samples and coupons for other products of Amalgamated Industries.

Sincerely,

> When legal liability is a possibility, take great care with wording.

Jack Danna
Director, Customer Service

Sample 11: A Response to a Complaint That Shows Sympathy Without Assuming Responsibility.

Dear Mr. Martinez:

I was sorry to learn that when you unpacked your recent order from us we had shipped the wrong item. Furthermore, I was upset to learn that when you called us to correct the situation, you received a rude, unresponsive answer.

I can understand your anger and disappointment with this level of service. Please know that it represents a sharp departure from the way that we usually treat our customers.

To ensure that we are shipping the proper item in the future, we have changed our procedures. We now have a final check of paperwork and product by a shipping clerk at the point of departure (rather than in the department doing the packing). We have also reprimanded the employee who treated you rudely and have refreshed his knowledge of the fundamentals of customer service.

As a token of my regret over this entire situation, I have enclosed a new invoice reflecting a 25% discount off the original amount you were billed. Please discard our original invoice and process this one (provided you see this gesture as fair).

Again, I am sorry that the level of service you received from us this time was not up to our usual standards. I hope that you give us a chance to "get it right" in the future.

Sincerely,

> Mary backs up her apology with a tangible way of making the mistake up to the reader.

Mary Glover
Vice President, Sales

Sample 12: In Response to a Customer's Legitimate Grievance.

When your organization is clearly in the wrong, and especially if you have damaged a customer relationship through costly delays or poor treatment, you must:

➤ Show that you have taken steps to ensure that the situation won't happen again.

➤ Try to fully or partially restore the customer's faith in the company.

Most customer complaints are legitimate. It's human nature to foul up now and then. Every organization does. The best companies realize this and understand that the customers who complain do them a favor by pointing out shortcomings. It is the customers who don't complain and don't return, or who complain to other potential customers, who can wreck a business.

Trick of the Trade
Many good companies encourage dissatisfied customers to complain. One has the following blurb on its invoices: "If you don't like our service, let us know. If you do like our service, let your friends know." That's the best approach to complaints ever.

The Least You Need to Know

➤ Send written rejections when enough time has passed that you look as if you thought it over, but without thoughtless delay.

➤ You can be as personal or impersonal in a rejection as the situation requires, but always be cordial and never cold.

➤ When you have a high volume of submissions to reject (for example, resumes), an acknowledgment letter can replace a rejection letter.

➤ In written rejections and apologies, keep explanations brief.

➤ Respond to written customer complaints quickly, in writing, and with a explanation of how you will avoid similar problems in the future.

➤ When apologizing, send a "peace offering" if appropriate; when answering a customer complaint, try to make up for the injury or loss to the customer.

Chapter 22

Cover Letters That Open Doors

In This Chapter

➤ Using the cover letter for its proper purpose

➤ How to get your cover letter to stand out from the rest

➤ Conducting wholesale and custom job searches

A *cover letter* is really any letter that accompanies (or "covers") other material. In everyday language, however, it usually means the letter that you send with a resume. This chapter will show you how to write a cover letter that opens doors.

Breaking Out of the In-Box

The goal of the cover letter and resume is to get you an interview. That is the one and only goal of approaching someone with these tools. Without an interview, you can't get a job or an assignment, and without a cover letter and a resume you usually can't get an interview. Even if you call the hiring authority on the phone, they'll say, "Send me a resume" before having you in for an interview.

This is partly just procedure, but it's also to save time for the people doing the hiring. Resumes save time by letting companies screen out people who are clearly unqualified. At the resume stage, therefore, your goal is not getting screened out. During the interview stage, your goal should shift to getting selected.

This is a subtle difference but a real one. Most companies receive so many resumes, they mostly have to screen people out. But they interview few enough people for a job so they can actually select someone.

Four Rules for Cover Letters

Keep the following rules in mind as you write cover letters:

➤ A cover letter, no matter how well written, can't compensate for a poor resume.

➤ A cover letter should reveal your personality, writing ability, and interest in the job.

➤ A cover letter should be straightforward and brief.

➤ A cover letter and resume must be completely free of errors.

Let's briefly look at each of these principles.

A Cover Letter Can't Compensate for a Poor Resume

Many people seem to believe that the cover letter can explain why they're qualified for the job even though their resume shows that they aren't. They use statements such as "Although I lack sales experience, I am willing to learn" or "While I have never worked with computers, I am extremely interested in them." If the job qualification is sales experience or a background in computers, these statements highlight a *lack* of qualifications.

Trick of the Trade
The better you tailor your resume to the job specifications, the better your chances of being called for an interview. The best way to do this is to have your resume done on your computer, where you can quickly adjust it to highlight the experience you have that is most relevant to the job.

It's far better to use the cover letter to bring out any related experience. For example, if you want a sales position but lack sales experience, you should highlight any experience that involved customer contact, negotiation, or proposal writing. If you have it on the resume, you can say in the letter, "I believe my background in customer service has prepared me well for a career in sales."

See the difference? In one instance you're excusing a shortcoming—and drawing attention to it. In the other, you're highlighting a qualification for the job. But it has to be on the resume, not just in the cover letter. You will be judged mainly on your resume.

Be Personal, Write Well, and Demonstrate Interest

A resume is a fairly impersonal document. You don't mention the words "I" or "we" or "you," and you can't talk to the reader the way you can in a letter. Your cover letter is your chance to reveal the person behind the resume. So use a personal, but professional, style.

The cover letter is also your main chance to show off your written communication skills. Again, you can only do so much in a resume, because a resume is a formula. Yes, there are poorly written and well-written resumes, but a letter is a better vehicle for revealing your writing skills. Make the most of the opportunity.

Finally and perhaps most important, you can use the cover letter to tell the company why you are approaching them. This function of the letter is essential, especially if your qualifications are not exactly as specified in the help-wanted ad or if you're sending your resume unsolicited as part of a general job search.

If your resume is unsolicited, you should have a sentence somewhere that begins, "I am writing to you because…" or "I am interested in working at Company X because…" Forcing yourself to finish one of those sentences will help you answer a key question in the reader's mind, since he didn't run an ad.

> **What's That?**
> An *unsolicited resume* is one you send in the hope of finding an unadvertised opening, or of creating an opening. When you're on a job search, it's important to send unsolicited resumes to department managers in companies where you'd like to work, as well as resumes in response to ads.

Keep It Short and to the Point

All business writing should be straightforward and concise. With cover letters the point bears repeating, however, because if you really, really want the job (or if you're desperate), you may tend to write an overly long cover letter.

In a moment I'll show you a three- to four-paragraph outline that works.

Zero Errors Is the Goal

Again, it may seem to go without saying that your goal is zero errors. However, I've seen too many errors in cover letters and even in resumes to let this pass without comment. Furthermore, although the personal computer is one of the best helpers you can have in a job search, it does encourage certain kinds of errors.

For example, let's say you have an old cover letter on your computer and you want to use it to respond to a help-wanted ad. You copy the letter to a new file, give the file a new name, and then type in the new inside address with the name and title of the person you're responding to. *But* you forget to change the salutation from "Dear Mr. Anthony" to "Dear Mr. Abernathy" before you edit the body of the letter for your new target company. Then when proofreading, you blow past the salutation.

Another common error is to leave a "Mr." in when it should be "Ms." or leave the wrong company name in the body of the letter.

Remember: Because the goal of most readers is to screen people out, any excuse you give them will do. A single error of this nature is excuse enough for many readers.

An Outline for Cover Letters

Here is a general outline for a cover letter for a resume:

Salutation:

First paragraph: State why you are writing and mention the specific position.

Second paragraph: Discuss your qualifications and experience, and link them as directly as possible to the qualifications for the job.

Third paragraph: If appropriate, mention why you're interested in working for the company, including any events or people that brought you to them.

Fourth paragraph: Close on a positive, helpful note.

Use either your personal letterhead or the format for a personal business letter with your own inside address. Don't use your company's letterhead, because you are not writing on behalf of your company. If you are self-employed and have company letterhead, do not use it if you're applying for a position as an employee.

Watch Out!

In cover letters, be very clear about your objective. You may in fact be open to full-time, part-time, or freelance work, but you're usually better off with one approach to a company. Otherwise, they get confused or you appear desperate—or both.

Sample Cover Letters

Samples 1 and 2 are examples of letters in response to an advertisement. Each follows this outline. Sample 1 is written by someone with the exact qualifications mentioned in the ad.

Trick of the Trade
Don't be afraid to sell yourself on paper. Use positive adjectives and describe your work in glowing (but not outlandish) terms. As the saying goes, "If you don't toot your horn, nobody will."

In Sample 1, the writer does not mention his interest in the specific firm. Although there would be no harm in including a sentence or two about this, it's not necessary in this case. Since his qualifications are right on target, the writer's strategy is to use a very "soft sell." Sometimes not acting too eager can actually help.

In Sample 2, the writer's qualifications are not exactly what the company is seeking, so she has to sell herself a bit harder.

John Carlton
444 Fedilis Street
Westport, CT 09999

(203) 555-1111 (home)
(203) 555-8889 (office)

Ms. Jayne Harris
Director of Recruiting
Hot Shop Advertising
555 Madison Avenue
New York, NY 10000

John draws attention to the best parts of his resume.

Dear Ms. Harris:

I enclose my resume in response to your advertisement in the *New York Sunday Times* for a senior copywriter with a specialty in consumer packaged goods.

As my resume shows, I offer five years of experience writing compelling copy for nationally known brands. These best-selling brands include Happy Nut peanut butter, Just Ducky children's products, and Zip Zippity toothpaste and mouthwash. I have worked in all phases of campaign development, from initial concept to final production, and in both print and broadcast media.

You can reach me at my office during business hours or at home during evenings and weekends. Thank you for your consideration.

Sincerely,

John Carlton

Sample 1: Cover Letter by Someone with the Perfect Qualifications.

99 Pleasant Street
Hanover, NH 09999

Mr. Lyle Emerson
Director of Human Resources
Everclear Spring Water Co.
888 Glen Ellen Road
Portland, ME 99999

It is generally a good idea to mention specific reasons for your interest in the company.

Dear Mr. Emerson:

I am writing in response to your advertisement in the *Sun* for a sales representative.

My interest in Everclear has grown out of a desire to sell for a company that is a leader in its industry. My research tells me that Everclear is such a company and that your sales force is among the best in the industry.

As my resume shows, my background includes experience in marketing, market research, and key-account analysis. At Mason Building Products, I worked closely with our sales reps to resolve customer problems while staying focused on the bottom line. I also have first-rate prospecting and closing skills, thanks to successful volunteer fund-raising experience.

I would appreciate having an opportunity to meet with you to discuss the contribution I could make to Everclear. Thank you for your consideration.

Sincerely,

Lorraine Fernald

Sample 2: Cover Letter by Someone with Good, but Not Perfect, Qualifications.

In Sample 2, Lorraine includes a paragraph about her interest in the company because she has to support a switch across industries and from marketing to sales, but she wisely keeps attention focused on her resume.

Trick of the Trade
Volunteer work can help you gain skills and fill gaps in your paid work experience. Be sure to mention any that you have if it's relevant to the job you're seeking.

When selling yourself, it's better to highlight experience than to just go on about how aggressive or bright you are. Such comments sound self-serving, while statements supported on the resume sound factual. The exception is when you're starting your career and your resume is too light to offer much support. Then a statement in the cover letter about your energy or ability to learn fast can help.

In your cover letter, don't mention the reasons you want to leave your present position. Instead, focus on the contribution you want to make to a new employer.

A Few Words on Timing

The best time to respond to an ad is mostly a matter of luck. As a rule, though, I believe it's better to respond a bit later rather than too soon. The heaviest volume of resumes comes into the company in the first two weeks after the ad appears.

If your resume hits the company early, they may not be ready yet to evaluate it seriously. If it hits them in the high-volume days, it faces stiff competition for attention. But if it comes in on the late side, you may face less competition, and they may not have seen many resumes that they like. In that case, yours may be seen as a standout.

How to Make a Cover Letter Stand Out

There are three basic ways to make a cover letter really stand out:

➤ Write something that's self-revealing and positive.

➤ Show genuine interest in the company.

➤ Use the right kind of humor.

We'll look at each one of these in a moment.

Most cover letters begin with the usual, "I am writing in response to…" This more-or-less stock sentence tells the reader that you're responding to her ad. After that first sentence, you must show some personality if you want to stand out. You may want to stand out by mentioning someone you know at the company. It can work, but be careful: Your contact could be an enemy, instead of an ally, of the hiring authority. Tactfully discuss this with the person whose name you're thinking of using. If you're not sure, you may be better off not using it.

Write Something Self-Revealing

To get beyond the "boilerplate," you can say something personal about your background, your reason for pursuing this opening or this company, or your current situation. Just be sure that it is positive. This is not the time to write about your recent divorce, rehab, or unemployment experiences.

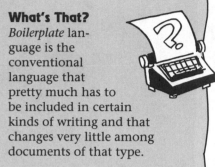

Statements about geography are fine. You can mention that you are new to (or would like to return to) an area, or that your spouse is taking a job there. Don't make it sound like the only reason for pursuing the job. But if it's a nice or exciting area, the desire to be there is something you'll have in common with the reader.

A career change can be an interesting personal topic. If you discuss it in a positive way, you can begin addressing the barriers to making such a change. For example, if you want to move from a business career to a teaching career, you might say, "My years in management have given me experiences and 'war stories' that will enable me to bring the material to life for students." If you were moving from nursing to business, you could mention your people and decision-making skills, and grace under pressure.

A major interest, accomplishment, or life change can help you come alive on paper. Just be sure to connect it to one of the job qualifications. For example, "As an avid whitewater rafter, I know the value of teamwork," or "As a former dancer, I've developed confidence and poise in front of groups."

Show Genuine Interest in the Company

The best way to show genuine interest is to do research on the company. Don't parade a bunch of facts, but show that you know the company by mentioning how you can make a contribution based on what you know.

For example, try to use statements such as, "My experience in testing and rolling out new products could help me to contribute to your product development efforts," or "Given that the company is retrenching, my experience in cost control and outsourcing could be quite useful."

Another way to show interest is to say that you're excited by the possibility of joining the company. Of course, you can say this whether or not it's true, yet it tends to work best when you really feel that way.

When I was a corporate manager, I received a letter in which the applicant said: "I am literally almost out of my mind with enthusiasm over the potential of the information industry." The guy was young and, in a charming way, naive. Despite his lack of experience, we were interested in him for his enthusiasm.

Sometimes if you have no other cards to play, sheer passion, enthusiasm, and persistence can work. Those qualities can't be faked. This strategy works best if you're young, or at least youthful. Few people pursue a job with raw passion, so it's impressive when you see it. It's not a substitute for experience, but it's the next-best thing. Actually, in some cases it's even better.

> ### Trick of the Trade
>
> How do you research a company? Many libraries have materials on publicly held companies—companies with publicly traded stock. Business libraries always do. There are business libraries in every major city and at business schools, which often extend privileges to visitors. Also, any company will send you their product literature, newsletters, and such if you ask. Always request an annual report from a publicly held company before you interview there.

Use the Right Kind of Humor

One way to stand out is to use humor, but be careful. As always in business, there is appropriate and inappropriate humor. The standards for "appropriate" can be very tight, particularly when a new hire is at stake.

In creative businesses, such as advertising and entertainment, humor can help your cause. People in these businesses like to be around people who are fun and who have an offbeat take on things. Even here, however, you need to be careful.

The first rule of using humor is this: If you can't be funny, don't try. Let's face it, some people are funnier than others. If you're not funny and you try to be, you may do more harm than good. Most of us do have a sense of humor, though, and letting it show can help you connect on a personal level and stand out from the 105 other people who sent a resume that week.

Humor on paper is largely a matter of tone. With the right tone—ironic, world-weary, light-hearted, whatever—a remark about the weather or a commute can seem funny. With the wrong tone, of course, it all falls flat.

Keep in mind that you're not auditioning for *Comedy Central*. You're just trying to show there's a human behind the resume. Try for a light remark that's natural to the situation. Humor in the following categories tends to be viewed as "appropriate" in business.

➤ The weather: "I look forward to hearing from you, even if Chicago winters can still freeze your eyeballs."

➤ Commuting: "It took me years to escape L.A.'s commutes, but for Disney I'd hit the freeway on a bicycle."

➤ Insider industry developments: "With loans at a record high and a recession due within a year, I've got my pencils out and I've got them sharp."

Beyond these categories, you're on your own. I grant you, these examples are not knee-slappers. They don't have to be. They just have to show you're human.

Key point: If you do use humor, all you need is one humorous remark in the cover letter—and, of course, none at all in the resume.

The Wrong Kind of Humor

Don't use self-deprecating humor—making yourself the butt of your own joke—or you may come off as having a poor self-image. Don't refer to unemployment or idleness or anything derogatory about yourself, even if you think you've got a hilarious slant on it.

Scratch anything even remotely politically incorrect, as well as wife, husband, children, in-law, divorce, religion, or money jokes. If you're of a certain age, don't make references to the 1960s.

Don't write things in parentheses that flag the fact that you just "made a funny," such as (Ha!), (Just kidding!), or (Yuk Yuk).

This is probably a good time to mention that when you sign a cover letter, if you have an "i" in your name you shouldn't dot it with a circle. Trust me on this one.

> **Watch Out!**
> Avoid "novelty" or "grabber" openings. I saw a letter begin, "As you go through an endless pile of resumes, looking for someone to interview, you now come across someone truly unique." Most business people see applicants who write these kinds of letters as oddballs.

Two Job-Search Approaches: Wholesale and Custom

In addition to answering help-wanted ads, you should also send your resume and cover letter unsolicited to companies that have not advertised a position. But be aware that answering ads (especially "blind" ads, if you choose to answer them) is a low-percentage game.

People do get jobs through ads, but many jobs are not advertised. So you have to get out there in other ways if you need a job or want to change jobs. Aside from answering ads, there are two basic types of job search. I call them wholesale and custom.

> **What's That?**
> A "blind" advertisement is one that does not identify a company (or even an employment agency) and asks respondents to reply to a post-office box. Many people won't answer these ads. If you have a job, your employer may have placed the ad and may be upset to know you're looking. It's a good idea to know where your resume is going before you send it; and when you respond to a blind ad, you just don't know.

The Wholesale Search: Paper the World

In a wholesale job search, you target companies broadly, send out lots of resumes, and play a "numbers game." If you mail 300 resumes, you'll probably get six to nine requests to come in for an interview.

The actual number you get will depend on your age, salary, industry, level in the organization, geographical area, and economic conditions. It will also depend on your experience and accomplishments and how well you get them on paper.

Although horror stories abound (people mailing 500 resumes and getting no responses), you can pretty much expect a response rate of about 2–3 percent. That's if you do it right and the economy is in decent shape.

Watch Out!

You can open your cover letter with "Dear Sir" or "Dear Sir or Madam," but it's much better to use a name and title on the inside address (and the envelope!) and a personal salutation. This means you'll need the name of that person (which means a phone call), plus a computer or a resume service.

To get the name of the person to write to, call the organization and ask to be connected to the department in which you would like to work. Ask whoever answers for the name and title of the manager of the department. If they ask why you want to know, tell them. Be sure to get the spelling of the manager's name and the correct address.

Because mass mailing demands a lot of target companies, you have to target them broadly. So broadly, in fact, that you're actually targeting an industry, such as banking or advertising, or a position common to most companies, such as accountant or salesperson. Most people using this approach also target a geographical area, but some go nationwide.

Sample Letters for the Wholesale Search

Samples 3 and 4 are letters for situations in which the applicants are mailing unsolicited resumes as part of a wholesale job search. When you're not applying for an advertised position, you have to work harder to get the company to think about you—to consider having you in for an interview or to pass your resume on to a colleague.

When you're sending an unsolicited resume to a company, should you send it to the Personnel department or to the hiring authority? If you send it to Personnel, there is a chance that they'll route it to the hiring authority—but there is a good chance that they will not.

If, for whatever reason, you can't find out who the hiring authority is, send your resume to a specific person in Human Resources. However, it's better to mail to the hiring authority or a senior person in the area in which you want to work.

Sample 3 is a "broadcast letter" from a financial analyst doing a mass mailing to Human Resources departments.

In an unsolicited cover letter, don't be afraid to ask for an interview. This is usually phrased in the form of "an opportunity to meet and…" or "an opportunity to discuss…" Although asking for a meeting hardly guarantees that you'll get one, it makes sense to ask because that's why you're writing.

The broadcast letter in Sample 4 has a slightly different spin, because the applicant is just beginning his career.

What's That?

The *hiring authority* is the person who can hire you. In most large organizations, several people have "input" into a hiring decision, but one person usually has the power to say "yes" or "no." That person is the hiring authority. They're almost always the person the job reports to.

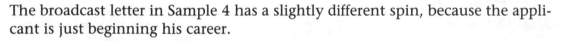

Trick of the Trade

In many letters, but especially those in which you are selling yourself, it's easy to overuse the word "I." One way to check on this and make it less noticeable is to make sure that you don't begin every paragraph with "I." Also say, "You can reach me…" instead of "I can be reached…" and "Please consider meeting with me to discuss…" rather than "I would appreciate your meeting with me to discuss…"

Dear Ms. Emery:

I am a financial analyst with 24 years of experience in manufacturing. I am seeking a position as a senior financial analyst and have enclosed my resume for your review.

As my resume indicates, much of my work has focused on analyzing large investments in productive capacity. These include major projects such as new plants, plant expansions, and acquisitions. I also offer solid international experience, particularly in analyzing the effects of exchange rates, currency controls, and changes in tax policy.

Your company is of interest to me because, given my skills and experience, I want to join an organization committed to international growth. Having known the thrill and challenge of contributing to overseas expansion, I believe I could assist your company in this arena.

I would appreciate your giving me an opportunity to discuss my qualifications and to learn about your needs. If you agree this may be worthwhile, or if you wish to discuss any aspect of my background, please call me at 212-555-9999.

Thank you for your consideration.

Very truly yours,

> Since a broadcast letter is not specific to the company that receives it, hundreds can be sent.

Susan Haver

Sample 3: A Broadcast Letter to a Human Resources Department.

Dear Ms. Ozkar:

I am a recent graduate of Pleasantville College's business program, and I am seeking an entry-level position in accounting with a substantial industrial firm.

While earning tuition money during my first two summers of college, I was a part-time assistant to the bookkeeper at the Tammymack Country Club in Glenridge. I also served a summer internship at a local accounting firm between my junior and senior years.

I am considered detail-oriented, energetic, and motivated, and have been told that I have excellent problem-solving skills and that I work well with others.

Your company is among those that I am targeting because of your reputation, industry position, and history of success. I would like a chance to do all that I could to learn your business and contribute to that success in the future.

Please give me an opportunity to meet with you to discuss my qualifications and the role I might play in your accounting function. You can reach me at the above address or at (999) 555-1234.

Thank you for your consideration.

> There are graceful ways to mention your strengths.

Sincerely,

Mike Cambridge

Sample 4: Broadcast Letter from a Recent Graduate.

The Custom Search: Research, Then Write

People do get interviews and jobs with the wholesale method, but these days the custom method (also known as the "guerrilla" job search) yields better results. It takes more work, but it prepares you much better for the interview.

In a custom job search, you target companies carefully, research them well, decide what role you could play and what contribution you could make, identify the hiring authority, and approach that person. Target no fewer than six companies. Eight or ten is a good number. As you do your research, you'll quickly develop a favorite target company or two, if you don't have one at the outset.

Some career counselors suggest that you send a letter simply requesting an "interview for information" to the hiring authority or to a contact. Many also suggest heavy networking to locate unadvertised jobs or to get more interviews for information.

Frankly, I prefer a direct approach based on your desire to work for an outfit, your knowledge of the company, and what you have to offer them. The interview for information can be seen as a ploy. Why be coy? If you want to work there, apply for a job—or help them create one for you.

The key is to show that you offer value. That's much easier to do if you've done solid research on the company, know what you can contribute, and show motivation to work there.

> **Trick of the Trade**
> The more research you do on a company, the more confidently you will approach them. Even if you don't display a tenth of what you know about the outfit, knowing it will vastly improve your performance in the interviews.

Sample Letters for the Custom Search

Samples 5 and 6 are letters written for a focused, custom job search. Sample 5, for example, is by a fairly seasoned middle manager.

Sample 6 is for a recent graduate on a guerrilla job search. It takes an aggressive approach to the request for an interview. Doing your homework can help get you to this point of self-confidence.

Some businesses, such as law, entertainment, finance, and sales, are more open to an aggressive approach than others. In Sample 6, aggressiveness is coupled with a bit of intellectual idealism that, if sincere, will speak to many people. This kind of letter, along with a strong performance on the telephone, very often opens doors.

> An opening that expresses long-term interest in the company will usually interest the reader.

Dear Mr. Grimes:

I have been following Amalgamated Industries for some time and have long felt that I could some day make a contribution to the company. Now that Amalgamated is moving into the telecommunications business, I believe that day may have arrived.

My interest in Amalgamated grew out of a desire to be affiliated with a growing firm that could consistently reinvent itself. Regardless of current economic or market trends, Amalgamated maintains strong growth and a leadership position. Quite frankly, it is the kind of company I would like to work for.

As my resume reveals, I offer 32 years of management experience in the telecommunications equipment business. This experience has been concentrated on the operations side of the business. As senior operations manager, I have managed plant start-up, retooling, and all phases of operations. Cost control and just-in-time inventory management are particular strengths of mine.

Please consider meeting with me to discuss ways in which I could contribute to Amalgamated's thrust into this exciting business. You can reach me at the above address or by calling (999) 555-3333.

Thank you very much for your consideration.

Sincerely,

Rob Ringelstein

Sample 5: Letter for a Custom Job Search.

Dear Ms. Garribotto:

Having made a study of the major East coast firms engaged in product liability law, I have of course researched Sparks Manhower & Weeks. I would very much like to be considered for a junior associate position at the firm.

My interest in product liability law is an extension of studies and volunteer work I did as far back as my undergraduate days. The tension between the risks of open capitalism and the need for public safety has always been fascinating to me. I see product liability law as a major way in which our society manages that tension.

As a leader in that area, Sparks Manhower would offer me an opportunity to play a role in this important arena. In return, I would do everything in my power to contribute to the firm's record of growth and excellence.

After you have had a chance to review the enclosed resume, I will take the liberty of calling you with the purpose of arranging an interview. Please give me the opportunity to at least meet with you to discuss the potential contribution I could make to your firm.

Meanwhile, thank you for your consideration.

Sincerely,

> Many people will respect this kind of aggressive effort.

Rudy Grenoble

Sample 6: Letter from a Recent Grad on a Guerrilla Job Search.

Letters That Work Get You Interviews

Ultimately, the only measure of a "good" letter and resume is whether they get you interviews. People reading resumes are people, and what hits one as healthy aggressiveness will hit another as unhealthy obnoxiousness. One person may see a wimp where another sees a gentleman.

Sometimes you get only an exploratory phone call. Be ready for these. While most companies phone when they want to interview you, some will call before deciding to have you in just to see if you sound as good as you look on paper.

A good letter definitely helps get you in the door. After that, it takes pluck and luck, as they say. Timing and chemistry also play a huge role in the hiring process. But a good cover letter and resume give you the best edge over the competition.

The Least You Need to Know

➤ Have the best resume possible, tailored to the position you're applying for, before you worry about the cover letter.

➤ The ideal cover letter will reveal your personality, emphasize your qualifications, and describe your interest in the job.

➤ A broadcast letter is a general letter for a mass-mailing of your resume. Letters you write after you research an organization tend to be more effective.

➤ Ask for an interview, and don't rule out a passionate or aggressive approach. Many people take the person with the "fire in the belly" over those too shy to put themselves across.

Chapter 23

Networking with Thank-You Notes and "Flower Mail"

In This Chapter

➤ The role of writing in networking and relationships

➤ When to write a thank-you note

➤ Keeping in touch with "flower mail"

The telephone and e-mail—and the pace of life today—threaten to do away with the personal note. The very rarity of a note, however, makes it stand out all the more. It's a warm way to stay in touch and to set yourself apart from the pack. This chapter will show you how it's done.

An Update on the Art of Networking

Networking has come to be viewed skeptically by many business people. Networking has always gone on, but until recently it didn't have a name and wasn't viewed as a big technique for success. Rather, it was based on personal relationships and shared interests or institutions, such as schools, clubs, or professional associations.

In the past 15 or 20 years, however, networking has become an end in itself for some people. Many people work at developing networks instead of relationships and at gaining contacts instead of friends.

The best way to "network" is to take a genuine interest in other people. If you're interested in others, you wind up playing more of a role in their lives and their thinking. When they see a situation that may be an opportunity for you, they'll think of you and call. If you're out of work, they'll care and want to help. If they meet someone who can help you, they'll mention your name and tell you to call that person.

In other words, there is "networking for success," and then there is cultivating genuine relationships. Writing can help you focus on genuine relationships, particularly in the long run.

The Role of Writing

Writing a personal thank you or other note doesn't take a lot of time, but it takes enough so that many people don't bother. When you take the time to write a note of thanks or support or congratulations, you're saying that you care about that person. (And you're saying it more sincerely than any greeting card could.)

Over time, the notes you send help forge a chain, just like all the telephone conversations and face-to-face meetings and lunches and drinks and other contacts and gestures. That chain helps form the relationship.

The Thank-You Note

The business (as opposed to personal) thank-you note can be typed or handwritten. Most often it is typed on company letterhead—formatted, of course, as a letter rather than a memo.

By a business thank-you note, I mean a note written to thank someone for:

➤ A favor you requested

➤ An outpouring of effort or a job particularly well done

➤ A business gift

Here is an example of each.

Dear Jim:

Thanks so much for driving those materials to the FedEx office at the airport for me last night. I know you were beat and that you wanted to get home, so I appreciate it all the more.

Best,

Mike Ross

Dear Pamela:

Just a note of thanks for all your effort on the General Industries project these past couple of weeks. As I think you know, this project would not be on track (or profitable) if not for your hard work and professionalism.

It's great working with you.

Regards,

Donna Laswell

Dear Mr. Herskowitz:

Thanks so much for the beautiful fountain pen that you presented to me after my keynote speech at your convention this past Thursday. It is one of the nicest I've ever seen and I'll remember the occasion—and your generosity—as I use it in the years to come.

I appreciate it.

Best wishes,

Gabriella Mattheson

Writing a thank-you note is a straightforward matter. There's no need for an outline because the note is short and should genuinely express your gratitude. As with all forms of writing, you should be concise, complimentary, and tasteful.

The need to write a more personal thank-you note often arises in the course of business. These notes are in response to more personal favors or gestures, such as dinner invitations or expressions of support during difficult times. These can be typed on letterhead, but it is often more appropriate to write them by hand on notepaper.

Here are two examples:

Watch Out!
As something of a formal practice, thank-you notes do have their little "rules." For example, after a couple has dinner at the home of another couple, the thank-you note should be written by the visiting woman to the hostess.

Dear Louise,

Thank you so much for having us out to the beach house this past weekend. John and I—and Jimmy and Jennifer—are all "water rats" from way back, as I think you noticed. That is a beautiful spot you have there, and it was great to get to spend that kind of time with you and Steve.

Warmest wishes,

Joyce Myers

Dear Bill,

Just a thank you for your recent note of support and for being such a friend during Kate's recent illness. You and Joan are the greatest.

We'll all be seeing more of each other again, when Kate is back on her feet (which should be in another three or four weeks).

Thanks again,

Jerry

These kinds of thank-you notes are considered a bit formal by today's standards but haven't gone out of style. Returning kindness with kindness will never go out of style. These notes have merely fallen by the wayside, probably temporarily, as we hurry on.

Thank-You Letters After Job Interviews and Client Meetings

Believe it or not, people often fail to write a thank-you note after a job interview or a business development meeting with a client or potential client. Always, always, always write a note of thanks in these situations because:

➤ It's good manners to thank people who give you their time when you ask for it.

➤ So many people don't do this that you automatically stand out from the crowd.

➤ You get an opportunity to build a relationship and do a bit more selling.

Thank You for the Interview

Thank-you notes for job interviews should be on personal letterhead or formatted as personal business letters.

> **Watch Out!**
>
> Get thank-you notes for interviews and business development meetings in the mail fairly quickly, by the next business day or the day after that. It's courteous and the meeting will still be fresh in both your minds.

Samples 1 and 2 offer examples of the personal letterhead kind and the personal business letter kind, respectively.

As Sample 1 demonstrates, you don't have to thank every person you interview with in a session, but it is nice to mention each one. Address the letter to the hiring authority, and extend thanks to each person who interviewed you.

Be sure to use the opportunity to reinforce your main message, which should be your major area of interest, your main qualifications, or both. Don't go on and on. Three short paragraphs are enough.

Watch Out!
If the interview went badly, there is not much you can do to fix it in a note. If you made a poor impression you can try to correct it, but raising the issue again may just reinforce the original impression.

Lisa Russell
9 Deer Hollow
Middleville, IA 99999
(999) 555-1212

Ms. Diane Sollars
Vice President
Campo Company
222 Second Avenue
Sioux City, IA 99999

Dear Diane:

Diane scores points by being specific about her interest and qualifications.

Thank you for having me in for the round of interviews yesterday. I enjoyed meeting you and learning more about Campo. Please convey my thanks to Charles and Donna as well.

I was particularly interested in the national expansion effort that you are planning. That is where I believe I could potentially contribute the most to the company. As I mentioned, I was instrumental in Babbo Corporation's expansion beyond the Pacific Northwest. Timothy Miller at Babbo can tell you more about the role I played in coordinating our nationwide initiative.

Again, thanks for giving me such a clear picture of Campo. It is a company that I would love to join. I look forward to hearing from you soon.

Sincerely,

Lisa Russell

Sample 1: Thank-You Letter for a Job Interview.

4 Rubicon Lane
Yonkers, NY 99999
(914) 555-3333

May 7, 1998

Ronald Kerry
Director, Management Information Systems
First National Bank
One First National Plaza
New York, NY 10001

> Don't be shy: Say why you want the job.

Dear Ron:

Thank you for meeting with me this past Tuesday regarding career opportunities in MIS at First National. Frankly, I was very impressed with your shop and would love to be part of your team.

Although I have never worked in an environment as fully networked as yours, please know that I see the possibility of doing so as motivating, to put it mildly. All of us in technology thrive on new challenges, and I believe that in the course of my career I've shown that the times when I've had to meet a challenge are those when I've contributed the most.

The possibility of joining First National's MIS department is exciting to me. Thanks again for having me in and for your consideration.

Sincerely,

Mike Montgomery

Sample 2: Another Thank-You Letter for a Job Interview.

Thank You for the Meeting

If you're in sales or running your own business, thank-you notes are extremely important after you meet with a potential client.

Sample 3 is a letter of thanks after a sales call. This kind of letter should go on company letterhead.

After a sales presentation, thank the prospect for the meeting, emphasize the advantages of your product or service, and nail down the next steps. Never just leave the prospect "hanging" regarding what you're going to do next. Instead, try to create some anticipation.

Trick of the Trade
Build bridges, don't burn them. If you are around long enough, you'll find that you'll ultimately do business with many people who wouldn't deal with you at the outset.

Sample 4 is a thank you from a freelance desktop publisher who pitched a piece of business but was rejected because his price was too high. This would go on letterhead and have an inside address.

As Sample 4 shows, you can use a thank-you note to good advantage after a meeting in which you don't get a deal. You can show you're a professional, leave the door open, and reinforce the message that if there's a way to do business with them (without abandoning your position), then you want to do business with them.

Perfect Health Programs Inc.
1000 Commercial Street
Midway, MD 99999
(999) 555-0909

Ms. Becky Jones
President
JMP Inc.
444 Dorset Avenue
Baltimore, MD 99999

Dear Becky:

Thank you for giving me the opportunity to meet with you this morning to discuss your employee health plan needs. Please thank Jim and Merry for me as well.

While the plan you currently have is certainly adequate for your company's needs, I believe that we may be able to offer you very competitive coverage with equally fine providers at a lower total cost. And we can do this without shifting more expense to your employees.

> Always mention next steps.

As we discussed, I will have a formal proposal prepared for JMP by the end of next week. That proposal will show the cost and coverage of both the Gold and the Platinum plans that I presented today, as well as those of your current plan. I know that you will see a clear difference—and, I believe, the advantage that Perfect Health can provide.

Please look for our proposal early the week of the 12th. And thank you for giving us the opportunity to submit it.

Jayne Neuberger

Senior Sales Representative

Sample 3: Thank-You Letter for a Sales Call.

Dear Kelly:

Thank you for giving me the opportunity to meet with you and tell you about InstaPress Services. Thank you also for you candor regarding the potential for InstaPress to work with you folks.

While I grant you that our pricing is at the higher end of the range, I believe this reflects a higher level of quality and service. I would still like to work with you at some point and show you what we can do.

Should the need arise, please let me know. I would be happy to work on your toughest, most exacting "rush" job, so please keep us in mind.

Sincerely,

> Leave the door open, even if you lose the sale.

Myra Aronson

Sample 4: Thank-You Letter After a Rejected Bid for Business.

All About "Flower Mail"

"Flower mail" can mean anything from a thank you to any of the various notes we'll cover in the rest of this chapter. I use "flower mail" as the all-purpose term for the many other notes you can write to business contacts, associates, and friends, including:

➤ Congratulations

➤ Support

➤ Jokes and gags

➤ Notes to be with interesting articles, book reviews, or catalogs

Here is an example of each, which could be either formatted as letters on letter-head or handwritten on note paper.

Here's a note of congratulations:

Dear Brian,

Congratulations on your well-deserved promotion to District Manager. It could not have happened to a more deserving (or nicer) guy. Although I know you won't need it, I wish you the very best of luck in your new position.

Let's get together so I can buy you a beer some day next week.

To your continued success,

Larry

Here is a note from a loyal writer expressing support for a friend or an associate coping with a business-related problem, such as legal charges:

Dear Marty,

Please know that I am with you all the way during this difficult time. As the saying goes, "What doesn't kill you, makes you stronger," and I know you'll come out of this stronger than ever.

If there is anything I can do to help you, please let me know.

My very best regards,

Michael Weathers

269

Don't underestimate the power of an old saying during times of trouble. Notes like this one are a source of comfort and support to people having tough times, and they are not forgotten.

The following note is one I sent along with a wanted poster for a bunch of white-collar criminals, mostly embezzlers, to a friend who is an executive recruiter.

> Dear Jory,
>
> I know you're always looking for aggressive, bottom-line oriented guys, so I thought I'd you send this sheet of candidates. Most of them would need a benefits package that included immunity from prosecution, but I think they've got the right stuff.
>
> Don't forget my finder's fee if you place any of them.
>
> Keep on dialing,
>
> Tom

Most jokes travel by e-mail these days, but if you have something to send in hard copy, like a cartoon you've clipped from a magazine, it's a chance to write a note.

That brings up a topic related to relationship building and networking: finding reasons to write.

Finding Reasons to Write

If you're in business for yourself, it makes sense to stay in regular touch with your prospects and customers. Often, however, you want to keep in touch in some way other than a sales letter, some no-pressure form of communication that keeps them aware that you exist, but does not ask for a piece of business.

Thank you and welcome-aboard letters are one way to do this. Here's an example:

> Dear Mr. Haines:
>
> Thank you for your recent initial order. Jim McMurray, your account executive, tells me that we stand a good chance of doing more business with you folks now that we have an office in Memphis.
>
> I hope that's the case, and if there is anything that any of us here at Consolidated can do to keep you happy, please let me know.
>
> Sincerely,
>
>
> Deane Smith
> President

This note is a bit more personal in style than the usual welcome-aboard letter, intentionally so. Too often those letters sound like—and are—impersonal form letters. If you finally get to do business with an outfit after months or years of soliciting them, take a moment to welcome them warmly and get things off on a good footing.

You can only thank someone for becoming a new customer once. So aside from thank-you notes and sales letters, what can you send to customers and prospects by way of keeping in touch?

Many companies use newsletters, but I think a lot of that material goes unread, and it sure isn't personal. I think that sales people, small-business people, and freelancers do better by sending a copy of an article or a book review that the person would find interesting along with a short note.

Here's an example of what I mean:

Dear Ms. Yudkin:

Here is a copy of an article from a recent issue of *Fortune* that you might find interesting. It is about a reversal of the recent boom in outsourcing. It seems that many companies are now finding that they can save money by bringing certain formerly outsourced functions back in-house.

The article isn't clear on whether this reversal is due to some real change in the economics of the situation or to a new fad in management thinking.

Either way, knowing that you've always been skeptical of outsourcing, I thought you'd like the piece.

Regards,

Larry Crisp

It's a nice way to stay in touch, isn't it? Of course, it takes personal involvement to do this, and from a practical standpoint you can't do it for many people. But for important prospects or major accounts, or if you are a sales person with a small book of business, it may be worth it to track the interests of decision-makers and send them an article of interest along with a note now and then.

In fact, it may be worth it to integrate these kinds of contacts into your regular program of sales letters, which we discussed in Chapter 17.

Do's and Don'ts of Thank-You Letters and "Flower Mail"

The letters we've been talking about in this chapter are a simple form of business writing, but there are several things to remember.

Do:

➤ Keep notes short and to the point.

➤ Write sincerely.

➤ Realize that, although some people may be surprised or think you're being formal, they'll enjoy receiving notes anyway.

➤ Use notes to forge relationships and stay in touch.

Don't:

➤ Write a personal note to someone you don't know well enough.

➤ Be overly familiar or cute in a note.

➤ Write a thank-you note for every little thing someone does.

➤ Expect to get notes in return; you may, but most people don't write them.

➤ Expect notes to work miracles; they are a small part of building a relationship.

The Least You Need to Know

➤ Writing thank-you notes and staying in touch by mail can help you build relationships.

➤ A note of thanks to an employee putting out extra effort is a great idea, because most employees feel underappreciated and many are never thanked.

➤ Notes of support and offers of help in times of trouble can lead to friendship.

➤ Writing a thank-you note or letter after a job interview or client meeting is a must.

➤ Notes should be personal in style. They offer a real opportunity to write it the way you would say it.

Chapter 24

...I highly recommend...

Writing Letters of Recommendation

In This Chapter

➤ When *not* to write a reference

➤ How to respond when someone asks you to write a reference

➤ Writing the reference you really want to write

At a supervisory or managerial level, you will occasionally be asked to write letters of reference or recommendation. This is a normal and usually reasonable request, but one that can put you on the spot or in an uncomfortable position. This chapter will show you how to handle such requests and how to write a letter of reference or recommendation.

The words *reference* and *recommendation* are pretty much interchangeable. One difference is that a reference is usually for business purposes—a job reference or a credit reference—while "recommendation" is the word used more often in the academic world. People need letters of recommendation when applying to college, for example.

This chapter will also briefly cover letters of introduction. These are not as common as they once were, but they still exist and they are a kind of reference.

Who Is Asking and Why?

The first issue is: Who is asking you for the reference and why are they asking?

The person asking for the reference is your first reader. It's a funny situation because he's asking you for an opinion of himself, presumably an honest one. However, honest opinions are not always what someone really wants. (If you've ever heard the question, "Do I look fat to you?" you know what I mean.)

You will probably be asked to send the reference directly to the institution that requires it. If you don't give a copy to the person who is the subject of the reference, it can leave that person feeling "in the dark." Also, under freedom-of-information regulations, the subject of the letter is often entitled to see his files. To be on the safe side, your best policy is to assume that the subject will see any reference you write for him. It is a (more-or-less expected) courtesy to give him a copy.

Reference requests are a bit of a social game. People who ask you for a reference have been asked to supply one by a college, graduate school, employer, club, or lender. It's a social game because no one is going to ask someone to write a reference if they think they'll write a bad one. Actually, the institution is saying to the applicant, "Do you know two or three literate people who will vouch for you? If not, we don't want to know you either."

But it does go a bit deeper, because there are good references and then there are *glowing* references. A glowing reference is completely and enthusiastically positive. Everyone who asks for a reference wants a glowing one, but not everyone who is asked wants to write a glowing one (or knows how).

Before getting further into good and glowing references, let's discuss negative references.

What About Negative References?

I'm not going to show examples of negative references because I don't believe in writing them. I would give a negative reference only verbally and then only in special situations. For example, I would want to warn a prospective employer of a violent individual or a compulsive thief. But even then I would do it in a subtle way.

What's That?
Libel means untrue, negative written statements about another. *Slander* refers to untrue, negative spoken statements.

Giving references is mainly a case of "If you have nothing nice to say, don't say anything." There are potential legal issues, including the possibility of you or your company being sued for libel or slander. Even if you can prove in court that your negative reference is true, it's expensive and time consuming.

Then there is the social aspect. If someone asks you for a reference and you agree to give them one, they expect it to be a good one. If you can't agree to give them a good one, then don't agree to give them one at all.

How Do I Refuse to Give a Reference?

Refusing to give a reference or recommendation to someone who asks can be awkward. It's best to handle it honestly, either when they ask or soon afterward.

When someone asks you for a reference and you need time to think over your answer, say something like, "I take writing a reference very seriously so I always like to think about it before agreeing to give one. Let me get back to you in a day or two." If they ask why, explain that it's nothing personal. It's just your policy. You can even say you got burned once. Just don't agree to give a reference that you're not comfortable giving.

To refuse, be straightforward and say something like, "I'm very sorry, but I really wouldn't feel comfortable doing that. I think that, given your performance (or "our working relationship" or "our history together"), you would be better off asking someone else." This can lead to a difficult moment or a conversation you'd rather not have, but it beats giving a reference you'd rather not give.

What If They Didn't Ask?

If someone uses you as a reference before asking you to write one, you still have a right to refuse. They either grossly misinterpreted your opinion of them or they should have cleared it with you first. In either case, they created the problem and it is theirs to solve. Their best move is to say that you are an outdated reference or you're out of the country, "indisposed," or whatever. In any event, it is *their* problem.

A verbal (as opposed to written) reference is another story. Although it would be helpful to ask you or alert you, someone who worked for you should be able to use you as a reference without asking.

> **Watch Out!**
> To save yourself time and trouble, you may be tempted to tell someone to write their own reference for you to sign. Or they may suggest this. It's a bad idea. It can easily place you in the position of either signing off on a letter that is too complimentary or editing out their over-the-top compliments. Either way it can be awkward.

Help, I Need a Reference

Let's look at a few situations in which people ask for references, and at some samples of written references.

Employment References

References for employers are the most serious. Employers who check references want an honest assessment of the applicant. Some employers, and some executive recruiters and industrial psychologists involved in hiring key people, will take the person giving a reference through a serious, detailed interview designed to get the truth.

People who are asked for references know the applicant and usually want them to get the job. They usually have little reason to say anything negative. If they did, they could create legal liability, which is why some companies have a policy of not letting managers supply references. Employers calling for references are directed to the Human Resources department, which will verify only dates of employment, job title, and salary.

Think about it: If you were to say that so-and-so is not a team player or often missed deadlines and it gets back to the applicant who was turned down for the job, you may be sued. Do you have documented proof that they're not team players? How often is "often" when you say they missed deadlines?

It's no joke. Of course, if the person you have been asked to supply the reference on was a fantastic employee, that's another story. But then, what if the person fails or does something dishonest on the new job? Could you be liable? See how involved this can get?

The best advice is to avoid writing employment references. This is easy to do, since most employment references are checked by telephone. Be as bland or as enthusiastic as you want to be, but be careful of negative statements. If a former employee was a real problem and still used you as a reference (some do), the best strategy is to "damn them with faint praise"—give them a polite but unenthusiastic recommendation. The lack of enthusiasm implies a negative opinion. An example would be if you were asked about an ex-employee and said, "He was consistent." You may mean he was consistently bad.

Blanket Recommendations

It is likely that the only written employment reference you'll ever be asked to write is a *blanket recommendation* for future employers, in which you state how you know the person and that you know they are reliable, honest, hard working, and competent (or excellent). Here are two examples of such letters.

Watch Out!
Be careful when writing references if you have a high-profile position. Many business frauds have occurred because the con man presented written references from well-placed people.

A departing employee will often ask for this kind of letter because they're not sure where you'll be when they need a reference. It's up to you to agree or refuse. You can always refuse by saying, "I like to give references on a case-by-case basis."

Sample 1 is a "glowing" recommendation.

Re: Mary Wares

To Whom It May Concern:

Mary Wares joined Amalgamated Industries in the finance group in 1989. She reported to me, in my capacity as Director of Financial Services, from then until she was promoted to Controller in 1993. In the five years Mary worked for me, first as Assistant Treasurer and then as Treasurer, she was an absolutely first-rate professional in every way.

Mary's key strengths include highly developed analytical and problem-solving skills. She repeatedly displayed an ability to cut to the heart of an issue, clarify our options, and implement the best one. Our treasury function is large and complex, and Mary thrived on both the size and complexity. She brought the same energy to resolving the most minute operational problems as she did to major policy questions.

Mary is an excellent manager of people. That is why I fully supported her promotion to Controller, a position in which she managed 18 senior accountants, and managed them well. (At that point she reported to our then Vice President of Finance, as I did.) Before that, as Treasurer reporting to me, Mary managed four assistant treasurers excellently.

Finally, Mary brings a sharp, but never unkind, sense of humor to the job. She works as long as it takes to get the job done, and displays the team spirit, maturity of mind, and scrupulous honesty so necessary in the finance function of a major company.

I enthusiastically recommend Mary Wares for any position or endeavor for which you may consider her.

Very truly,

> Frank's letter is strong on specifics.

Frank Squire
Vice President, Finance

Sample 1: A Glowing Recommendation.

The salutation "To Whom It May Concern" is traditional for references. You really don't know who will be reading them, and they go into the file that the outfit creates on the person.

As Sample 1 shows, you want to say things that are complimentary and related to the person's professional role.

For any written employment reference, you should:

➤ Mention your relationship to the subject.

➤ Mention how long you've known the subject.

➤ Mention the subject's strengths.

➤ Give examples of the strengths.

➤ Mention what you recommend the subject for.

Also, try to point out personal qualities that are useful on the job, such as a sense of humor and energy.

Watch Out!

When you write a glowing reference, show the person as balanced. Otherwise, the reader can misinterpret a compliment. For example, unless balanced by another comment, "detail-oriented" may mean "lacking imagination." Similarly, "imaginative" can mean "flighty" unless balanced by a phrase like "but realistic."

Sample 2 is a nice, but not glowing, reference.

Sample 2 is somewhat subdued in its praise. Saying he did a "fine job" does not imply that he was excellent. Adjectives like "hardworking" and "diligent" imply that he showed up and did his job, but was not brilliant and didn't make much effort to go the extra mile. The letter is light on specifics, does not convey great enthusiasm, and is limited to "any sales position." All in all, it gives the impression that Ted was a solid employee but not a star.

To Whom It May Concern:

I have known Ted Marks for the three years he worked for me as a salesperson at Amalgamated Industries. I am the Southeastern District sales manager and I hired Ted.

Ted did a fine job during his time at Amalgamated. He was hardworking and diligent in executing his duties and represented the company well. Customers also liked Ted.

He also performed well in terms of his level of sales, typically making, and occasionally breaking, his quota. His knowledge of our products and how to apply them to solve customers' problems was very good. Ted was good at resolving any difficulties that came up internally at our company, such as late deliveries.

I recommend Ted Marks for any sales position for which you may be considering him.

Very truly yours,

Marcia's recommendation is moderate rather than glowing.

Marcia LaPine

Sample 2: A Moderate Recommendation.

Character References

At times you may be asked for a so-called character reference for a friend or an acquaintance. You may not know the person professionally but you may be asked to vouch for their general character. This can come up in the course of someone's getting a loan, being admitted to a club, or even entering a profession (for example, an attorney applying to the bar association). Character references are often handled by telephone, but the need to give one in writing occasionally arises.

Sample 3 is an example of a character reference for a friend written to a potential lender.

Most character references should mention reliability, stability, sound personal habits, and honesty. When possible, it's not a bad idea to throw in references to the stereotypical middle-class symbols of these qualities, such as marriage, children, home ownership, and sports.

To Whom It May Concern:

I have known Edwin Runyon for eight years as a friend and as a friend of his family. I can say without qualification that Ed is reliable, honest, and a person who keeps his commitments.

He is a man who sees his responsibilities clearly and discharges them faithfully. I have seen this in his relationships with his wife, Lorraine, and his children, Ed junior and Maggie, and with his neighbors and friends.

Ed is balanced, law-abiding, responsible, and sober, but he enjoys a good time, particularly on the golf course (handicap: 12).

I recommend Edwin Runyon to you without qualification for any endeavor or responsibility for which you may be considering him.

Sincerely,

Kate Merrill

Sample 3: A Character Reference.

> Remember to say how long you've known the person you're recommending, and in what capacity.

Recommended Style for References and Recommendations

Note that the style of references is rather formal. That's as it should be, because you don't know the person you are writing to and your view of the subject—the person you're writing about—is supposed to be objective. Although everyone knows you are not objective, that is how it's supposed to sound.

A formal style also suits the formality of the process. The person asking for the reference is making a formal application, so a formal letter is what the situation demands.

Trick of the Trade

Occasionally, of course, you too may find yourself needing a reference. In our economy, references are becoming more important as job tenure becomes shorter and temporary and contract work become more common.

Try to get blanket letters of recommendation when you can, and build a portfolio of work samples, if that's possible in your profession.

Academic References

Business employees often take a leave of absence in order to further their education in college or graduate school. Although you may not like losing a good employee, there is nothing you can or should do to stop it. The employee deserves your support.

As in Sample 4, you want to stress qualities such as intelligence, analytical ability, and hard work.

Always close a letter of recommendation with a clear statement of support. Naming the individual and the institution they're applying to lends a nice touch and emphasizes the strength of your recommendation.

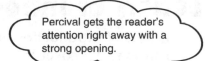

Percival gets the reader's attention right away with a strong opening.

Dear Admissions Committee:

It is with great pleasure that I write to you in support of Clara Goodleaf's application to your Graduate School of Business.

I have known Ms. Goodleaf for all five years that she has worked at Amalgamated Industries. I interviewed her when she applied to the company after she graduated from Smith, and I supported her hire as an entry-level market researcher. Two years later, she was promoted to manager of product development, reporting directly to me. I am vice president of marketing at the home products division at Amalgamated Industries.

Ms. Goodleaf is certainly one of the brightest and most insightful people I have had the pleasure to work with in a 27-year career. Her ability to grasp the abstract issues in a business situation while staying focused on concrete practicalities is unmatched in my experience. Most people can do either one or the other. These twin intellectual abilities are the main reason she moved from an analytical position (at which she excelled) into product development (where she also excelled).

Ms. Goodleaf quickly gains the respect and the cooperation of everyone she works with. This is partly because she herself respects and cooperates with others, and partly because people are attracted by her ability to focus on what is important and then act.

I have known for some time that Ms. Goodleaf would be leaving the company to pursue a graduate business degree. While as a manager I hate to lose such a qualified staff member, I enthusiastically recommend Clara Goodleaf for admission to Harvard University's Graduate School of Business.

Sincerely,

Percival Merrin
Vice President

Sample 4: Academic Letter of Recommendation.

Letters of Introduction

Letters of introduction are mostly a thing of the past, thanks to the telephone. However, I'll cover them briefly because they are a form of reference and they still exist.

A letter of introduction is a recommendation written to a specific individual to get help for the person being introduced. These letters are most often used to introduce someone who is visiting or moving to another city or country to someone there who could be of help.

Sample 5 is an example of a letter of introduction.

Remember, such letters should be personal in style, since you know the person you are writing to.

22 East Meadow Drive
East Meadow, NY 12222

May 22, 1997

David Ostin
President
DOE Productions
25000 Pacific Coast Highway
Malibu, CA 90265

> The inside address is in the personal business format.

Dear David:

The young fellow presenting this letter to you, Joe Hamlin, is the son of my long-time attorney and good friend, Jack Hamlin. I've known Joe since he was in grade school, and over the years have watched him develop into the ambitious, hardworking, intelligent man he is today.

As you realize, I don't know much about your business, but I do know that Joe seriously wants to get into the movies in some beginning capacity. If raw desire and willpower are any qualification for a career in Hollywood (and I've heard they are), this fellow is on his way.

All I ask you to do for Joe to is to give him an hour of your time and see if you can help him in any way. He's a good listener as well as a good talker, and I would appreciate anything you can do to point him in the right direction, help him avoid the classic mistakes, get to see a good agent, and so on.

Thanks much, David. I appreciate it.

Best regards,

Greg Garrison

Sample 5: A Letter of Introduction.

Final Recommendations About References

Most people usually find writing recommendations a chore. While they're happy to help out, it can be troublesome to express your opinion of someone on paper, except when you get to write a glowing recommendation for someone you really respect and want to help. Such situations do arise.

The rest of the time, writing references will be an obligation you can discharge quickly by following the models in this chapter. If you really feel uncomfortable about the whole thing, it would be better to use the phone or refuse altogether.

The Least You Need to Know

➤ Writing references and recommendations more or less comes with the job of being a manager, although it may happen infrequently.

➤ Unless you can give an enthusiastic and unreserved recommendation, it's a good idea to think it over for a day or two before agreeing to write a reference.

➤ Employment references can raise organizational and legal considerations, so be careful what you write or say.

➤ In a reference, mention your relationship to the subject, how long you've known her, her relevant qualities, and whatever you are recommending her for.

➤ Use a formal style for most recommendations.

Part 5
Now What Do I Do with It?

You've finished your letter or memo, and it looks and reads like a great letter or memo.

Now what?

Now you send it, but that's not as simple as it used to be. You now have choices and, as in many other areas of life, choices can cause confusion. How should you send it? Is overnight delivery really necessary? Does the other guy have a fax machine? What about the costs? What about envelopes and labels?

Then there's keeping track of what you've written. There are those follow-up steps that you promised yourself you would take if the letter didn't get action. How will you remember them?

All of these letters and memos you've learned to create have to go somewhere. You need a filing and follow-up system that makes sense. With the amount of paper you are now equipped to produce, it's something to think about and put in place.

We'll deal with all of this in Part 5.

Chapter 25

Getting the Message Out

In This Chapter

➤ Your options for sending a document

➤ U.S. mail, courier, fax, e-mail, and overnight mail—pros and cons.

Your choices for how to send a document used to be limited to the United States Postal Service, messenger, or interoffice mail. Now the post office has competition on all sides. And technologies like the fax machine and electronic mail mean that you can deliver the message, if not the document, almost instantly.

Given all these choices, you want to make the right one. That's what this chapter is about.

So Many Options, So Little Time

The major options for delivering letters, memos, and, depending on their length, other documents, are:

➤ Electronic mail (e-mail)

➤ Fax

➤ Interoffice mail

➤ Regular U.S. mail (including bulk rate)

➤ Priority (two- to three-day) delivery

➤ Overnight delivery

➤ Messenger or courier

Each of these has its pluses and minuses. But before we look at these individually, let's look at what drives the decision about which one to use.

What Drives the Delivery Decision?

The considerations driving the decision of which delivery system to use for a particular letter or memo are:

➤ Urgency and time-sensitivity

➤ Length of the document

➤ Number of copies you must send

➤ Need for hard copy

➤ Appearance and "production values"

> ### What's That?
>
> The term *production values* is used in the movies and theater to indicate the way a film or play looks. Does it look well put together, or shabby and cheap?
>
> In letters and memos, the quality of the stationery, whether you used printed or hand-lettered labels, and other aesthetic considerations all come under the heading of production values.

Urgency and Time-Sensitivity

Ask yourself, seriously, how quickly the document must get to the other person. Many people just use the fastest means possible. This can undercut the production values—for example, a fax is not as "nice" as a hard-copy letter—and sometimes creates a false sense of urgency.

The problem with creating a false sense of urgency is that your readers will soon come to the conclusion that you think everything is urgent. If you think everything is urgent (or if they think you think that), they'll stop treating any of your projects as urgent.

Time-sensitivity differs from urgency. Time-sensitivity means that some documents *must*, for legal, scheduling, or organizational reasons, be at a certain place by a certain date. For example, you may need to send a confirmation letter to a supplier by a certain date in order to get a discount. A filing date for a legal motion can be critical. Or you may need to reserve a place for a conference by a certain date or another party may get it on a stand-by basis.

Urgency and time-sensitivity are related, of course. We all have so much to do that getting things done in a timely manner often creates urgency. Be realistic about how long things take. You can save yourself and others a lot of rushing around if you schedule realistic amounts of time for research, analytical, and writing tasks. The key is to manage your work so that not every letter and memo becomes urgent.

Length of the Document

Some documents are just too long to send by fax. E-mail is only for short messages.

Even when you're using hard copy (paper, as opposed to a computer file), length can determine mode of delivery. When you send hard copy through the U.S. Postal Service, if the document is long enough and weighs enough, it may make sense to use two-day service instead of first class.

When considering length, be sure to consider any attachments and enclosures.

Watch Out!
Many people are irritated by long faxes. And if the person receiving the fax does not have a plain-paper fax machine, but one that uses thermal paper, she will get a poorer image and curled paper. Faxes longer than five pages are just too long, in my opinion, unless they're extremely urgent.

Number of Copies You Must Send

The more copies you have to send, the more complex and costly the delivery becomes. The cost of sending out 12 copies of a document by overnight carrier instead of first-class mail can add up.

The issue of multiple copies raises other questions. Do some people need their copy tomorrow, while others can wait two or three days?

Hard Copy

Some letters cannot be faxed, let alone sent by e-mail, because they must be signed and returned. With other letters, you may simply want to make the kind of impression only hard copy can create.

Bear in mind that if your readers are going to file the letter, most would rather file a true non-faxed copy than a faxed copy. For one thing, thermal fax paper yellows and fades much faster than regular paper.

Appearance and "Production Values"

Faxes and e-mail simply don't look as good as hard copy sent in an envelope. The envelope, stationery (perhaps with color in the letterhead), and your actual signature all make an impression on the reader.

Many people see the delivery mechanism itself as part of the production values. They believe that if something arrives by overnight carrier it will stand out in the recipient's in-box. This may or may not be true, depending on how much mail and how much overnight mail the person receives.

In any event, it is always worth considering the impression your document is going to make on the reader. Many readers will be affected by the means of delivery you choose.

There is also the issue of cost control. Several years ago, *The Wall Street Journal* reported that a survey had found that over 50 percent of the mail sent overnight does not really have to be in the recipient's hands the next day. Most of this unnecessary overnight mail was sent either out of habit or to impress the reader. Be sure you make this decision wisely, because the costs add up.

Choosing the Right Delivery System

Let's look at the pros and cons of these delivery systems.

Electronic Mail

Electronic mail, or e-mail, is fast and offers other benefits, but also has drawbacks. Here are some of each (we'll discuss them all in Chapter 28):

Pros	Cons
Speed of delivery	Usually not suitable for a letter or memo
Can be saved to computer disk	Recipient needs a PC and e-mail software
Can be forwarded to another reader	No hard-copy original or signature
Inexpensive	Not completely secure and confidential

On most e-mail systems, you can often check whether your message was received and when by requesting a receipt.

Many e-mail software programs enable you to "attach" a document in a word processing software file to an e-mail message. This allows you to send the original document in a computer file to the recipient. You are still not sending an actual hard copy with your signature, but when the recipient prints the document, except for your signature and perhaps your letterhead, it will look exactly like the original letter.

This e-mail attachment method is especially effective for memos within your company where e-mail and word processing software are likely to be compatible and where the lack of a signature is not an issue.

We'll talk more about e-mail (including its limitations on attachments) in Chapter 28.

Faxes

Using a fax machine has many of the advantages, and some of the disadvantages, of e-mail. Although documents delivered by plain-paper fax machines are easier to read than those on thermal paper, you often don't know which kind of machine your recipient has. As noted, most people do not like to read long faxes delivered through machines using thermal paper.

What's That?
Although you know what a fax machine is, you may not be aware that "fax" is short for "facsimile." A *facsimile* is a copy of something, not an original.

Pros	Cons
Speed of delivery	Fax isn't an original with a "real" signature
Can reach multiple readers at the same time	Recipient must have a fax machine
Can be sent from your computer (with the right setup)	Can be difficult to read
Very inexpensive	

To send a fax from your computer, you need special communications software and a fax modem. Many, if not most, new computers sold for business use from the mid-1990s on come fitted with a fax modem. Even if that's not the case with the person you are writing to, your fax will still get through, by way of the recipient's fax machine.

Incidentally, one useful tactic is to e-mail or fax a copy of the document and then follow up with the actual document by first-class mail.

What's That?
A *modem* is equipment that enables a computer to access telephone lines and send and receive data, messages, and documents to and from other computers. A *fax modem* can reach fax machines and other computers with fax modems.

Interoffice Mail

Interoffice mail in large companies is fast, inexpensive, reliable, and delivers originals complete with your signature. There is only one drawback: It reaches only the people in your organization.

Provided that your interoffice mail system is reliable and secure—and most are—this is the delivery system of choice for internal memos unless you need the instant delivery of e-mail.

First-Class U.S. Mail

Despite the spread of e-mail and faxes on the one hand and overnight delivery on the other, the U.S. Postal Service's regular first-class mail remains the major delivery system for business documents. It still offers tremendous advantages and few disadvantages.

Pros	Cons
No equipment required by either party	Each piece is created and sent separately
Every recipient gets a signed original	Usually the slowest means of delivery
You can request return receipts	
More personal to some people than fax or e-mail	
Inexpensive	

A *return receipt* from the postal service is a postcard attached to the envelope or package you are sending. That postcard is signed by the recipient, stamped by the mail carrier with the date and time of delivery, and sent back to you as your receipt.

What's That?
In the world of the U.S. Postal Service, *first-class* means regular mail service, as opposed to their more expensive *Priority* or *Express* service. *Second-class* is a less expensive bulk rate for large mailings such as direct-mail programs. *Third-class* is the even cheaper book rate that enables people to send books through the mail at low cost.

With regular mail, which e-mail fans call "snail mail," no electronic file is delivered, unless you include it on a disk. In some cases, the lack of an electronic file can be an advantage. Electronic files are convenient—they can be stored on the recipient's computer and forwarded to someone else at a moment's notice—but they are also easy to alter. Fortunately, this is not common. However, there are some documents that you may just not want forwarded electronically.

The U.S. Postal Service's first-class delivery remains an extremely cost-effective way of sending letters outside your company. Delivery often occurs on the next day within a local area and within two or three days within a region. Coast-to-coast delivery can take as little as three days, although it's safer to allow four or five.

Watch Out!
Whenever you use any mail delivery system, even an overnight service, there can be delays created by the internal mail system in the organization you're sending mail to. In many cases, it's wise to allow an extra day for a piece of mail to reach someone in a large outfit, bearing in mind that the piece will go to the organization's mail room first.

Priority Mail Service from the U.S. Postal Service

The U.S. Postal Service's Priority Mail service offers two- to three-day delivery of envelopes and packages weighing up to two pounds for a flat rate of $3 (as of this writing). This service has the benefits of first-class service, plus added speed. In my experience, most of this mail is delivered within two days, or on the next day within the state.

You do not get a detailed receipt with a tracking number, as you do with overnight service, but you do get a special red, white, and blue envelope that makes your piece stand out in an in-box.

Overnight Delivery Service

Overnight delivery as it now exists was created by the Federal Express company (FedEx). Other entrants into the business soon followed, and the U.S. Postal Service developed Express Mail (and Priority Mail) in response.

In practice, overnight delivery services provide "guaranteed" overnight delivery at a rate of about three to four-and-a-half times the price of Priority Mail—and about 30 to 40 times that of first-class mail.

"Guaranteed" in the case of FedEx and DHL, a major competitor of FedEx, means that if the piece is not delivered the next day (or by the designated time the next day), you don't pay. That can be small consolation if for some legal or financial reason the document had to get there on time, but the reliability of these services (particularly FedEx) is very high.

These services offer all the pros and cons of first-class mail, except that delivery is much faster (a major pro) and much more expensive (a major con). One other advantage, which can be significant, is that material delivered by overnight or express often gets priority from recipients. You also get a tracking number with this service, so that you can always find out where your envelope is. FedEx now publishes these numbers on their Web site, so you can look it up yourself!

Note that for security reasons, some overnight delivery services, including Federal Express, will not deliver to a post office box. The U.S. Postal Service, however, will.

> **Trick of the Trade**
> If your company is large enough and sends enough overnight mail, you can negotiate discounted rates with the overnight services.

Messenger or Courier

For the ultimate in service, you can have your document (or package) picked up and delivered by hand. Within a city or a metropolitan area, this is called a messenger service. When the distances are greater or span national borders, it is called a courier service.

These are a very expensive means of delivery. You must pay the courier's travel expenses. Most business letters and memos do not call for hand delivery. Less expensive but just as convenient, if you're sending something within a city, is to send your package or document by cab. Many taxi services will function as a messenger for the price of the cab fare plus tip. If you absolutely need same-day service, this is a good way to go.

Appearances Count

Remember, appearance is often an issue when it comes to delivery systems. Overnight delivery services often function more to emphasize the importance of a document than to ensure rapid delivery. (Much of what I've received overnight was simply not very urgent.)

People are affected by production values. Most still like hard copy. A nice, crisp letter on letterhead with a signature in ink makes a more personal impression than e-mail or a fax. A printed address label looks much better on a Postal Service Priority Mail envelope than a handwritten one. Such details make a difference.

Many professionals will place their document in a properly addressed company envelope and then into the envelope provided by the overnight delivery service, rather than placing the letter directly into the Priority envelope. It's extra work, but it certainly looks better.

Cost/Benefit Analysis

The business world has become extremely fast-moving and time-sensitive. In many enterprises, deals, relationships, and money can be won or lost on the basis of speed of response. But many people in business have a tough time knowing when rapid response is necessary and when it is not.

The costs of responding rapidly even when it's unnecessary can be high. It can be stressful for people and can make your outfit appear rushed.

It can also cost you money. If only two letters a week go by overnight service at $10 when they could have gone by first-class mail at 32¢, the company will be wasting over $1,000 a year. As of this writing, you can buy two high-quality plain-paper fax machines for that amount and get change back!

Be conscious about the costs and benefits of your means of delivery. Consider your purpose for writing and the impression you are likely to make on your reader. You should not always use the cheapest means of delivery any more than you should always use the most expensive. Instead, use the one that makes the most sense.

The Least You Need to Know

➤ Today you have more ways of sending a document than ever, ranging from extremely inexpensive to very expensive.

➤ Each delivery method has pros and cons. A con can even eliminate a choice; for example, your reader may not have e-mail.

➤ Cost, timing, and the form of the document that the reader likes or needs are the issues to consider when chosing a mode of delivery.

➤ Because so many rapid means of delivery are now available, it's easy to assume that speed is necessary even when it's not.

Chapter 26

Winning the
Paper Chase

In This Chapter

➤ How to create and maintain a filing system

➤ What a tickler file is and how to use one

➤ Tips on staying organized

You have planned, outlined, written, edited, and sent your letter or memo. Surely now you're finished, right? Uh, not quite.

A letter or memo is often the start of something, or at least it is intended to be. As you know by this time, however, you will sometimes have to write follow-up letters or memos, and you'll need to refer to what you have already written. Sometimes you'll even have to produce copies of correspondence.

It comes down to keeping track of what you write. This chapter will show you how.

Remember What You Wrote?

You will often be called on to remember what you put in writing. During a phone conversation or a meeting, someone may ask you for specific details from some piece of correspondence. Or you may have promised to do something in a letter, which means that you'll have to remember to do it. You may need a copy of the document to bring to a meeting or even for legal reasons.

If you're like most people, you probably find it hard to remember exactly what you wrote. Most of us write too many documents with too many details to remember them all. We also have dozens of little things to do every week and we can't remember them all, particularly the little things we may mention in passing in a memo.

You need something other than your memory. You need a system.

Even if you don't write all that many letters and memos, you need a system for keeping track. This is about staying organized. It's about organizing paper and having a system for following up. In business, files are the beginning of organization.

Watch Out!

Some people seem to be disorganized by nature. One theory is that some of them have Attention Deficit Disorder (ADD), a condition that makes a person seem scattered and unfocused but also creative and, at times, "hyperfocused." If you think you may have ADD, talk to a psychologist or doctor about medication and counseling.

Whether you have ADD or not, if you're always disorganized, you must address this in your business life. One strategy is to avoid jobs that call for a lot of organization, such as administrative positions. Another is to have well-organized people working for you. Another is to use "tricks" like checklists and color-coded files, tools that are useful even to the most organized.

Types of Files

Leaving aside computer files and computerized calendars for the moment, here are some of the kinds of hard-copy files you will need:

➤ Archives

➤ Historical files

➤ Working files

➤ Tickler files

Archives are files that you no longer have to refer to, but have to keep for tax, legal, or organizational reasons. Companies often store archives (or archival files) off-site.

Historical files have to do with the more recent past. In these files you store documents you've written and may need to refer to soon.

Working files have to do with the present. That is where you keep papers you need on a daily or perhaps weekly basis for quick reference.

Tickler files have to do with the future. They represent a system for storing reminders about next steps, follow-up measures, or things on your "to-do" lists.

Behind this fourfold filing system is the idea that a document always has a place, even if that place is the "circular file"—the trash can! A document may move from a working file, where you may have to refer to it at any moment, to a historical file, where you have to be able to locate it quickly but not very often, to an archival file, where it is stored on another floor of your building or perhaps miles away.

This process has to be managed. If your working files are clogged with historical documents or you send something to the archives too soon, this system won't work.

> **What's That?**
> A *tickler* is a reminder to do something on a certain day. It can be as simple as a notation on your calendar or as sophisticated as a computerized reminder linked to the date-and-clock function in your PC.

> **Trick of the Trade**
>
> Almost any business should have a document retention schedule that tells everyone in the company how long various types of papers should be kept. This is a guide to which papers should be retained, when they should be sent to the archives, and how long they should remain there.

Archives

The two most important things about archives are first to have them and second to use them.

Many companies, particularly smaller ones, do not have archival files. Instead, they let papers pile up in historical files. This is a problem, because the more papers there are in a given file, the more disorganized the file becomes, and the less chance you will have of finding what you need when you need it.

Almost any business, even a one-person shop, should have at least a section of files designated and stored as archives. Larger companies need entire rooms devoted to archives. Document storage services can maintain archives off-site if space is an issue.

Many larger companies have archives but fail to use them properly. Most commonly, they let too much paper pile up in the historical files before weeding them. It takes discipline to be organized, and that discipline includes regular weeding.

> **What's That?**
> *Weeding* is the process of going through a file and deciding which documents to keep there, which to move to the archives, and which to discard.

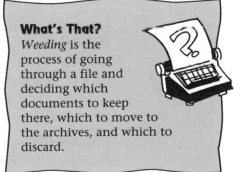

Historical Files

Historical files are those you keep in your office or department. You can set up historical files for letters and memos:

➤ By subject, activity, or project

➤ By the company or person you wrote to

➤ By some method of your own devising

To set up a file on a subject, activity, or project, simply label a file folder with that subject, activity, or project and place related documents in that folder.

Sounds simple, right? Unfortunately, it's not that simple.

It's very easy to create a confusing or useless file by making its title—the subject, activity, or project—either too broad or too narrow. If you make the title too broad, the folder will get too thick too fast. Worse, it will contain documents related to too many different things. Picture a person managing a department of 18 people with a folder labeled "Employees." Eighteen folders would probably be a better idea.

Watch Out!
The most dangerous titles for a file are "Other" and "Miscellaneous." While those titles seem sensible, in a few weeks or months you often have no idea what's in those files. If you do use these titles for files, at least make them as specific as possible, for example "Sales Letters—Other" or "Miscellaneous Equipment Problems."

If, however, you make the title of the folder too narrow, you will quickly create more files than you can manage. Picture our manager of 18 people with 18 folders labeled "Jean Smith's Vacation Day Requests," "Mark Jones' Vacation Day Requests," and so on, and another 18 labeled "Jean Smith's Reviews" and "Mark Jones' Reviews," and so on.

Only you can decide on the scope and titles of your folders. But if you are going to err in either direction, you're generally better off with files that are too large. At least you then have fewer files to keep track of and you have a general idea of where to locate an item. You can subdivide files that tend to get large quickly, such as those with labels like "Sales Letters" or "Equipment Problems," by adding dates. For example, you can have files labeled "Sales Letters—January," "Sales Letters— February," and so on, or "Equipment Problems, First Quarter," and so on.

Filing your letters and memos by the person you wrote to works best if you write frequently to a manageable number of people. That way you wind up with files labeled "Letters, Amalgamated Industries" and "Memos, Marketing Department." The danger, however, is in creating too many small files containing one or two letters. Of course, you can have a file labeled "Other Letters" or "Miscellaneous Correspondence," but that can easily get out of hand.

You are free, of course, to come up with your own method of organizing your files. If something works for you, go with it. There is no right way to file, although there are innumerable wrong ways. Use common sense.

Working Files

Some people don't distinguish between historical and working files. While the two may contain similar materials, a working file usually contains documents that you may have to refer to very quickly. For example, if you write a memo asking people to get back to you about the subject by telephone, it would be good to keep a copy at hand in a working file.

Another definition of a working file is a file you keep on a current project. That's the file you bring to meetings on that project and the one where you keep the most relevant (as opposed to background) information on the project. There is no problem having both a working file and an historical file on a project. Another distinction is that you may keep working files in a file rack on your desk or credenza, and historical files in your drawer or cabinet.

Trick of the Trade
A working file can be a subset of an historical file and help keep papers organized. For example, you can have a working file labeled "Amalgamated Industries Billing Problems" and move information from that file into a larger "Billing Problems" historical file once the problem is resolved.

Tickler Files

Tickler files tell you what to do in the future. A tickler system in a datebook or on a calendar instead of in a filing system will do the same thing.

To set up a ticker file, take 31 blank, empty files, either plain file folders or the hanging type. Number each from 1 to 31, one for each day of the month. When you must remember to do something on a certain date, write yourself a reminder and place it in the folder for that date— or insert a copy of a letter or memo with the follow-up action circled or highlighted.

Trick of the Trade
A tickler file may not be essential in your job. You may be able to get by just writing reminders to yourself in your calendar or datebook. However, a tickler file does help many people to do proper follow-up.

Take another 12 folders and label them with the months of the year. Place reminders for upcoming months in the appropriate folders. At the beginning of each month, transfer the reminders for that month into the files labeled 1–31. Don't forget to write the date on the reminder so that you know exactly when it needs to be done.

Get Good Files

Choose a style and brand of folder that complements your filing system. The hanging variety is especially popular. It allows great flexibility and works well with file folders, which can be slipped directly into a hanging file.

Color-coded tabs and colored dots that you stick on documents also work well for many people. For example, red could mean documents having to do with employees, green could be for customers, blue could be for suppliers, and so on.

The Care and Feeding of Files

Once you set up a filing and tickler system, you need to maintain it. There is a wonderful saying about mail that also makes sense for other documents: *Touch each piece of paper only once.* It's great advice but hard to follow. There's a great temptation to postpone a decision about a piece of paper and to let paper pile up. I advise against it. Strongly.

Here are some hints on the care and feeding of files:

➤ Get into the habit of attending to files at a certain time. For example, each time you finish and send a memo, file a copy, or file the day's memos just before you leave at night.

➤ Weed your files on a schedule, for example every other Friday for working files and at the end of June and December for historical files.

➤ Make good use of the "circular file" by asking yourself, "Will I really ever need this piece of paper?"

Too many of us create disorganized, confusing work environments for ourselves. Take the time to maintain some order in yours. You'll feel—and you'll be—more on top of things.

Running Your Calendar

Ever hear someone referred to as a "follow-up king" or a "follow-up queen"? It's a nice compliment and one that you will hear if you do the following:

➤ Commit to do only things that contribute to your long- and short-term goals and that are suited to your skills.

➤ If you are a manager, delegate as much authority and responsibility to your subordinates as you can, and do it in writing.

➤ When you commit to do something, or when you delegate, *always* schedule it in your tickler file or your calendar or datebook.

➤ Do things when they are scheduled instead of procrastinating.

➤ Plan and schedule on an annual, monthly, weekly, and daily basis, and when you plan, be sure to evaluate and check off what you've completed in the past.

➤ If there is going to be slippage on a schedule, always call before you are past due, discuss the delay, and reschedule the due date.

Watch Out!

Most people wait far too long before rescheduling something that they know is going to miss the deadline. Buy yourself time—and good will—by calling the person you owe the work to as soon as you know it's going to be late.

Get Organized

Business runs on paper. Time is money. These sayings became clichés because they're true.

When you put the two statements together, you understand the link between keeping your paper and your time organized. It all adds up to money. So if you're not organized, get organized. If you are organized, stay organized.

The Least You Need to Know

➤ A good set of files is essential to managing both the documents you create and those that come from others.

➤ By maintaining archives as well as historical, working, and tickler files, you can control office paper according to how often you need it.

➤ Label your files with titles that are neither too broad nor too narrow.

➤ Learn the value of the "circular file."

➤ The time and energy it takes to get organized are worth it. Disorganization is what really wastes resources.

Part 6
Screen Writing—Letters, Memos, E-Mail, and Your Computer

The personal computer has revolutionized business writing. Secretaries and dictation are becoming things of the past. Everyone now must be able to handle a keyboard. Today, each of us is running the equivalent of our own printing press.

But there are better and worse ways of using this remarkable tool. Some business writers hobble along in an uneasy alliance with their machines. Some have been dragged away from their old ways kicking and screaming. Others "kind of" know what they are doing, but "kind of" don't. Still others readily adopt the technology and all it can do and quickly learn how to do it all.

Also, now that almost all computers are electronically linked, e-mail is everywhere. Most of us are embracing this newest form of business communication. Even if you're not, there is no way to avoid it. And there is no good reason to.

Unfortunately, there is a lot of poorly written e-mail traveling the networks. And some of those who are hippest to the computer are producing some of the worst e-mail. For business purposes at least, there's a way to do e-mail and a way not to.

So whether you are a novice still trying to figure out your keyboard or an expert slinging e-mails around the globe, there is something for you in this final part of the book.

Your PC Is Your Private Printing Press

In This Chapter

➤ How to boost your writing productivity with your personal computer

➤ Using templates and style sheets

➤ Using mail merge for business development and job searches

The personal computer is so useful for producing letters, memos, and other documents that it has just about done away with the typewriter. With good word processing software, a personal computer can enable you to write faster and, I believe, better than you can using any other method. If you're in business and you have to write, you are putting yourself at a real disadvantage if you're not writing on a personal computer.

Many of us, however, get far too few of the benefits our personal computers have to offer us as business writers. This is due partly to lack of knowledge, partly to habit and, I think, partly to laziness. If you think you could be getting more "word power" from your personal computer, this chapter will show you that you're probably right.

How to Get More from Your PC

In this chapter, I'll assume that you are writing your letters and memos using word processing software on a PC, if only at a beginner's level. (In general, I'll be using Microsoft Word for Windows® as my frame of reference, but WordPerfect®, Word's major competitor, has most of the same features.)

If the question is, "How do you get the most from your PC?" the answer has to be "By knowing how to apply as many of the features of the software as possible to the work you do."

Entire books have been written on how to use Word and WordPerfect. Training programs teach people how to use these word processing packages at the beginner, intermediate, and advanced levels. This is not one of those books, nor can any book teach you to use software the way a live trainer can. But I can alert you to the major features that can make writing letters and memos less troublesome and more productive.

In general, the way to learn to use the PC to maximum advantage is to:

➤ Allow yourself extra time to learn a new task or feature, realizing that the investment in time will pay for itself down the road.

➤ Use the "Help" feature and the user manual when you have a new task to do and learn to do it the right way.

➤ Follow the instructions in "Help" or the user manual precisely.

➤ Write your own instructions if you learn something from a friend or colleague.

➤ Have patience when you are learning a new feature.

It is tempting to keep doing things in one incorrect and cumbersome, but workable, way on the PC. You may feel that learning a different method of doing something just isn't worth the trouble. But these are not the roads to high productivity on the PC. Knowing what you are doing is the true route to success.

Three Productivity Boosters

Three major features that can really boost your writing productivity are:

➤ Templates

➤ Styles

➤ Mail merge

Let's look at each of these individually.

Using Templates to Stop Reinventing the Wheel

If you write a lot of letters and memos, you should definitely use templates. A *template*, or document template, is a framework or blueprint for a document. Think of it as a mold that you "pour" your document into. A template resides on your computer until you call it up and use it. There are two types of templates: those that come preloaded in your software and those you create yourself.

A template saves you from having to deal with issues of spacing, margins, what goes where, and even some wording and page numbering. Once you have a template that produces the letter or memo you like, keep using it. Why reinvent the wheel?

The following are two examples of memo templates that I created in Microsoft Word for Windows to resemble those that come preloaded in the software:

Memorandum

Date: {date goes here}
To: {recipient's name goes here}
From: {sender's name goes here}
Re: {subject goes here}

cc: {name(s) of those receiving courtesy copies go here}

{Begin typing body of memo here}

Memo

Date: {type date here}

To: {type name(s) here}

From: {type name here}

Subject: {type subject line here}

Distribution: {type name(s) here}

{type message here}

Sample 1: Two Document Templates for Memos.

All you have to do with these templates is delete the information in the brackets, and type in the text that goes in those areas. In an actual preloaded template in Word for Windows, the date is automatically inserted by means of a link to the computer's internal calendar.

The following are two examples of business letter templates that I created in Microsoft Word for Windows to resemble those that come preloaded in Word:

{Company Name}
{Company Street Address}
{City, State Zip code}

{Date}

{Recipient's Name}
{Recipient's Title}
{Recipient's Company Name}
{Company Street Address}
{City, State Zip}

Dear{Recipient}:

{Begin typing letter here}

Sincerely,

{Your name}
{Your Position}

CC: {Name(s)}

Enclosure

{Your Name}
{Street Address}
{City, State Zip code}

{Date}

{Name}
{Title}
{Company Name}
{Street Address}
{City, State Zip}

Dear {Name}:

{Type letter here}

Sincerely,

{Your name}

Sample 2: Two Document Templates for Business Letters.

The first of these two sample templates is for a business letter, while the second is for a personal business letter.

As with the templates for memos, you delete the material in brackets and type the text into the proper areas. If a line like "CC" or "Enclosure" does not apply, you simply delete it.

> **Trick of the Trade**
> There are several other templates (which Microsoft calls "Wizards") that can make your life easier. Especially useful ones include templates for a fax cover sheet, an invoice, and press releases.

Creating Your Own Templates

As you can see by the fact that I created these templates, you are not limited to the ones that come loaded into the software. Being able to create your own templates enables you to (among other things) design your own letterhead, save it in a template, and call it up whenever you want to use it for a new letter. With your own templates, you can create a very consistent look for your business communications.

If you have a company or a person at a company that you write to often, you can also create a template with your letterhead or your inside address, plus their name, title, inside address, and the salutation; you'll have a real time-saver.

> **Watch Out!**
> It's tempting to simply copy over an existing letter to a new file and use that as the basis of a new letter to the same outfit.
>
> This is what I call a "sort-of template." It's OK to do this, but be careful not to leave in incorrect text (such as the wrong person's name) when you create the new letter. You're better off creating a real template with just the parts you know you'll use repeatedly.

If this business of templates seems mysterious to you, don't fear. The preloaded ones are extremely easy to use and it is almost as easy to create and use your own templates. If you write often to the same people, it's worth knowing how to use templates.

Save Time with Styles

Like templates, styles in word processing software speed up the task of formatting a document. A *style* is a preformatted way of presenting text. A style can apply to an entire document or to a single paragraph or line (or even a single word).

Basically, a style tells the computer to format that document or paragraph or line in a certain way. This can mean with a certain spacing in a certain font in a specific size, either plain or with an effect such as underlining or italics, and so on.

A style automatically applies all the decisions that you could make manually about how a letter, section, header, or line should look. That's how it saves you time.

A template has styles imbedded into it. In a sense, a template is a "map" of the styles that should apply to that type of document. If you type the text of your document, and then afterward apply a template to that text (instead of typing the text into the appropriate areas of the template), the text will be formatted into the style of that template.

Trick of the Trade
When you create templates and styles, have a system of naming them that will make sense to you. It is easy to forget what you named a template or style after several days or weeks of not using it.

You can create your own styles and store them in a "style gallery," which is a collection of styles. Then you can apply them automatically to text that you highlight with your mouse.

Whenever you come up with a format for text that you believe you will want to use again, store it in the style gallery. You will not only have it for later reference, but you'll be able to apply it automatically in future letters and memos.

Mail Merge Magic

As a time-saver, nothing in word processing beats mail merge. The *mail merge* feature enables you to create a letter once and then run as many personalized copies as you want, each with the individual recipient's name, title, and address on his or her copy. It also enables you to automatically create a personalized envelope for each letter. If you're a freelancer, independent contractor, or small business owner, you can run full-blown sales campaigns by mail. If you're a job seeker doing a mass mailing, or even specialized mailings of cover letters to potential employers, mail merge can save you hours.

To use mail merge, you create a mailing list and a letter to send to the people on the list. Both the mailing list and the letter can be used over and over again. (Just be sure to put a new date on the letter before you do.)

The mailing list resides in a database in a table in the word processing package, in a spreadsheet, or in actual database software. You create a letter with an inside address and salutation similar to the example in Sample 3, and it goes on your company letterhead.

What's That?

A *database* is a set of information separated into small components and stored in software. A database for a mailing list would include Mr. or Mrs. or Ms., first name, last name, street address, city, state and ZIP code. Each of these items would be in a separate field—an accessible section of the software—where it can be read by the program and pulled into the correct spot on the letter.

```
«Title» «First» «Last Name»
«JobTitle»
«Company»
«Address1»
«City», «State» «PostalCode»

RE:  The Sale of a Lifetime

Dear «Title» «LastName»:

I'm writing to tell you about the sale of a lifetime in
which can save you up to...etc. etc.


Sincerely,



Chris Como
President
```

Sample 3: Mail-Merge Setup for a Sales Letter.

When you run mail merge, the software goes through the mailing list and extracts the correct information from the list and plugs it into the proper spots in the letter you created. The result is a letter that looks exactly as if it were created just for that reader.

Envelopes or mailing labels are created in the same way, except that you key the information into a mailing label template on the screen. At your command, the program creates the envelopes or mailing labels from the mailing list.

Watch Out!
A mailing list will quickly become outdated unless you weed it of "nixies" (pieces of mail returned as undeliverable). Recent estimates have it that information will change for about 10 percent of the people on a mailing list in an average year.

Other Useful Features for Letter and Memo Writers

There are several other productivity boosters worth mentioning.

Spelling Checker

Use it. Use it. Use it. Use it before your final edit and then any time you touch the document again.

AutoCorrect Feature

Many people underuse the AutoCorrect feature in the spelling checker, but it's very useful. I have the AutoCorrect feature set to fix teh (the), compoany (company), and taht (that), among dozens of other words that I frequently mis-key. If you can't train your fingers, why not have an automatic fix?

What's That?

The *AutoCorrect* feature in Word will automatically change a mis-spelling to the correct spelling as soon as you type the word, saving you the trouble of doing it manually with the spelling checker. But you first have to designate the misspelling as a word to be automatically corrected.

Automatic Envelope and Label Feature

From the inside address on any letter, Word for Windows will create and print an envelope and a label automatically—including your return address—on command. This feature is completely independent of mail merge.

The Care and Feeding of Electronic Files

Like paper files, electronic files must be maintained. These files do not necessarily break down into working files and historical files, but it's a good idea to have archival files stored off your hard disk so that you don't clutter it.

You maintain computer files by keeping your directories and subdirectories organized (and weeded). You must also name files in a way that will make sense to you even after you haven't accessed the files for several weeks or even months.

What's That?

A *directory* on a computer is a collection of files or subdirectories. A *subdirectory* is one of several collections of files within a directory.

Think of your computer's hard drive as if it were a file cabinet. The directories are like drawers in the cabinet and the subdirectories are like hanging files. You can also create sub-subdirectories that are analogous to the manila folders within those hanging files. Within either subdirectories or sub-subdirectories there are document files, which are like hard-copy documents inside a hanging file or a manila folder.

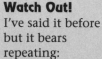

Trick of the Trade

A tickler system works extremely well on a computer if you make sure that everything you need to do is in the system and you check it each morning. The clock and calendar almost guarantee that you will be "tickled." I say "almost" because computers can break down.

Power Up

You must, of course, get to know the features and commands of your particular word processing software. If your software and computer are anything close to the current state of the art, you will have most of the features I've mentioned in this chapter. If you are using out-of-date equipment and you do a lot of writing, you'd probably find it worthwhile to upgrade.

Watch Out!
I've said it before but it bears repeating: Always, always, ALWAYS back up your files onto a floppy or other portable disk and keep back-up copies off-site in case of fire, flood, theft, or vandalism.

Speed and ease of use boost your productivity and make life less frustrating. Business—and business writing—is tough enough without hampering yourself with Stone Age equipment.

The Least You Need to Know

➤ Many people do not get all they can out of their word processing software. Get to know your software and stop doing things the hard way.

➤ The more you use templates and style sheets, the less repetitive writing you have to do and the more time you save.

➤ Mail merge can help you paper the world with your message or your resume.

➤ If you haven't updated your equipment in three years or so, you can probably boost your productivity with an upgrade to your computer, your software, or both.

Chapter 28

Electrifying E-Mail!

In This Chapter

➤ The basics of electronic mail

➤ When e-mail works and when it doesn't

➤ How to write an effective e-mail message

Now that the world—the business world, anyway—is wired, e-mail is everywhere. E-mail is here to stay and, although it should be kept in its proper place, it has its uses.

Unfortunately, there is a lot of bad e-mail floating around the ether. Perhaps the medium encourages sloppy writing, which of course has no place in business. I say this because I know people who write great business letters and memos but seem unable to send me a coherent e-mail message.

E-mail should be written to the highest standards, and this chapter will show you how.

What's That?

E-mail (electronic mail) is a message sent electronically from one computer to another over telephone lines or a private network. Since the message is created on and sent by the computer, there is no need for a hard-copy (paper) version.

Elementary E-Mail

To create and send an e-mail message, you and the person you're writing to each need two things in addition to your computers: communications software that enables your computers to interface, and an account with an online service, such as America Online (AOL) or CompuServe, or with an Internet service provider (ISP).

You do not need to have the same brand of communications software or the same service provider or even the same kind of service provider. That is, one of you can be on AOL and one of you on an ISP. These companies merely provide links to the system that enables computers to communicate. Of course, if you work in the same company as the person to whom you are sending the e-mail, you are probably connected through the company network and can assume that the other person has the same kind of software that you do.

The communications software must be loaded onto your computer (or your network, if your company has one). This software lets you compose e-mail and gives you access to the communications system.

What's That?

Online means that your computer is actively hooked up to a network giving you access to online services such as weather reports or games. Think of it as being on the telephone, which it is, since you are using phone lines to communicate. You are being charged for this, though at much cheaper rates than for talking on the telephone.

Off-line means that your computer has the capability to be online, but is not using that capability.

E-mail is a lot like the postal system, except that delivery is usually within minutes, or at most a few hours. You write on what you should think of as a postcard. You send it to another's electronic mailbox where it resides until the message is opened and read. An *electronic mailbox* is software and storage space on a computer's hard disk. Messages are stored in this space and the software notifies you when you have new messages. And like regular mail, the message can be forwarded to others.

Watch Out!

E-mail sometimes goes undelivered, usually because of problems with the network, the software, or the recipient's computer. Unfortunately, you may not find out that the message was not delivered. If the message is an important one, it's a good idea to check the "return receipt" box before you send the message, if your e-mail service has such a thing, to verify that the message was received.

The Pros and Cons of E-Mail

In this book I will discuss e-mail strictly as a business communication tool. This chapter is not about using e-mail for personal communications, for entertainment, or to "flame" people who irritate you. (A *flame* is the electronic equivalent of hate mail, an angry or outrageous message.)

For business communications, e-mail has several major pros and cons:

Pros	Cons
Fast and easy delivery	Not seen as proper for "official" business
Very personal tone	Format is often lost in recipient's copy
Can reach many readers at once	Not completely secure and confidential
Users can print a clear hard copy	No "real" original hard copy with signature
Reader can save message in a file	Message must be very short
Easy for readers to reply	Recipient needs a PC and e-mail software
Inexpensive (compared to overnight mail)	
Can be forwarded to another reader	

Without a doubt, speed and ease of delivery are the major advantages of e-mail. Although a fax offers these too, the print quality of a fax is often poor.

E-mail has other advantages over a fax. A fax from a fax machine (as opposed to one sent to a computer) cannot be stored electronically. Unlike a fax machine, which may not be near the person you're writing to, the computer that receives the message is probably sitting on the recipient's desk, and will notify her that she has a message as soon as she goes online—or with some systems, even when she isn't online.

E-mail is easy because there is no hard copy to deal with. It's great for reaching a lot of readers—for example, all 23,000 employees in a large company—at once. E-mail can be sent internationally far more easily and cheaply than a letter.

Remember, though, that there are some "hidden" charges that can make e-mail more expensive than first-class mail. Although you are not charged a fee by your online service or Internet Service Provider (ISP) (unless you write the e-mail online), the person who receives the e-mail usually is. This can be a per-piece charge, and a user may not appreciate your message costing them money.

Trick of the Trade
To save money, always write e-mail messages off-line, then go online to send them.

E-mail is fast and convenient, but when you get rid of paper, you may get rid of other things along with it, such as format. Because of the variety of communication software packages, the format of an e-mail message often gets scrambled in transmission. Sentences are often cut short and dropped to the next line, which can be irritating, and effects such as spacing, centering, special fonts, or bold or italic type are usually not reproduced—or worse, come through in garbled form.

Watch Out!
It's best to keep your text very plain and simple in an e-mail. When you get fancy, you create unwanted effects at the reader's end. When you keep it plain, you pretty much know what the reader is going to see.

There is a lot of clutter in electronic mailboxes. This is true of regular mailboxes and in-boxes, of course, but it seems to be a special liability of e-mail. Those who receive dozens of e-mail messages a day quickly learn to delete those that seem unimportant.

The absence of a piece of paper you can hold in your hand hurts e-mail in a way. A piece of paper says, "Slow down and take a moment," while e-mail begs for a quick look so you can get to the next one. In a way, the benefit of e-mail is also its drawback.

E-Mail Is Not Secure

Many companies openly admit that they monitor employees' e-mail. Of course, they may just be saying this to get people to cut down on personal e-mails. Many e-mail messages concern jokes, gossip, sports, or plans for the softball game. Companies are legitimately concerned about the huge volume of this kind of e-mail. Of course, companies may also be snooping.

Either way, when I say to think of an e-mail as a postcard, I mean it: Potentially anyone can read it. Aside from corporate snoops, there are "hackers" who make a game of breaking into computer networks. You simply don't know who has access to your electronic mail.

I'm not saying never to trust e-mail. Most messages are not read by anyone else and, as with a postcard, you probably don't care if they are. But for certain communications, including many proposals and most communications about the careers and finances of others, you must consider the confidentiality issue.

When to Use E-Mail

Use e-mail for a business message when:

➤ You need to reach a lot of people quickly with a fairly short message.

➤ You have a short, personal message and don't require the "official" aspects of hard copy such as a signature.

➤ Security and confidentiality are not important.

E-mail is more a substitute for the telephone than for letters and memos. Many people send and receive so many messages a day that it becomes almost a way of life, just like the phone.

E-Mail in Action

For actual business messages, e-mail is ideal for setting up meetings among a number of people with busy schedules to coordinate. It is also ideal for quick, simple directives to a subordinate or requests for information.

Here are some examples of internal e-mail messages (messages within the company). These examples reflect both the proper style and form as well as typical situations where e-mail beats a letter or memo.

To: All Department Heads

From: J. McNamara

Subject: Meeting on Capital Budgets

We need to meet regarding the capital budgets for next year. I expect that it'll take about three meetings for us to get numbers on the table and then work things through to the final allocations.

I'd like to hold the first meeting on Oct. 15 or 16.

Would you please get back to me via e-mail by close of business Friday at the latest on the times on those days that are good for you?

Thanks,

Jim

To: All Consulting Personnel

From: C. Delise

Subject: Stop Servicing Amalgamated Industries

CC: J. Brion

Effective immediately, PLEASE STOP SERVICING Amalgamated Industries.

After three years as clients paying us an annual retainer, they dropped their contract as of the end of last month. Therefore they are not entitled to any more service. But word has not gotten around all of Amalgamated, since we keep getting calls from them.

I realize this may be awkward, since many of us have built up relationships with people at Amalgamated. But we clearly cannot service a company that is no longer a client. Please explain this to anyone who calls from there.

If any caller from Amalgamated wants to discuss this, please refer them to me at ext. 2333 or to John Brion at 2343.

Thanks in advance for your cooperation.

To: All Headquarters Personnel

From: G. Tiliston

Subject: Missing File on Harrison Corp.

We cannot locate the credit file on Harrison Corp. If you borrowed it or have found it or have any idea where it might be, please call me ASAP at ext. 810. Thanks.

To: M. Redding

From: F. Pollack

Subject: Thank You!

CC: L. Cincotta

Mike,

Thank you for all your great work on the Lewiston project. As you know, this was a really big one for our group and it was thanks to you that the project got out the door on time.

I and everyone in the Northeast district truly appreciate and applaud your work.

Best regards,

Frances

These are all examples of business situations in which e-mail can be highly effective. For reaching a group of people with a quick, informal request or directive, e-mail is the way to go.

You can also direct e-mail outside the organization, for example to freelancers or even clients, as in the following examples:

To: L. Ropier

From: B. Blanchard

Subject: Report Covers Not Delivered

Lisa,

You were going to have the final versions of the report covers delivered to me here at Consolidated yesterday. They never arrived.

Please get in touch with me ASAP. We need those covers!

(I left a voice mail for you this morning as well.)

Barbara

To: T. Winick

From: T. Silveira

Subject: Today's Meeting

Dear Tim,

Thanks for a great meeting today. Donna and I now have what we need to work up a very competitive quote for you folks.

Thanks again for your interest.

Cheers,

Terry

Most clients who are wired for e-mail are happy to receive e-mail messages. In fact, many prefer them to the phone.

Writing E-Mail Messages

Remember to be businesslike at all times, as in the examples shown. I believe in maintaining high standards of written communication in e-mail. This means clarity and effectiveness. It means writing Standard English (for the most part). And it means being courteous.

Conciseness is even more important in e-mail than in regular mail. The volume of these messages can be high, so people want you to get right to the point. These messages also take up space in mailboxes and on hard disks—another reason to be brief. Finally, nobody likes reading long documents on a computer screen.

E-mail software provides a simple template with "To," "From," and "Subject" already inserted so you can fill them in. It automatically inserts the date and time of the message. After you fill out the "To," "From," and "Subject" lines, you then move the cursor to an open space below and write the message. *After you review it,* you click on the icon that sends the message.

You can (and should) maintain an address book for people you send e-mail to frequently. If you work for a company, your e-mail administrator maintains an internal address book, so you can easily send messages to co-workers.

Watch Out!
Remember, an e-mail puts something in writing. So be careful what you write about. For example, if you're confused about what was said at a client meeting, call to clarify it rather write an e-mail that says you're confused.

What's That?
An *address book* in an e-mail system is a set of names and e-mail addresses in a database. From the database you click on names to transfer them to the "To" area on your message. This saves you from looking up and keying in the names and addresses.

In most systems, you can create your own custom lists so that you can just click on the name of the list (for example, All Marketing Personnel) and they all get the message.

Don't Get Sloppy!

I stress that you send your message *after you review it* because a lot of e-mail is clearly going out unedited. A lot of it is unclear and confusing. A lot of it reflects poorly on the writer's ability to sound professional.

Actually, e-mail is one area of business writing that doesn't call for a whole lot of planning, but I strongly recommend at least some.

One good way to plan is to jot down on the screen the points you want to cover and the order in which you want to cover them. You can delete these points after you write the actual message. Or you can do this brief plan on paper. If, like me, you've seen a lot of second (and even third) e-mail messages sent to correct earlier ones, then you know that planning an e-mail can help.

I believe that a salutation, even if you omit the "Dear," is worth including if you are writing to one or two individuals. It makes the message more personal. It also lets anyone who is "cc'd" on the message, or who gets it forwarded to them, know right away who the message was for originally.

Many people omit the "signature" as well as a close. I always "sign" my e-mails and at times use an informal close such as "Regards" or "Cheers."

Do's and Don'ts of E-Mail Style

There is a lot of poor business writing out there, and e-mail often adds to it. Please don't make matters worse.

Here are some "Do's" and "Don'ts" for e-mail style:

Do	Don't
Plan briefly what you'll cover	Write in a "jabbering" fashion
Be brief and to the point	Try to persuade or sell at length
Ask for action or information	Clutter up mailboxes with a lot of nonsense
Use Standard English	Get too cute or overly breezy
Tell people where to get more information	Upload long or numerous attachments
Use initials and acronyms	Use all caps or many font effects

Some popular initials and acronyms are useful, particularly the standard ones such as FYI (for your information), ASAP (as soon as possible), and COB (close of business). I'm less a fan of the newer Web-driven ones such as IMHO (in my humble opinion), BTW (by the way), and FWIW (for what it's worth). That's because these statements aren't usually worth including even as initials. One handy acronym in circulation is FAQ (frequently asked question).

Whatever you do or say, please be sure your reader understands it.

Watch Out!
Business people who are not fascinated by the online world often find cyberculture cuteness tiresome. Meanwhile, those who dwell in cyberculture find it hip and amusing. As always, rule number one is: Know your audience.

Smileys

No discussion of e-mail would be complete without touching on "smileys," also known as "emoticons," which people use to express emotions in e-mail. Smileys are faces formed with keyboard characters; to "see" them, turn your head sideways and read the colon or semicolon as the eyes of the face. I find smileys a bit too cute. A lot of other business people do too, but here are some examples:

Smiley	Meaning
:-)	A smile or happiness
:-(	A frown or unhappiness or disapproval
;-)	A wink or "just kidding"
:-)(-:	A kiss or "love ya"

There are books with hundreds of these symbols as well as collections that make the rounds on e-mail. Use them if you like them, but I'd avoid them in any actual business messages.

Attaching a Letter or Memo to an E-Mail

Most e-mail software allows you to attach a computer file—including a file containing a letter or memo—to an e-mail message, meaning you can send an actual letter or memo by e-mail. After receiving the file, your reader can print it and read it on hard copy. It won't have your signature, but it's the next best thing. You can always send signed hard copy later.

Watch Out!

Be careful when you send a letter or memo as an attachment. If your reader doesn't have the same word processing software as you, he may not be able to convert the document to his software, and so may lose the format or even the entire text.

Very long files can also be "compressed" automatically for faster transmission. This too often leads to software compatibility problems, since the recipient needs the same decompressing software as the sender to decompress the file.

It's a good idea to telephone and talk these things over before trying to attach a file.

Faster, Faster

Like overnight delivery and the fax machine, e-mail is both a cause of and a response to the increasingly rapid pace of business. These days, it's important to remember that quality will usually win out over speed. Doing something quickly, but badly, just doesn't make sense. So when you write an e-mail message, it can often be useful to take a few extra moments to print it out and edit it before you send it.

Stay on top of e-mail. Be sure to check your messages once a day at least. It's best to answer or forward them right away. Otherwise, they pile up and defeat the purpose of e-mail, which is speed.

The Least You Need to Know

➤ E-mail is a wonderful technology, but it hasn't taken the place of letters and memos.

➤ Your writing style for e-mail can be more personal and breezier than your style for letters and memos, but maintain businesslike standards.

➤ You don't need to do much planning for an e-mail message, but a little will help a lot.

➤ E-mail is NOT confidential.

Index

Q-R

When You're Smart Enough to Know That You Don't Know It All

For all the ups and downs you're sure to encounter in life, The Complete Idiot's Guides give you down-to-earth answers

The Complete Idiot's Guide to Learning French on Your Own
ISBN: 0-02-861043-1 ▪ $16.95

The Complete Idiot's Guide to Dating
ISBN: 0-02-861052-0 ▪ $14.95

The Complete Idiot's Guide to Hiking and Camping
ISBN: 0-02-861100-4 ▪ $16.95

The Complete Idiot's Guide to Cooking Basics
ISBN: 1-56761-523-6 ▪ $16.99

The Complete Idiot's Guide to Learning Spanish on Your Own
ISBN: 0-02-861040-7 ▪ $16.95

The Complete Idiot's Guide to Choosing, Training, and Raising a Dog
ISBN: 0-02-861098-9 ▪ $16.95

The Complete Idiot's Guide to Gambling Like a Pro
ISBN: 0-02-861102-0 ▪ $16.95

The Complete Idiot's Guide to Trouble-Free Car Care

ISBN: 0-02-861041-5 ▪ $16.95

The Complete Idiot's Guide to the Perfect Wedding

ISBN: 1-56761-532-5 ▪ $16.99

The Complete Idiot's Guide to Getting and Keeping Your Perfect Body

ISBN: 0-286105122 ▪ $16.99

The Complete Idiot's Guide to First Aid Basics

ISBN: 0-02-861099-7 ▪ $16.95

The Complete Idiot's Guide to the Perfect Vacation

ISBN: 1-56761-531-7 ▪ $14.99

The Complete Idiot's Guide to Trouble-Free Home Repair

ISBN: 0-02-861042-3 ▪ $16.95

The Complete Idiot's Guide to Getting into College

ISBN: 1-56761-508-2 ▪ $14.95

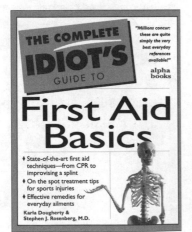

You can handle it!